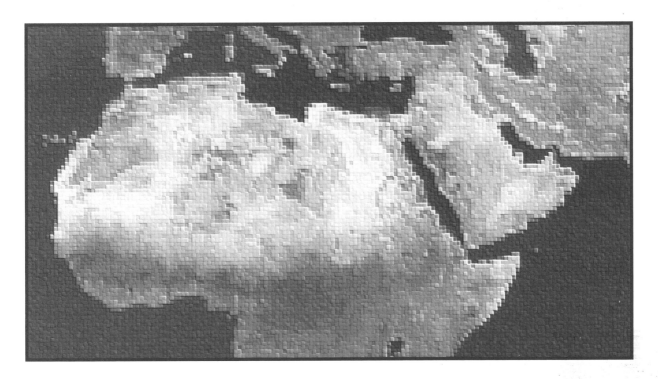

Arab World Mosaic

A Curriculum Supplement for Elementary Teachers

2nd Edition

**SCHOOL OF EDUCATION
CURRICULUM LABORATORY
UM-DEARBORN**

Written by
Lars Rodseth, Sally Howell and Andrew Shryock

Edited by
Sally Howell and Andrew Shryock

Illustrated by
Michelle Gallagher

Published by
The ACCESS Cultural Arts Program

Graphic Design by
IRIS Design & Print, Inc.

About ACCESS

The Arab Community Center for Economic and Social Services (ACCESS) is a human service organization committed to the development of Michigan's Arab American community in all aspects of its economic and cultural life. Our staff and volunteers have joined forces to meet the needs of low income families, to help newly-arrived immigrants adapt to life in America, and to foster among Americans a greater understanding of Arab culture as it exists both here and in the Arab world. To achieve these goals, ACCESS provides a wide range of social, mental health, educational, artistic, employment, legal, and medical services. ACCESS is dedicated, in all its efforts, to empowering people to lead more informed, productive, and fulfilling lives.

The Arab Community Center for Economic and Social Services
2651 Saulino Court
Dearborn, Michigan 48120
(313) 842-7010
(313) 842-5150 (fax)

About the Authors

Sally Howell was Cultural Arts Director at ACCESS from 1987-1995. She wrote many of the stories and lesson plans which appear in the *Arab World Mosaic*; she also served as editor and general director for the project. Howell has done ethnographic research in Yemen, Jordan and Detroit. She has published several articles on the artistic and cultural life of Arab Detroiters. Howell was Executive Producer of *Tales from Arab Detroit*, a documentary video on the cultural identity of Detroit's Arab American community. She is currently curator and project director for the *Community between Two Worlds: Arab American in Greater Detroit* exhibition which will travel to six cities through 2001.

Lars Rodseth has done field research in Nepal and Micronesia and has published articles on gender systems and the biological dimensions of human social behavior. Using interviews with Arab Americans as a guide, Rodseth wrote many of the original stories and lesson plans that appear in the *Arab World Mosaic*. He is currently Assistant Professor of Anthropology at the University of Utah.

Andrew Shryock has done ethnographic fieldwork in Yemen, Jordan and Detroit. His books include *Nationalism and the Genealogical Imagination* (1997) and *Arab Detroit: From Margin to Mainstream* (2000). Shryock wrote the cultural notes for the *Arab World Mosaic* and served as editor for the project. He is currently Assistant Professor of Anthropology at the University of Michigan.

2nd Edition Copyright © 2000 The Arab Community Center for Economic and Social Services
1st Edition Printing 1994
Printed in the United States of America.
ISBN: 0-8187-0222-2
Library of Congress Card Number: 94-74372

Acknowledgments

The *Arab World Mosaic* is the product of ideas, energies, and talents drawn from a variety of sources. This wealth of resources would have meant nothing, however, without financial backing. I should begin the pleasurable task of giving thanks by expressing our special gratitude to the individuals and funding agencies whose generosity sustained (and occasionally revived) this project:

Khalid and Sally Al-Turki
ARAMCO
The Ford Motor Company
The Michigan Humanities Council
The National Endowment for the Humanities
The Olayan Group
The US Outreach Fund

Work on the *Arab World Mosaic* began in 1992, when ACCESS organized a consulting team of teachers, curriculum specialists, and Middle East scholars to discuss the pressing need for elementary level curricular materials on the Arab world. This group defined the scope of the project, selected appropriate topics, and identified approaches that could be used effectively in classrooms. Special thanks go to Marcy Faiz, Reema Haugen, and Maura Sedgeman, all of the Dearborn Public Schools, who spent the summer of 1992 working with ACCESS to review existing materials, develop the lesson plan layout used throughout the *Arab World Mosaic*, and sample lesson ideas in the classroom. Marcy Faiz also wrote preliminary drafts of over a dozen lesson plans.

We are additionally grateful to Megumi Sunako, a University of Michigan graduate student who interviewed over 30 Arab immigrants about life in their countries of origin. These interviews provide the background for the many original stories and exercises that fill the *Arab World Mosaic*.

For the weighty task of assembling this information in coherent and easy-to-use forms, we turned to Lars Rodseth. Lars reviewed provisional drafts of the *Arab World Mosaic* and wrote original stories and entirely new lesson plans based on provisional ideas and the interviews with Arab Americans we had recorded in 1992.

Andrew Shryock was called in to write the cultural notes that accompany the lesson plans. Andrew later became co-editor of the project and worked with me to create new lessons and stories that would complement materials already in place. Rodseth and Shryock brought to the project a much needed emphasis on explanatory frameworks and representational strategies that would make the *Arab World Mosaic* accessible to teachers not familiar with the Arab world. We thank them both for their interpretive insights.

Annette Vanover, the former Cultural Arts Coordinator at ACCESS and currently the Art Projects Coordinator at Focus: HOPE, was involved in the project from its inception. A master of the subtle art of planning, Annette inspired and channeled the efforts of the numerous consultants, scholars, and artists who contributed to this project. Her steady contribution of useful ideas and materials kept the *Arab World Mosaic* fresh, and her thorough scrutiny of every new draft made our editorial work more efficient.

The wonderful illustrations that grace the *Arab World Mosaic* were drawn by Michelle Gallagher. Although an Arab American herself, Michelle has never been to the Middle East, and her illustrations demanded a good deal of background research and consultation with project staff and scholars, a process which, we are glad to say, did not dampen Michelle's creativity. Indeed, we are delighted with the results, and we thank Michelle for the care and patience she showed both ACCESS and her work.

We have also been fortunate, during every stage of this project, to benefit from the advice of Betsy Barlow, Outreach Coordinator at the Center for Middle East and North African Studies at the University of Michigan. As always, she has given this project her unstinting support. Several teachers reviewed and assessed the *Arab World Mosaic*, including Gloria Ankeny and Santina Buffone, both of the Dearborn Public Schools, who encouraged us to think beyond the K-3 boundaries we had originally set for ourselves. I also thank the participants in the "Arab World Workshop," sponsored by the Institute for Global Education in Grand Rapids, Michigan. The suggestions made by members of the workshop were a last-minute jolt of encouragement and good sense.

The most important contribution to the *Arab World Mosaic*, however, was made by the dozens of Arab Americans who reviewed early drafts, gave us their childhood memories to use in stories and lesson plans, and always made themselves available to answer questions about their lives in the Middle East and America. This list of names would include (among many others): Layla Abdul 'Aziz, Adil Al-Ghazali, Salih Al-Harathi, Arwa Al-Mawari, Wegdan Azzou, Mohammed Farrag, Maha Freij, Hoda Hussein, Iman Hussein, Miriam Hussein, Nahida Ismael, Ibtisam Jabarah, Maha Jammal, Mansur Marea, Adel Muhammed, Michelle Musallam, Fadya Naji, Ahmed Obaid, Hamsa Roummani, Nehmet Sabra, Nadir Seif, and Anton Shammas.

To those of you who asked to remain anonymous; to those whose names I have overlooked; and to the dozens of ACCESS staff members and friends who contributed to the project in less obvious, but no less important ways, I extend my heartfelt thanks.

Sally Howell

Special Contributors

Marcy Faiz, Resource Teacher,
 Dearborn Public School

Annette Vanover, Art Projects Coordinator,
 Focus: HOPE

Principal Consultants

Reema Haugen, Resource Teacher,
 Bilingual and Compensatory Education
 Program, Dearborn Public Schools

Maura Sedgeman, Resource Teacher,
 Bilingual and Compensatory Education
 Program, Dearborn Public Schools.

Betsy Barlow, Outreach Director,
 Center for Middle Eastern and
 North African Studies,
 University of Michigan

Additional Consultants

Gloria Ankeny, 8th Grade Teacher,
 Dearborn Public Schools

Dr. Santina Buffone, 4th Grade Teacher,
 Dearborn Public Schools

Ann Chin, 4th Grade Teacher,
 Oakland Intermediate School District

Dale Donaldson, 3rd Grade Teacher,
 Dearborn Public Schools

Bernadette Donohue, Music Teacher,
 Rochester Schools

Sammar Farhat, 1st Grade Teacher,
 Dearborn Public Schools

Alison Jones, artistic consultant

Paul Ragheb, VISTA volunteer

Dr. Anthony Russo, Social Studies Coordinator,
 Dearborn Public Schools

Sarah Spice, project researcher

Megumi Sunako, project researcher and
 interviewer

Dr. Janice Terry, Professor of History,
 Eastern Michigan University.

Nancy Unis, 3rd Grade Teacher,
 Detroit Public Schools

Introduction

America has always been a diverse nation made up of peoples from around the world. Only recently, however, have Americans accepted the idea that our schools should reflect this diversity, not only in the make-up of their students, but also in the knowledge our children are taught in the classroom. Across America, educators, parents, and children are searching for new ways to explore a world in which cultural diversity has become an everyday fact of life. It will probably take decades for this changing mentality to be fully integrated into school curricula; what teachers need now are multicultural materials they can use independently and without great inconvenience to themselves. Positive steps toward a more global curriculum are being made every day; nonetheless, smaller ethnic groups (and newer ones) are still very likely to be left out of this process. The *Arab World Mosaic* was designed to help teachers include information about the Arab world, a politically sensitive and much misunderstood place, to students at the earliest levels of education.

The *Arab World Mosaic* is a curriculum *supplement*. It is designed to enrich what children are already learning in school. Our first four chapters, which are intended for K-4 students, arrange information in a series of concentric circles, beginning with the self, then moving to the family, the home, the neighborhood, the community, and the natural world. Each ring adds to the complexity of the cultural images developing in the student's mind about the Arab world. You should not present this hierarchy of images as an exotic world unrelated to our own. Instead, the lesson plans are designed in ways that allow you to weave cultural knowledge into ordinary classroom activities that teach reading, basic math, and writing skills. In other words, *Arab World Mosaic* does not insist that you treat its content as something separate, something unique, something to be taught over and above everything else you teach. It is intended to add new dimensions to the body of knowledge American teachers already impart to their students. This, we believe, is a more constructive way to introduce children to family patterns in the Middle East, the kinds of houses, towns, and cities Arabs are likely to live in, how Arab Christians and Muslims celebrate holidays, and so on.

In the rapidly expanding market for multicultural curricula, the *Arab World Mosaic* stands out in two respects. First, it tackles the delicate issue of cultural difference early in the educational process. We believe that children can make sense of human diversity at a very young age, and that exposing them to a more diverse range of human possibilities is something that should be done sooner, not later. In our review of existing materials on the Arab world, we were encouraged to discover that a great deal of energy has already been devoted to multicultural arts and crafts projects, or math and science activities. Many of the elementary curriculum supplements now available are very helpful. In particular, we recommend *The Arabs: Activities for the Elementary School Level* by Audrey Shabbas, Carol El-Shaieb and Ahlam An-Nabulsi, and *Lands, Peoples, and Communities of the Middle East*, by Juanita Will (Soghikian) Swedenburg.

Nonetheless, we felt the need to pass along more in-depth *cultural* information than these materials contain. It wasn't until we began creating our own lesson plans that we realized how difficult it is to convey cultural knowledge to young children and teachers without over-generalizing or stereotyping the very people we were trying to represent. Using an anthropological approach — which seeks to understand cultural difference by relating it to problems all humans share — we have worked hard to create a product which one teacher has described as "the first real-life, how-and-why resource on Arab cultures I've seen." This anthropological approach, we believe, is a special strength of the *Arab World Mosaic*.

The *Arab World Mosaic* offers another advantage to its users: namely, the genuine diversity and cultural authenticity of its *content*. The *Mosaic* was compiled in Dearborn, Michigan, heart of the largest, most highly-concentrated Arab community in North America. Over 200,000 Arab Americans live in the Metro Detroit area. This unique community, drawn from all corners of the Arab world, is made up of individuals from peasant, bedouin, urban, and cosmopolitan backgrounds; moreover, the community is evenly divided between Christians and Muslims. More than 30 Arab Americans from Metro Detroit were interviewed for this project: Yemenis, Syrians, Lebanese, Palestinians, Jordanians, Iraqis, Moroccans, Saudi Arabians, Egyptians, and Omanis. Using the flood of biographical detail they provided, we have written more than 20 original stories for the *Arab World Mosaic*. With few exceptions, the information included in the *Mosaic* is based on the lives of real people; their recollections of childhood in the Arab world are the tools we use to illustrate how real Arab communities tell stories, celebrate holidays, decorate their homes, prepare their foods, and raise their families.

The Arab immigrants who shared their memories with us have led fascinating lives. They have seen more of the world than most Americans ever see; they speak many languages; they have crossed boundaries; and they can look at themselves from multiple points of view. We hope that the *Arab World Mosaic* will teach your students some of the lessons learned by immigrants in *all* times and places. When used creatively, the *Arab World Mosaic* will help your students realize that the world is an exciting place filled with interesting places, unusual images, and all sorts of people. It will teach them that people in other parts of the world are just like them in many ways, and not like them in many others. Most important of all, the *Arab World Mosaic* will help children learn early in their lives that being different is a natural part of being human.

Using the Arab World Mosaic

Keeping things in perspective — The *Arab World Mosaic* is carefully laid out along schematic and progressive lines. Its six units are meant to accumulate in the minds of your students, and we recommend that you incorporate each lesson plan in the order we have given it. When used in this way, the layers of meaning we have laid down will accumulate gradually, adding to the richness of your students' views. It is equally possible, however, to adapt lesson plans to fit more flexible schedules. Each lesson plan is capable of standing on its own. The *Cultural notes* located at the end of most lessons are indispensable to the proper use of this supplement. Not only do they fill in background information you are not likely to know, they also provide comparative frameworks that will help you make sense of the diverse cultural patterns that surface in each unit.

A word about language — The Arabic language is written in a different alphabet from English; not all Arabic sounds are present in English; and Arabic dialects differ greatly among themselves. This makes transliterating Arabic into English difficult. Scholars have their own transliteration systems, which are helpful to people who understand both languages, but these are not likely to help teachers and students who do not know Arabic. Thus, we have tried to spell Arabic words in ways that will allow you to pronounce them consistently and reasonably well. Sometimes we even resort to the "rhymes with" technique. Those of you who are familiar with Arabic and find our system a bit over-simplified, please feel free to acquaint your students with more precise models of pronunciation. If there are Arabic speakers in your community (or your classroom!), ask their advice on how to pronounce certain words. They will be pleased to help you.

A good way to start — Even if you plan to use only a few lessons from the *Arab World Mosaic*, we recommend that you begin with the **I have a name** and **I have a language** lessons in Unit 1. Allowing students to pick an Arabic name, and teaching them the meaning of the name, is fun even for kids in upper grade levels. From then on, whenever you use lessons from this supplement, you can call your students by their Arabic names. Likewise, the greetings in the language lesson can be taught and used whenever you deal with Arab topics. Many American children, especially African Americans, are already familiar with Arabic names and phrases. Encouraging your students to identify themselves with Arab culture on this basic level will pique their interest in other, more complex features of the Arab world.

Spreading the work around — We began the *Arab World Mosaic* with a "whole language" approach. As a result, many of the lesson plans are oriented toward math, science, reading, and writing problems, as well as the more conventional concerns of social studies. This is a convenient system for teachers who handle several subjects at once. If, however, you teach only English, or only social studies, and you do not have time to prepare math exercises, please recommend a pertinent lesson to your students' math teacher. In this way, teaching about other cultures can be worked into the wider curriculum. We have designed lessons that would be appropriate for most of your school's teachers. If your school is spending a week or month focusing on the Middle East, our lesson plans can be used in a variety of classrooms.

Traps to avoid — Please remember that no single unit or lesson is intended to sum up (or stand for) all of Arab society. We have taken great pains to provide you with a diversity of images. Please avoid the twin sins of multicultural education: (1) accentuating the exotic at the expense of the familiar and (2) accentuating similarity at the expense of difference. If you use a broad range of lessons from all six units, the *Arab World Mosaic* will, by its very design, help you avoid these all-too-common tendencies. If you use only a scattering of lessons at odd times throughout the year, it will be harder to protect your students from stereotypical ideas and assumptions about the Arab world.

Books you ought to buy — We have supplied the written materials you will need to carry out all but seven of the 42 lesson plans which comprise the *Arab World Mosaic*. The seven exceptions require story books set in the Middle East which, because of their high quality and general appeal to children, we strongly recommend that you buy.

These titles include:

The Day of Ahmed's Secret,
by Florence Parry Heide and Judith Heide Gilliland, Clarion Books

Nadia the Willful,
by Sue Alexander, Dragonfly Books

Sami and the Time of the Troubles,
by Florence Parry Heide and Judith Heide Gilliland, Clarion Books

Sitti and the Cats: A Tale of Friendship,
by Sally Bahous, Roberts Rinehart Publishers

Sitti's Secret,
by Naomi Shihab Nye, Four Winds Press

All of these books are available in paperback from Amazon.com and Borders Books and Music. We also recommend a book which is currently out of print. Please check with Borders when you make your purchases to find out if *Amina and Muhammad's Special Visitor*, by Diane Turnage Burgoyne, Middle East Gateway Series, is once again in print.

Get Arab families involved — The best resources a school district can call upon are the families of its students. If you have Arab students in your classrooms, or are aware of any Arab families in your school system, you might want to invite these people to help you teach lessons from the *Arab World Mosaic*. Arabic speakers can teach you to pronounce greetings correctly. Arab cooks can help you prepare the special dishes described in the lessons. Parents can read folktales to the class and share other stories and poems they remember from childhood. There is no limit to the ways in which Arab and Arab American parents can help you with your work.

Other sources of information and assistance — There are several universities around the country which host federally-funded outreach programs on the Middle East. By calling the program nearest you, you can learn about upcoming educator workshops on the Arab world, about materials available for loan or purchase, and about local scholars who can provide you with more direct services. A list of Middle East Outreach Centers is given in

Appendix A. It is beyond our means to list the many non-profit, unaffiliated outreach centers now operating across the country. Your local university should be able to help locate these groups. In Michigan, call the ACCESS Cultural Arts Program at (313) 842-7010 or the Center for Middle Eastern and North African Studies, the University of Michigan, at (734) 769-4142, or contact their website at www.umich.edu/~iinet/cmenas/. The Middle East Outreach Council also has a helpful website with information about university and non-profit outreach programs nationwide. They can be reached at www.link.lanic.utexas.edu/menic/meoc.

Middle Eastern Materials for Teachers, Students and Non-Specialists, a comprehensive, annotated list of books, articles, audiovisual and other teaching materials, can be purchased from the Middle East Studies Association (MESA) for $10. For more information, write to Middle East Studies Association, University of Arizona, 1232 North Cherry Avenue, Tucson, AZ 85721, or call (602) 621-5850, or contact the MESA website at www.mesa.arizona.edu.

Table of Contents

Table of Contents continued

Objectives

1. To stress the importance of writing

2. To have the students practice writing their names

3. To help the students imagine themselves as members of another culture

Materials

1. *The Day of Ahmed's Secret*, by Florence Parry Heide and Judith Heide Gilliland

2. World Map (optional)

3. Writing paper and pencils

4. Attached list of Arab names. The American and Egyptian lists of names were taken from *The Best Baby Name Book in the Whole Wide World*, by Bruce Lansky

5. Drawing paper and crayons

Procedures

1. Locate Egypt on the world map.

2. Read *The Day of Ahmed's Secret*.

3. Discuss Ahmed's secret. Why is it important for Ahmed to be able to write his name? Ask the students if they remember when they first wrote their own names.

4. Have the students practice writing their names.

5. Ask students about their names. Are they named after a relative or someone important? Do they like their names? Do they have nicknames? Middle names? What is their favorite name? Ask why people have names.

6. Read some of the popular American names listed below. See if students know the meanings of these names. Next, ask them what their own names mean. If the students cannot answer this question, explain that most of the names Americans use come originally from other languages.

7. Read the popular Arab American and Egyptian names listed below. Discuss the customs of naming in the Arab world (see **Cultural notes**).

8. Have each student pick an Arab name from the list provided.

9. The students may now draw self-portraits and label them with their Arab names. In some cases, a portrait may reflect the meaning of the name. "Najma," for example, may choose to draw herself beneath a starry sky. Students might also draw themselves in an Egyptian setting, such as the marketplace or the Great Pyramids. For more ideas, students may consult the illustrations in *The Day of Ahmed's Secret*.

The Most Popular American Names (in 1986)

Brittany	Jessica	Christopher	Joshua
Kristin	Sara	Michael	Nicholas
Heather	Amanda	Matthew	Brandon
Stephanie	Ashley	Ryan	Robert
Lindsay	Jennifer	Andrew	Daniel

Popular Arab American Names

Miriam — Mary	Hassan — beautiful one
Leila — dark as night	Naadir — exceptional
Nuura — light	Imaad — pillar
Sawsun — lily of the valley	Ashraf — ascending, lofty, noble
Yasmeen — Jasmine flower	Saamer — good companion
Maha — small deer	Yuusuf — Joseph
Nawaal — reward	Taalib — seeker of knowledge
Nasreen — white rose	Waleed — newborn
Ameera — princess	Azeez — beloved
Saamia — pure	Mahsin — charitable

Some Popular Names in Egypt

Azeeza — cherished	Gamaal — beauty
Ofra — earth-toned	Abdulla — servant of God
Faatima — daughter of the	Ahmed — highly praised
Haleema — gentle	Ali — lofty
Hoda — calm	Mahmood — praised
Haala — halo	Mohammed — praiseworthy
Intisaar — victory	Naasir — triumphant
Nabeela — noble	Sa'eed — happy
Nimma — delight	Saami — royal
Rakeeya — refined	Tawfeek — success
Sameera — entertaining	Yahya — John

Cultural notes

1. Vocabulary from *The Day of Ahmed's Secret*:

    Butagaz, or butane gas, is used to fuel stoves, ovens, and hot water heaters in many parts of the Arab world. It comes in large metal cannisters that are hooked up directly to the stove by a rubber hose. The cannisters must be refilled once every week or so, and there is often a butagaz man who drives around the neighborhood exchanging empty cannisters for full ones.

    Rosewater is water in which rose petals have been steeped (see the **Cultural notes** at the end of the following lesson, **I have senses**).

2. Arabic names have well-known meanings. Jameela, a girl's name, means "beautiful." Hakeem, a boy's name, means "wise." Other names have religious significance. Among Muslims, for instance, it is common to create boys' names by combining the Arabic word "servant" (abd) with words describing God or the attributes of God. Thus, Abdullah means servant (abd) of God (Allah), and Abdalkariim means servant (abd) of the generous (al-kariim). Christian and Jewish names are also popular throughout the Middle East.

3. Arab parents often name one of their children after a grandparent or great-grandparent. This way, the names of cherished ancestors are kept alive in the family for many generations.

unit one

1

me

I have senses

Objectives

1. To develop the student's awareness of colors, sounds, and smells

2. To develop the student's vocabulary for sensory experience

Materials

1. *The Day of Ahmed's Secret*, by Florence Parry Heide and Judith Heide Gilliland

2. Blackboard or chart paper and marker

3. Herbs and spices (e.g., mint, cloves, sage, cinnamon, aniseed, oregano, cardamom)

4. Perfumes and incense — e.g., essential oils, rosewater, frankincense, camphor, myrrh, sandalwood — available at health food or import stores

Procedures

1. Read *The Day of Ahmed's Secret*.

2. On the blackboard or chart paper, write the three categories of **Colors**, **Sounds**, and **Smells**.

3. Discuss the colors in the story.

   What colors were woven into the donkey's harness? [blue, green, and gold]

   What color was the cart where Ahmed bought his lunch? [red and yellow]

   At sundown, what happens to the colors of the day?

4. See how many colors the students can name in the classroom. Those wearing bright or unusual colors may be asked to stand up. See how many different names for the same color can be listed on the blackboard or chart paper.

5. Now discuss the sounds in the story. Ahmed heard "trucks and donkeys, cars and camels, carts and buses, dogs and bells, shouts and calls and whistles and laughter all at once."

   What sounds do trucks make? Donkeys? Dogs? Bells? Whistles? Laughter?

   What sounds did Ahmed hear that we usually don't?

   What sounds do we hear that Ahmed usually doesn't?

   What sound did Ahmed's cart make? [*karink rink rink, karink rink rink*]

   What sound did the rosewater man make? [He clicked two cups together.]

   What did Ahmed do after he ate his lunch? [He closed his eyes for quiet time.]

6. Now have the students close their own eyes for quiet time. Remind them of what Ahmed's father told him: "If there are no quiet spaces in your head, it fills with noise." When the whole class is quiet ask the students to listen carefully. Ask them to count to themselves how many different sounds they hear. After a minute or two, have the students open their eyes and raise their hands to tell what they heard. On the blackboard or chart paper, list all the sounds the class can remember.

7. Pass spices around for students to smell. Mint, cloves, sage, cinnamon, aniseed, oregano, and cardamom are all commonly used in the Middle East. You can use bottled spices, but fresh samples have more aroma and are more interesting to touch and study. After a minute or two, have the students describe what they smell. Are any of the scents familiar? Do they put these spices in the foods they eat at home? Mention some American dishes and candies that contain these spices. Write the name of each spice on the blackboard or chart paper, then ask students to describe the smell that belongs to each.

Procedures *continued*

8. Pass around samples of rosewater, frankincense, camphor, myrrh, sandalwood, or other types of perfume and incense. Ask students to close their eyes. Pass the samples under their noses one by one. Do they smell good or bad? Have you ever smelled them before? Tell students about perfume and incense. Why do people use them, and how? On what special occasions? Tell students about the different ways spices, perfumes, and incense are used in the Arab world (see **Cultural notes**).

Cultural notes

1. For many centuries, Arab merchants dominated the spice trade between Europe and Asia. This domination ended in the 16th century, when European sailors discovered new routes to the Far East; nonetheless, people in the Arab world and throughout the Middle East have maintained an intimate knowledge of herbs and spices. The spices listed in Procedure 7 are used to enhance the flavor of foods, and Arab dishes are, on average, much spicier than American fare. In Arab countries, sage (*maramiiya*), mint (*na'na'*), cinnamon (*girfa*), oregano (*zatar*), cloves (*granfal*), and aniseed (*yanasoon*) are regularly added to tea, while cardamom (*haal*) is added to coffee. It is also believed that these spices have medicinal qualities: some cure headaches, some relieve cramps, some help you sleep, and others clear the mind. These qualities are discussed in Unit 4, **Plants and Animals**.

2. Rosewater is a simple, versatile perfume made by steeping rose petals in water. When rubbed on the body, it refreshes the skin and gives off a lovely scent. In some Arab countries, guests are given rosewater to splash on their faces and necks as a sign of welcome. Because of its sweet, flowery aroma, rosewater is added to syrups, rice pudding, and holiday cookies as well. When drunk or inhaled as steam, it can even cure headaches and upset stomachs.

3. Incense is used as an air freshener throughout the Middle East. In Yemen, for instance, a host will pass a small incense burner from guest to guest, and each will breathe in the relaxing fumes. Sandalwood is a popular scent. Since ancient times, Yemen, Somalia, and Oman have been points of origin for the lucrative trade in myrrh, one of the finest and most precious varieties of incense. Frankincense and myrrh — which, according to Christian tradition, were offered as gifts to the baby Jesus — are made from tree sap. Each is harvested by cutting the bark of rare tree species found only in East Africa and Southern Arabia. The sap that oozes out of the bark is allowed to dry for several weeks. The result is an aromatic resin which is reddish-brown (myrrh) or amber (frankincense) in color. Among Arab Christians, frankincense is still used regularly in church services, where it symbolizes the presence of the Holy Spirit.

I have a body

Objectives

1. To develop the student's vocabulary for parts of the body

2. To introduce Arab customs of decorating the body with henna

Materials

1. Blackboard or chart paper and marker

2. Non-toxic, non-permanent magic markers (preferably reddish brown or black)

3. Construction paper or cardboard

4. Pictures of henna designs (see illustration 1.2)

Procedures

1. Draw the outline of a human body on the blackboard or chart paper (see illustration 1.1). Ask the students to name parts of the body, and write these names in their appropriate places on the figure.

2. Explain to the students that people in other countries have different words for these same parts of the body. As examples, the Arabic names for **hand**, **head**, and **eye** may be written below the English words (see **Arabic word list** below).

3. Now draw the outline of a hand. Ask the students to name the parts of the hand, and label the parts on the outline. Arabic words for **finger**, **thumb**, and **palm** may be written below the English words (see **Arabic word list** below).

4. Have the students practice the Arabic words a few times. Point to the hand, head, eye, finger, thumb, and palm and see if they can name each one in Arabic.

5. Discuss the Arab folk traditions associated with henna (see **Cultural notes**). Examples of henna designs may be drawn on the blackboard or chart paper.

6. Show the students how to make their own henna designs (see **Fun with henna** below). Because henna is often difficult to locate and stains the skin for several weeks, we recommend that teachers substitute magic markers with washable and non-toxic ink for the more authentic henna. Alternatively, the students may trace their hands on a piece of construction paper or cardboard and decorate these tracings with designs like those in illustration 1.2.

unit one

1

me

illustration 1.1

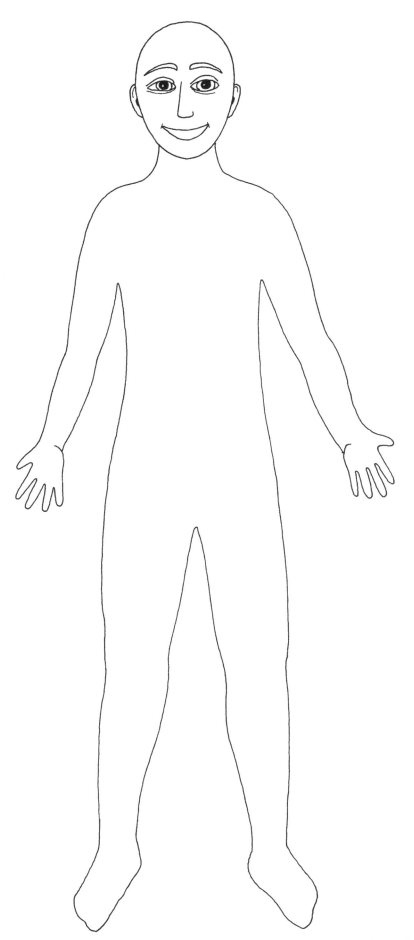

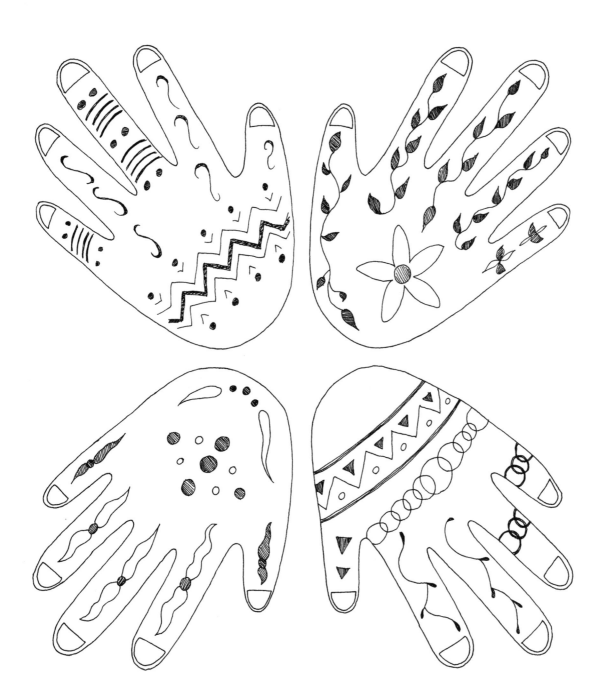

illustration 1.2

Fun with henna

1. Henna can be found in stores that specialize in Middle Eastern, Indian, or Pakistani imported goods. Some art supply and health food stores also carry it. Unless you are familiar with henna, or have children in your class whose parents know how to mix and apply it, you should substitute water colors or washable magic markers.

2. Explain the significance of henna to your students (see **Cultural notes**). Next, have them design a henna decoration on a tracing of their hand. They can model their design on the examples provided in illustration 1.2, or they can make new designs of their own. Encourage the students to create geometric motifs and abstract patterns. In Islamic cultures, these are preferred over pictures of people, places, or things.

Fun with henna continued

3. Children can draw their henna design on their own hands, but they will have more fun if they draw on the hands of fellow students. In the Middle East, henna is placed on the body by close friends and relatives, not by oneself. It is a joyful activity, and it is often accompanied by singing and dancing. Help your students organize a henna party (complete with sweets, drinks, and their favorite music) during which they can swap henna designs and draw them on each other's hands.

Arabic word list

hand	*eed*, rhymes with "need"	eye	*ayn*, rhymes with "fine"
finger	*oos-ba-a*, first syllable rhymes with "goose"	foot	*ka-dam*, rhymes with "bottom"
thumb	*ib-haam*, last syllable pronounced "ham"	leg	*ri-jil*, rhymes with "vigil"
		ear	*i-thin*, last syllable pronounced "then"
palm	*kaff*, rhymes with "stuff"		
head	*raas*, rhymes with "boss"	nose	*unf*, rhymes with "umph"

Cultural notes

1. The hands in illustration 1.2 are decorated with traditional designs dyed temporarily into the skin with a paste called **henna**. Henna is a popular natural cosmetic used throughout the Arab world to highlight hair, create temporary tattoos, color fingernails, and protect the skin. It is made by mixing the dried crushed leaves of the henna bush with water and a bit of lime juice. The resulting paste is a deep, reddish-brown color.

2. On special occasions, especially weddings and religious holidays, Arab women like to decorate each other's hands and feet with intricate henna patterns. These patterns are thought to be attractive and to make a woman's hands look delicate. Some people also think a henna design acts as a good-luck charm for the person who wears it. In many countries henna is associated with purity and with rites of passage such as circumcision and baptism. Young children, both boys and girls, have their hands and feet decorated with henna. It is so popular in some Arab countries that the night before a wedding is called *Laylat al-Hinna*, "the night of the henna." On this night the bride's relatives and friends gather for a party. The most talented artist in the neighborhood decorates the bride's hands and feet with elaborate designs. Since this delicate process may take several hours, the bride's family usually offers special food and drink to the guests. Young women and girls sing and dance around the bride to keep her entertained.

I have feelings

Objectives

1. To develop a vocabulary for emotions

2. To help the students understand what causes various emotions

3. To help the students interpret the emotions of others

Materials

1. Magazine or book illustrations

2. *Nadia the Willful*, by Sue Alexander

3. Blackboard or chart paper and marker

4. Paper plates

5. Popsicle sticks or tongue depressors

6. Tape or glue

7. Crayons

Procedures

1. Pick out some magazine photos or book illustrations showing various emotions. Include pictures from the Arab world and other cultural areas outside the United States. Whenever possible, include examples from the ethnic groups represented in the class.

2. Read *Nadia the Willful*, by Sue Alexander. Explain to students who the Bedouin are and how they live (see **Cultural notes**).

3. Discuss the emotions in the story. What led Nadia to feel the way she did? Ask the students what they think emotions are and where they come from.

4. Have the students name as many emotions as they can, and list these on the blackboard or chart paper. Ask the students to describe what

might give rise to each emotion. If the students need help, prompt them with phrases such as:

> I feel happy when...
>
> I feel angry when...
>
> I hide my feelings when...

5. Hold up each magazine or book illustration and have the students name the person's emotion. Add any new emotions to the list.

6. Pass out paper plates. Without telling the emotion, each student should draw a face displaying one of the emotions on the list. Glue or tape a stick on the back of each plate to make a puppet.

7. Have each student hold up their puppet and have the class guess which emotion is displayed.

Cultural notes

1. The Bedouin are desert nomads who tend herds of goats, sheep, and camels. Today, very few Arabs are nomads (perhaps only 1%), but many people throughout the Middle East are proud to claim descent from Bedouin tribes. Many of the values Arabs hold dear, such as honor, hospitality, courage, and family loyalty, are thought to be expressed in their purest form among the Bedouin. This image is somewhat romantic, as are many depictions of the Bedouin. In the modern era, Bedouin are not the camel-mounted, tribal warriors of old; instead, they are stock breeders, dairy farmers, and agro-business professionals. They are heavily invested in goats and sheep, not camels, and they produce wool, goat hair, and dairy products for sale on urban and international markets.

   Some Bedouin still live in tents, but most also own houses where they stay for several months during the year. In fact, it is common for Bedouin families to reside in a tent and a house at the same time, with members commuting back and forth by truck. *Nadia the Willful* takes place at some unspecified time in the past. It is an imaginary tale based on a real society. Be sure, however, to help your students understand that few Arabs ever lived this way — most have lived in villages, towns, and cities — and the total number of nomads in the Middle East is smaller today than it has ever been.

We are different; we are alike

Objectives

1. To help the student appreciate how all humans are both different and alike

2. To make a simple hat worn by children in Yemen

Materials

1. *Hats, Hats, Hats,* by Ann Morris

2. Blackboard or chart paper and marker

3. Felt or construction paper (11-1/2 x 14), crayons or magic markers for coloring, stapler

Procedures

1. Read *Hats, Hats, Hats.*

2. Ask the students what kinds of hats they wear, and list the different types on the blackboard or chart paper. Now list the various hats worn in Middle East (refer to illustration 1.3 and **Cultural notes**). Ask the students why they think people wear hats like these. Ask them which of the hats they would most like to wear.

3. People all over the world wear hats, but the hats are different in various times and places. Discuss other ways in which people are similar and yet different around the world and throughout history. Do all humans have names? Are names the same everywhere? Do all people speak languages? Do people speak the same language everywhere? Do all humans have eyes and hair? Are eyes and hair the same color everywhere? And so on.

4. Read the instructions for making a *gubba* that follow. Pass out a piece of construction paper or felt to each student. Help the students fold their material in half with the decorated side facing out (see illustration 1.4). Staple the two folds together at the top, sealing the "seam" tightly.

5. Have the students decorate their material with crayons or markers, using stripes and zigzags similar to those in illustration 1.4.

6. Ask the students to put on their hats and imagine the reasons people might wear *gubba*-s if they lived in a sunny place. If the hat were real and made of heavy cloth, would it protect children from the sun? If it were cold, would the hat keep children's ears warm? Ask the students if they ever wear hats to protect them from the sun or the cold.

illustration 1.3

A.

B.

C.

D.

E.

F.

G.

H.

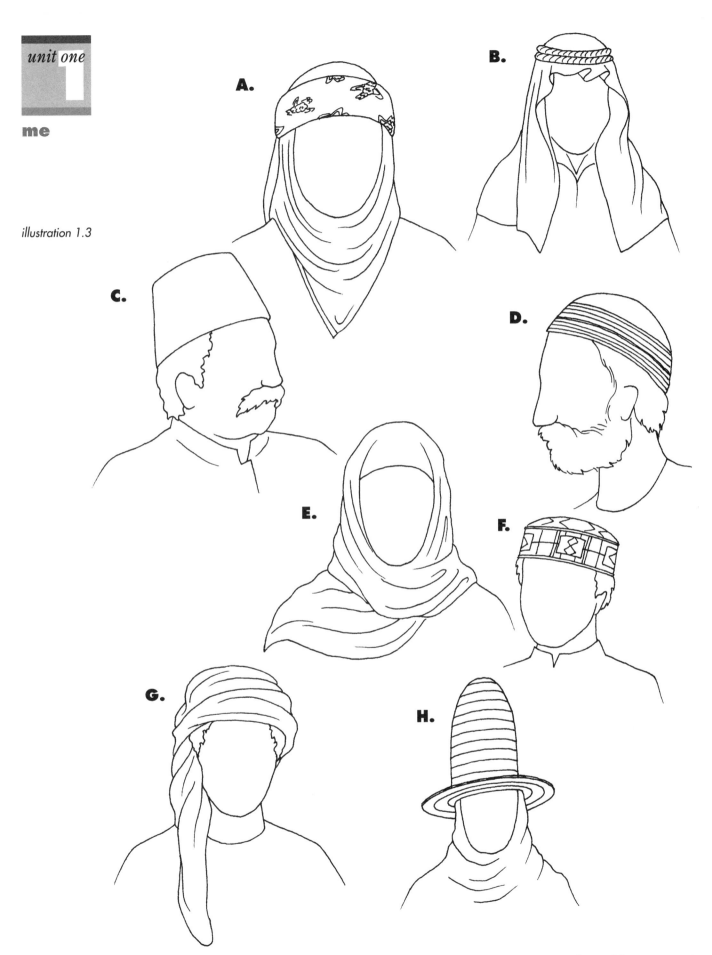

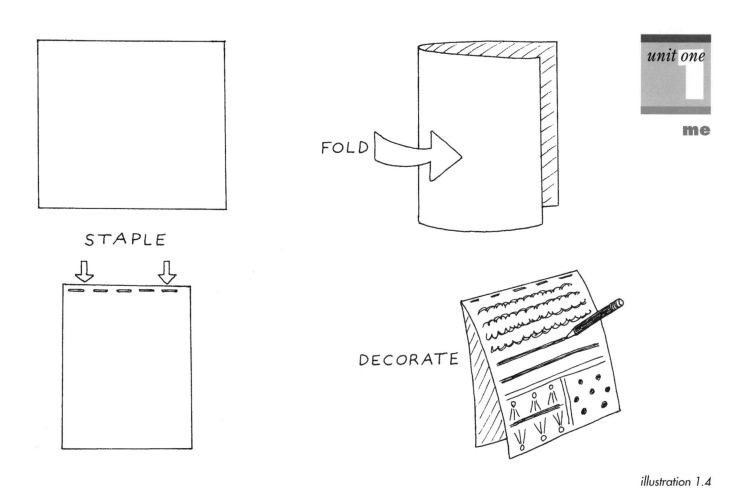

STAPLE

FOLD

DECORATE

illustration 1.4

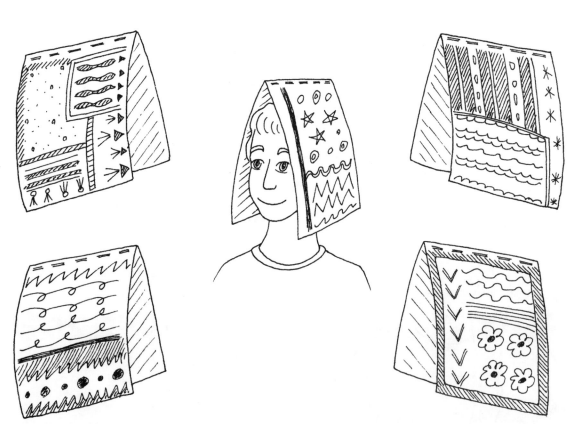

Cultural notes

1. *Gubba*-s are worn by children in villages and towns throughout Yemen and Saudi Arabia. In the winter, both boys and girls wear them to keep their ears and heads warm. In the summer, they help protect their wearers from the sun. They are usually made of recycled cloth and are carefully embroidered to make them bright and attractive. As children age, boys begin to wear different types of hats, but girls in rural areas will wear the gubba until they reach puberty.

2. A variety of head coverings are worn in the Middle East. In the summer months, most of the Arab world is very hot and receives little rain or cloud cover. People need to cover their heads, especially when working or travelling outdoors, in order to protect themselves from the sun. In winter, much of the Arab world is cold, and people cover their heads to keep warm, just as we do when we go outside in bad weather. But climate is not the only reason people cover their heads. Hats can also be used to make a social or religious statement. In the Arab world, it was once common for both men and women to cover their hair in public. This meant that you were a modest, respectable person. As customs and fashions have changed, the types of head coverings people wear (and the situations which call for hats) have changed as well. Nowadays, many Arabs do not cover their head at all; others wear hats and scarves that are different from those worn by their parents or children. The following list describes the hats displayed in illustration 1.3 above.

   A. The *asaaba* and *sharb* is a two-part head piece worn by rural women in Jordan, Syria, Israel, Iraq, and Saudi Arabia. It used to be common throughout this region, but in recent years it has come to be identified with older women. Young women prefer either not to cover their hair at all, or to wear a less distinctive type of Islamic scarf (see *hijaab* below). The *sharb*, a long piece of black gauzy material, is put on first by wrapping it around the perimeter of the face one and a half times. It is held in place by a thick, brightly decorated *asaaba*, a separate piece of woolen fabric which is wrapped around the forehead like a head band and tied firmly in back.

   B. The *kuffeeya* is one of the oldest kinds of head covering found in the Middle East. It consists of a single piece of white or checkered cloth, and it is very simple to wear. You just drape the *kuffeeya* over your head or wrap it loosely around your neck. It is worn by men and boys, and it can be tied in hundreds of different ways. Often, you can tell what country or region a man comes from by looking at the way he wears his *kuffeeya*, or its color and texture. Sometimes the *kuffeeya* is held in place by thick braids of wool that are placed like a ring over the cloth. These braids are called *agaal*. The *kuffeeya* protects the head from the sun and wind. When pulled across the face, it becomes a muffler.

Cultural notes *continued*

C. The *fez* (or *tarboosh*) is a cone-shaped hat, worn by men, that was once popular all over the Middle East. It was especially common in areas ruled by the Ottoman Empire, and today many people describe the *fez* as a Turkish fashion. It was usually red in color. Men who lived in cities and belonged to wealthy, educated families were most likely to be seen sporting a *fez*. After the fall of the Ottoman Empire in 1918, this kind of hat went out of style. Today it is worn only by very old men. Ask your students if they know of hats that only older people wear. Have they seen old movies on TV? Do the men and women wear hats that are now out of style? Do their parents and grandparents have old-fashioned hats at home? You might encourage students to bring these hats to school and show them to the class.

D. The *hajj* cap is worn by men who have made the pilgrimage to Mecca, the holy city of Islam. It is a sign of religious commitment and piety. Muslims who make the pilgrimage must live the rest of their life in accordance with God's will, and the *hajj* cap identifies them as upright members of the community who deserve respect. This kind of hat is usually worn by older men. Traditionally, people did not visit Mecca until late in life. But any man who has made the pilgrimage, whether he is young or old, is entitled to wear a *hajj* cap. You might ask your students if they know of any special hats that are worn to signify a noble achievement or change in status. For instance: Do boys and girls wear special hats when they graduate from high school? Do they wear special hats when they become Boy Scouts or Girl Scouts, or when they join a baseball team? Do people who join the Army or Navy wear special hats?

E. The *hijaab* is a scarf worn by women. Like the *kuffeeya*, it is a simple piece of square cloth that can be draped or tied in a variety of ways. Some *hijaabs* are made of expensive silk and adorned with elegant and colorful patterns; others are made of plain, white cotton. How a woman wraps, ties, or fastens the *hijaab* around her head can indicate which country, religious group, generation, or class she is from, just as does the rest of her clothing. The *hijaab* is called by many different names, depending on whether it is made of a light or heavy fabric. Americans tend to associate this scarf with Muslim women. It is true that Muslim women who cover their hair (especially young women) usually wear a *hijaab*, but older Christian women in rural areas sometimes wear them as well. Many women wear them in winter to keep warm or at funerals, worship services, and other traditional observances to symbolize their respect and modesty.

F. The *kufiya khazayraan* is a men's cap popular in Yemen. It is sometimes decorated with embroidered designs. It is especially popular with young boys, who keep their hair shaved close to the scalp so the cap fits snugly.

Cultural notes *continued*

G. Regional variant of B. Worn in Yemen and Oman, this kind of *kuffeeya* is elaborately folded, but seldom are braids (*agaal*) used to hold it in place.

H. This domed hat, woven of straw, is indigenous to the Tihaama, on the Red Sea coast of Yemen. Both men and women wear them when working in the hot sun to shade their faces and protect their heads from the heat. The woman shown here is also wearing a scarf to cover her hair. Are there other parts of the world where people wear straw hats to keep the sun off their faces? Can your students think of American hats that have bills or brims? For example: baseball caps, cowboy hats, the wide-brimmed hats women sometimes wear to church. Point out the similarity between the Tihaama hat and a fireman's helmet. Both are made for doing hard work in intense heat. How are they alike? How are they different?

I have a language

Objectives

1. To develop the students' awareness of foreign languages and sounds

2. To practice spelling and writing skills using common phrases and words

3. To learn a few Arabic greetings and expressions

Materials

1. Chalkboard or chart paper and marker

2. **List of Common Greetings**, attached

3. Pencils and writing paper

4. Optional, numbers in Arabic

Procedures

1. Before class, write the greetings from the **List of Common Greetings** on the chalkboard or chart paper. Practice pronouncing the Arabic translations.

2. When students arrive, read the English greetings aloud to the class and have the students repeat the greetings with you. Have the students spell out the words and practice writing them.

3. Discuss each greeting. Ask students which phrases they use every day, and which ones they use less often. Explain that all of these greetings are used by Arabs daily (see **Cultural notes**).

4. Once the students have practiced writing the greetings in English, teach them the Arabic translation for each greeting. Have them repeat the Arabic expressions several times, until each comes naturally.

5. Role-play an exchange of greetings with one or two students who are especially good at pronouncing the Arabic.

6. Ask the students if their parents speak a language other than English. Have they ever heard a friend or neighbor speaking another language? Have they ever seen a foreign language on television or heard one on the radio? How do they feel when they hear another language and cannot understand? Explain that in classrooms across the Arab world, students are learning to speak and write English greetings just as they are now learning Arabic ones.

7. If desired, have the students use the Arabic phrases in place of the English ones for the rest of the day. Instead of saying "thank you" and "good-bye," for example, the students should say "shukraan" and "ma salaama."

8. Ask the students if they enjoy knowing words and phrases from another language. If they want to remember the Arabic expressions, keep these on the chalkboard for the next few days or weeks. Have the students practice the phrases every morning or afternoon.

List of Common Greetings and Expressions

English	Arabic
Hello	**Mar**-*ha-ba*
Hello (response)	*Mar-hab*-**tayn** (literally, "two hellos")
Good morning	*Sa*-**baah** *al*-**khayr**
Good morning (response)	*Sa*-**baah** *an*-**nuur**
Good afternoon/evening	*Mi*-**saa** *al*-**khayr**
Good afternoon/evening (response)	*Mi*-**saa** *an*-**nuur**
How are you?	*Kayf* **haal**-*ak?*
Fine, praise be to God.	*Ti*-**maam**, *al*-**ham**-*du-li*-**laa**.
Thank you	*Shuk*-**ran**
You're welcome	**Af**-*wan*
Good-bye	*Ma sa*-**laa**-*ma*
See you soon (response)	**Il**-*la li*-**kaa**
My name is…	**Iss**-*mee*…
What is your name?	*Shu* **iss**-*mak?*
Yes	**Ay**-*wa*
No	*La*
Peace be upon you! *(The preferred greeting; more polite than "hello.")*	*Sa*-**laam** *a*-**lay**-*kum*!
And upon you be peace! (response)	*Wa a*-**lay**-*kum sa*-**laam**!
Welcome!	**Ah**-*lan wa* **sah**-*lan*!
Welcome! (response)	**Ah**-*layn*! (literally, "two welcomes.")

9. If desired, the students can learn to count to ten in Arabic. Read the Arabic pronunciation for each number and have the whole class repeat it out loud.

one =	**waa**-hid	six =	**sit**-ta
two =	ith-**nayn**	seven =	**saab**-a
three =	tha-**laa**-tha	eight =	tha-**maan**-ya
four =	**ar**-ba'a	nine =	**tis**-a
five =	**kham**-sa	ten =	**a**-sha-ra

With practice, the students will be able to count all the way from one to ten in Arabic.

Cultural notes

1. The Prophet Muhammad advised his followers to answer every greeting with a reply equal to (or greater than) the greeting received. So the traditional Islamic greeting, "Peace be upon you," is answered by, "And upon you be peace." The reply is equal to the greeting. You can also give a reply *greater* than the greeting: "And upon you be peace and the mercy of God and His blessings!" This would be a mouthful for your students, but the same principle can be seen in several of the greeting-pairs displayed above. The response to "hello" is "two hellos." The response to "welcome" is "two welcomes." Doubling the response is a traditional sign of friendliness and goodwill toward guests.

2. In some Arabic greetings, the first phrase is uttered by the person approaching. When entering a house, for example, it is the guest who says "Peace be upon you" and the host who says "Upon you be peace." Likewise, it is the person leaving who says "Good-bye" and the person staying behind who says "See you soon." The other greeting-pairs are used with more flexibility.

unit two

2

family

family family

family

I live in a family

Objectives _____

1. To identify the members of Arab and American families

2. To have the students recognize their own roles as family members

3. To learn the names for family members in Arabic

Materials _____

1. *Nadia the Willful*, by Sue Alexander, or *Sitti's Secrets*, by Naomi Nye

2. For background information: *An Arab Family*, by Roderic Dutton

3. Illustrations of tent (2.1) and house (2.2)

4. Drawing paper

5. Crayons

6. Scissors

7. Paste

8. Blackboard or chart paper and marker

Procedures _____

1. Read *Nadia the Willful* or *Sitti's Secrets*. Identify the members of the family in the story. Have the students describe the characters and their relationships. Discuss the sadness of the family at a time of loss (in the case of *Nadia the Willful*) or long separation (in the case of *Sitti's Secrets*).

2. Have the students draw and label the members of the family in the story. If desired, they may also draw a tent or house for the family and paste the family members inside, or paste them inside the attached illustrations.

illustration 2.1

illustration 2.2

Procedures *continued*

3. Have the students draw and label the members of their own families. If desired, they may also draw a house for the family and paste family members inside, or paste the family members inside the house illustrations provided.

4. Make a list of descriptive words for the members of a family. Discuss the variation in names for each member: "grandmother," for example, may be addressed by various names in different families.

5. The teacher and the students may enjoy learning the Arabic names for various family members. On the blackboard or chart paper, list the Arabic words for father, mother, brother, sister, etc. (see **Arabic kinship terms** below).

6. Have the students label their drawings with the appropriate Arabic names.

Arabic kinship terms

The Arabic word for father is *abu*, and for mother is *umm*.

The Arabic word for brother is *akh*, and for sister is *ukht*.

The Arabic word for grandfather is *jiddi* or *seedi*, and for grandmother is *jiddti* or *sitti*.

The Arabic word for son is *ibn*, and for daughter is *bint*.

The words for uncle, aunt, and cousin are different for father's side and mother's side of the family. As seen in the table below, these words follow a clear pattern:

	father's side	mother's side
uncle	'amm	khaal
aunt	'amma	khaala
male cousin	ibn 'amm or ibn 'amma	ibn khaal or ibn khaala
female cousin	bint 'amm or bint 'amma	bint khaal or bint khaala

Cultural notes

1. The Bedouin are desert nomads who tend herds of goats, sheep, and camels. Today, very few Arabs are nomads (perhaps only one percent), but many people throughout the Middle East are proud to claim descent from Bedouin tribes. Many of the values Arabs hold dear, such as honor, hospitality, courage, and family loyalty, are thought to be expressed in their purest form among the Bedouin. This image is somewhat romantic. In the modern era, Bedouin are not the camel-mounted, tribal warriors of old; instead, they are stock breeders, dairy farmers, and agro-business professionals. They are heavily invested in goats and sheep, not camels, and they produce wool, goat hair, and dairy products for sale on urban and international markets. Some Bedouin still live in tents, but most also own houses where they stay for several months during the year. In fact, it is common for Bedouin families to reside in a tent and a house at the same time, with members commuting back and forth by truck.

   The tent Nadia and her family live in is called a "house of hair" (*bayt sha`r*) because it is made of hand-woven panels of goat hair. Tents just like it still dot the rural landscapes of Jordan, Syria, Iraq, much of North Africa and the Arabian Peninsula. The "house of hair" is well-adapted to a mobile life. Almost everything in it can be folded, collapsed, wrapped up, or easily moved around. There is no bulky furniture, only mats, blankets, and cushions. These can be spread for guests and family members to sit or sleep on, then quickly stacked away. The rooms, too, are flexible: the same space can serve as a workshop, a bedroom, or a reception area for visitors at different times during the day. When guests arrive, they enter one or the other of the tent's two sections, depending on their sex and age. The *shig* is for adult men and older boys. The *hareem* is where women, girls, and young children sit. If the guests are relatives, or very close friends, the entire family will visit together in the *shig*.

   The men's side of the tent is associated with hospitality, and many of the items found there are used in entertaining guests: coffee grinders and roasters, teapots, cups, and the best mats and cushions. Nowadays, a large thermos of coffee is kept ready in the *shig*, lest visitors drop by. The women's side of the tent is the site of food preparation and other domestic chores. In it, you might find a portable millstone, a large metal sheet on which unleavened bread is made, and a loom for weaving rugs.

   Making a traditional "house of hair" takes time and skill, and the younger generation of Bedouin women have neither the patience nor the ability to spend long hours weaving tent panels. Hair tents are gradually being replaced by canvas ones, but the look and arrangement of the new tents is very much like the old. The Bedouin are adaptable people, and their material culture is constantly changing. *Nadia the Willful* takes place at some unspecified time in the past. It is an imaginary tale based on a real society. Be sure to help your students understand that few Arabs ever lived this way — most have lived in villages, towns, and cities — and that the total number of nomads in the Middle East is smaller today than it has ever been.

Cultural notes *continued*

2. The family portrayed in *Sitti's Secrets* is of peasant origin. In contrast to Bedouin, peasants are sedentary farmers who live in rural villages. Village ties are very important to Arab immigrants. Many Arab Americans, like Mona and her father, keep in touch with their family in the "old country." Some families send their sons or daughters back to their native village to find a spouse. Others organize village clubs here in America to preserve a sense of community they hope never to forget. The power of village ties is hard for Americans, living in a highly mobile society, to understand. The village portrayed in *Sitti's Secrets* is over a thousand years old, and the families found in it today have lived there for several generations. They are all related and intermarried.

Arab villages are diverse in appearance. In Yemen, they might consist of stone houses four stories tall, perched atop craggy mountain peaks. In Jordan, a village might be a jumble of cement houses, all of roughly the same shape and color, hedged around by olive groves and wheat fields. In Libya, it might be an oasis in the desert, where mudbrick homes lie almost invisible beneath a brilliant green canopy of date palms. What all these villages have in common is agriculture and a reliable source of water. All over the Arab world, being a villager means being a farmer. Those few villagers, such as teachers, government officials, and merchants, who are not directly involved in agriculture, spend most of their time socializing, doing business with, or providing services to local farmers. Metropolitan centers like Baghdad, Cairo, and Beirut could not exist without the fresh crops and dairy products brought to their markets daily from hundreds of villages in the hinterland.

Mona's grandmother lives in a village on the West Bank, in the Israeli Occupied Territories of Palestine, and the presence of agriculture in Sitti's life is very strong. Mona's account is laced with references to fruits, herbs, and vegetables; fields, orchards, and grazing lands. These are resources that hold a peasant family together. Mona is not a peasant herself, nor does she live in an Arab village; still, the ties that bind Mona to her Palestinian kin are strengthened by a shared relationship to the land.

Happy times, sad times

Objectives

1. To explore how families meet their needs, express emotions, and cope with problems

2. To learn about Lebanon as an example of a Middle Eastern society

3. To practice story-telling

Materials

1. *Sami and the Time of the Troubles,* by Florence Parry Heide and Judith Heide Gilliland

2. World map

3. Blackboard or chart paper and marker

4. Optional: *Just Like Daddy,* by Frank Asch

Procedures

1. Read *Sami and the Time of the Troubles.* Discuss the book's illustrations of clothing, transportation, and ways of life.

2. Locate Lebanon on the world map. Ask the students to describe the differences and similarities between Sami's world and their own. Their observations may be recorded on the blackboard or chart.

3. Discuss the troubles in Sami's family, emphasizing that there are happy and sad times in all families.

4. On the blackboard or chart paper, list some of the activities shared by members of a family. Examples might be eating dinner, celebrating a holiday, or going on a trip.

5. Instruct the students to write or tell a story about the happy or sad times in their own families. If they are having difficulty, the teacher may want to use prompts:

   I remember when my father...

   I helped my mother...

   My mother got angry when I...

   My favorite thing to do with my brother/sister is...

   I know my mother/father love me when...

   My mother's hugs make me feel...

6. With first graders, read *Just Like Daddy.* They may enjoy making up their own version of the story.

7. Discuss the similarities and differences between the students' stories and Sami's.

Cultural notes

1. Sami lives in Beirut, the capital of Lebanon. During the 1970s and 1980s, Beirut was torn by civil war. Violence and danger have changed Sami's life in countless ways. They have also changed the city in which he lives. Before the "time of troubles," Beirut was a wealthy, robust, and cosmopolitan place. Its inhabitants cultivated an urban life-style that was very different from that led by peasants and nomads. All the conveniences of the city were close by: modern hospitals, excellent universities, government offices, glitzy shops, and open-air markets stocked with the finest goods. Sami has never experienced this Beirut; he knows about it only from the stories his mother and uncle tell him.

    A healthier view of urban life in the Arab world can be glimpsed in *The Day of Ahmed's Secret*, a book you have already read to your students (see Unit 1, **I have senses**). Ahmad lives in Cairo, and the sights he sees as he completes his daily rounds show the vibrant character of Middle Eastern cities during times of peace. Most of Ahmad's time is spent in the hustle and bustle of market places. All cities in the Arab world have at least two sorts of public spaces: markets, called *suuq*s, and mosques, which are houses of prayer and worship used by Muslims. For more information on the *suuq*, refer to Unit 3, **Roads to a market, Cultural notes**. For more general information on urban landscapes, see Unit 3, **Homes in a neighborhood, Cultural notes**.

Alphabetical families

Objectives

1. To practice alphabetizing
2. To explore some differences between Arab and American families
3. To practice drawing

Materials

1. Index cards or paper cut to 3" x 5"
2. Blackboard or chart paper and marker
3. Construction paper
4. Paste
5. Crayons

Procedures

1. Pass out five index cards to each student. On each card, have the students write the name of a family member. They should start with family members who live at home, but those students with small households may include the names of distant relatives or friends.

2. Divide the class into small groups. Each group should cooperate to place the cards in alphabetical order.

3. Check the cards to make sure they are alphabetized correctly, and have the students number them 1-5.

4. Now ask students to compare their own families with the family of a little girl in Yemen. Read the following story about Layla's family and show students illustration 2.3.

5. Now have the class alphabetize the names of Layla's family members. On the blackboard or chart paper, write the names in the order they are mentioned in the story. Then ask the students which name would come first in alphabetical order, which would come second, and so on. The two lists should be:

Layla	Abu Musa
Musa	Ahmed
Hoda	Hala
Hala	Hoda
Zaynab	Layla
Miriam	Miriam
Ahmed	Musa
Yusif	Um Musa
Abu Musa	Yusif
Um Musa	Zaynab

6. Ask the students about the similarities and differences between Layla's family and their own. Altogether, there are ten people living in Layla's house. Ask the students if any of them have ten or more people living in their own house.

illustration 2.3

Layla's family

My name is **Layla**. I am nine years old. I'm from the country of Yemen. I have been in the United States for only three days. I came here with my father, **Musa**. My mother is back home in Yemen. Her name is **Hoda**. I have three sisters and two brothers. My sisters are called **Hala**, **Zaynab** and **Miriam**. My older brother is named **Ahmed**, and my younger brother is named **Yusif**. My grandfather and grandmother also live in our house. I call my grandfather **Abu Musa** [father of Musa] and my grandmother **Um Musa** [mother of Musa]. Last year, my oldest sister got married in our village. I didn't have enough money to buy a wedding present, so my father bought a dress for me to give to my sister. All my relatives came to the wedding. I have many uncles, aunts, and especially cousins. After the wedding, my cousins and I played outside while the grown-ups danced and sang. It was a very happy day for my whole family.

Procedures *continued*

Then ask how many have nine, eight, seven, and so on. Keep count of the number of students with households of each size, and calculate the average size.

7. Explain that Arabs usually have larger households than Americans, although this is changing (see **Cultural notes**).

8. Hand out construction paper. Have the students fold the paper into fifths to make accordion-style books. The students may now paste the card for each member of their families in their books, keeping the names in alphabetical order. Below each name, the students may draw a picture of the family member. If desired, they can also draw (or cut out) the members of Layla's family (see illustration 2.3) and make a separate notebook for them.

Cultural notes

1. In Arab societies, the family is the most important social institution, and one depends on the aid and support of relatives throughout life. The characters in the books and stories you are reading in class would probably agree with the following statement: the more kin we have, the more confidently we can face the challenges of life, and kin are not of much value to us unless we keep them close, both emotionally and spatially. This world-view helps explain why Arab families tend to be much larger, and much more cohesive, than American ones.

    Most Americans are close to members of their immediate family: to their parents, siblings, and children. Sometimes we see our grandparents, our aunts and uncles, and our cousins during vacations and holiday seasons. When American children reach adulthood, they tend to leave their family, find work, and live on their own. Our parents, by and large, are left to fend for themselves in old age, or we place them in retirement homes. In the Arab world, it is uncommon for relatives to spend so much of their lives apart from each other. Often, cousins and siblings live together in the same neighborhood, and grandparents live with their children. When a son grows up, he tries to remain close to his father's household, even after he marries and has a family of his own. Daughters marry and become members of other families, but they maintain close ties with their father's household.

    It is also common in the Arab world for relatives to cooperate economically and socially. In rural areas, this might entail sharing a tractor or truck among several related families. In cities, it might mean a large group of relatives who work in the same line of business and agree to buy and sell among themselves at a special rate in order to improve their purchasing power and their ability to compete with other families. As in America, extended families will also pull together to celebrate weddings and holidays, or to help each other through difficult times. In these cases, Arab and American households look very similar, the only difference being that the size of the kin networks involved tends to be much larger among Arabs.

Family interviews

Note: This project is best for third graders.

Objectives

1. To collect information about a family member in an interview

2. To learn how to represent information in a bar graph

3. To explore cultural variation by discussing the differences between Arab and American families

Materials

1. Attached interview sheet

2. Yusif's interview (see attached)

3. Index cards or paper cut to 3" x 5"

4. Blackboard or chart paper and markers

Procedures

1. Hand out copies of the **interview sheet**. Have the students pick a family member to interview.

2. Read **Yusif's interview** of his mother (see below). This will help the students prepare for their own interview.

3. For each question on the interview sheet, the students should take one index card and write the number of the question in the upper right hand corner.

4. During the interview, the students should record the answer to each question on the appropriate index card.

5. When the cards have been filled out, demonstrate how to make a bar graph from one of the items in the interview. Favorite foods, for example, may be listed along the bottom of the graph. Draw a bar representing the number of responses for each type of food.

To compare Arab and American families, ask the students how many of their subjects said that *mansaf* (see **Cultural notes**) was their favorite food.

6. The students may now draw their own bar graphs. Collect the index cards and sort them by number, so that all the answers to each question are in one stack. Divide the class into small groups and provide one stack of cards to each group.

7. The group members should cooperate to compile the information and draw the graph for their item of the interview. Results may be summarized in class presentations.

8. Discuss the trends revealed in the interviews, and compare these trends with what was found in Yusif's family. Favorite foods, for example, in Yusif's home are likely to be very different from those in American households

Procedures *continued*

(unless, of course, the households in question are made up of Arab Americans!). Other common Jordanian responses to the interview questions Yusif asked his mother are discussed in **Cultural notes**. Discuss these different responses with the class.

9. If desired, make up responses to five imaginary interviews with Jordanians. Use information in the **Cultural notes** (and in previous lessons) for possible answers. Next, have students compile the results of these imaginary interviews and, repeating the techniques they learned earlier, create a bar graph summarizing the data.

Interview questions

Name:

This is my [mother, father, etc.]:

Age: Birthday:

Place of birth:

Where did you grow up?

How many brothers do you have?

How many sisters do you have?

What is your favorite food?

How and when is this food eaten?

What do you like to do best?

What was your favorite thing to do when you were my age?

Yusif's interview

Yusif lives in a town in Jordan. He is in third grade. His teacher asked the students to interview their family members. So Yusif went to his mother and asked her some questions. Here is what he asked, and what his mother answered:

Yusif: What is your name?

Mother: Yusif, you already know my name.

Yusif: I know, *umma*, but you have to say it for the interview.

Mother: Okay, okay. My name is Selwa.

Yusif: How old are you?

Mother: I am thirty-eight years old.

Yusif: Where were you born?

Mother: Yusif! You know perfectly well I was born right here in this town.

Yusif: Yes, *umma*, but just say it.

Mother: Oh, all right. I was born in Jordan, in the town of Zarga.

Yusif: How many brothers do you have?

Mother: I have five brothers. May God protect them.

Yusif: And how many sisters do you have?

Mother: Three living and one passed away. God rest her soul.

Yusif's interview *continued*

Yusif: What is your favorite food?

Mother: My favorite food is *mansaf*.

Yusif: Can you explain what *mansaf* is?

Mother: We just had *mansaf* for dinner tonight.

Yusif: I know, mother, but what if American children read this interview?

Mother: Don't they eat *mansaf* in America?

Yusif: Usually not. Except in Arab American homes.

Mother: How do you know so much about America?

Yusif: We learned it in school. Now please just explain about *mansaf*.

Mother: *Mansaf* is our national dish. It is made by boiling lamb in a thin yogurt sauce. When the meat is cooked, it's layered on top of a mountain of flat bread and rice. The yogurt is then poured over the meat and rice. Almonds, pinenuts and parsley are sprinkled on top.

Yusif: How do we eat *mansaf*?

Mother: We eat it with our right hands and tear off the best pieces of meat and almonds to place in front of special guests.

Yusif: And when do we eat *mansaf*?

Mother: Usually on special occasions.

Yusif: What was the special occasion today?

Mother: Today was the day you interviewed your mother!

Cultural notes

1. Some Arab responses to the interview questions will be very different from American responses. In Jordan, for example, "What is your favorite food?" is likely to elicit responses such as *mansaf, makloobi*, stuffed grape leaves, *filaafil*, and *tabooli. Mansaf* is described in Yusif's interview above. Here are brief descriptions of the other dishes:

Makloobi is the feast dish of Palestinians everywhere. It means "upside-down." *Makloobi* is made by filling a deep pot with layers of meat (usually lamb), followed by vegetables such as carrots, eggplant, and cauliflower, and finally rice seasoned with special spices. When the rice and meat are cooked and all the water is absorbed, the pot is upended and the stew is served on a large round tray with the meat on top.

Stuffed grape leaves, or *warag aynab*, is a dish common in many Arab countries. It is prepared by rolling a mixture of ground meat, spices, and rice in fresh tender grape leaves. The stuffed leaves are then simmered over low heat until the rice is fully cooked. Served with lemon juice, they are a favorite at parties.

Filaafil is a favorite snack or sandwich food. It is made by grinding chick peas with parsley and spices and shaping the mixtures into small rounds that are deep fried.

Cultural notes *continued*

Filaafil can be served with *tahiina* (sesame paste) for dipping, or it can be crushed open and rolled into pita bread with tomato, onion, and *tahiina*. Some people call *filaafil* the hamburger of the Middle East.

Tabooli is the preferred salad of the Lebanese. Made of a delicious blend of finely ground parsley, cracked wheat, tomato, and onions, and seasoned with olive oil and lemon, it is light and satisfying. Another popular salad is *fattoosh*, which looks more like a Western salad made of lettuce, tomatoes, and onions. In Lebanon, *fattoosh* is seasoned with olive oil, lemon, and sumac, and served with a bit of fried or dried pita bread to give it that special Middle Eastern taste.

2. Arab responses to other interview questions might not be too different from American responses. Common responses from Arab youngsters to the question "What do you like to do best?" might include:

watch television	take field trips (especially nature hikes)
play soccer	eat ice cream
play house (imitate mother's and father's activities)	

3. "How many brothers and sisters do you have?" Parents from the Arab world will tend to have more siblings than American parents. In Jordan, for instance, the average woman has 7.4 live births in her lifetime, and Jordan's birth rate is by no means the highest in the Middle East. In America, by contrast, a family with only four or five children is considered large. As Middle Eastern economies modernize, household size is beginning to shrink; nonetheless, the ideal of two children per family, which is embraced by many governments in the region, is still a distant goal.

4. "What was your favorite thing to do when you were my age?" American students and their parents will probably not differ radically in their responses to this question. In the Middle East, however, the similarities would be accompanied by some striking differences. Arabs near forty years of age — Yusif's mother Selwa, for instance — grew up in a society very different from the one we know today: in general, it was more agricultural, less urbanized, and had fewer of the conveniences of modern life. Yusif's mother and father might consider the following activities their childhood favorites:

embroidering dresses and pillows	riding horses
weaving rugs	listening to grandparents tell stories
visiting neighbors for tea	going to weddings
keeping a garden	playing siija, a game of skill which
taking care of farm animals	is played in the sand using small stones as pieces

Families are similar, families are different

Objectives

1. To identify some basic patterns of family life

2. To compare and contrast urban and rural families with a Venn diagram

3. To strengthen organizing and categorizing skills

4. To practice drawing

Materials

1. Chart paper and markers

2. Drawing paper and crayons

Procedures

1. Read the attached stories by Arab children and show students illustrations 2.4 – 2.7.

2. Make a chart with the following headings:

   Chores   **Play**

   Number of siblings **Kind of house**

   Mother's work   **Father's work**

3. In each category, list examples from the stories.

4. Draw a Venn diagram and help the students assign each of the listed examples to the urban families, the rural families, or both the urban families and the rural families.

5. Hand out drawing paper. Have the students fold the paper in half and then in thirds to make six equal-sized blocks. After labeling the blocks with the headings listed above, the students may fill each category with examples from one of the stories below. Have the students provide an illustration for each category: e.g., a picture of Naadir's mother working in the coffee shop.

6. If desired, ask students to draw a Venn diagram comparing their own family to any one of the families described in the stories below. The categories would be, for example, "my family," "Sameera's family," and "my family and Sameera's family."

illustration 2.4

Donkey trouble

My name is Aadil. I live in a farm town in Yemen. Yemen is a small country compared to America, but we are very proud of our country. Yemen has beautiful deserts and farms, and a long coastline where big ships come and go. My father works on an oil tanker. Sometimes he is gone for a long time, traveling to Saudi Arabia and other countries. When he comes home, I am very happy. My mother is always home; she takes care of me and my seven brothers and sisters.

My family lives in an old house with two floors. The first floor is for animals. We have cows, donkeys, sheep, and goats. They belong to my uncle. To get to the second floor, you have to go past the animals and up the stairs. In the living room, there are no tables or chairs; we like to sit on mattresses and cushions, which can be easily moved around on the stone floor. On the wall, we have pictures of my father, uncle, and grandfather, but not my mother or aunt or sisters because they are modest and don't want guests to see their pictures. There is also a picture of the President of Yemen and a big sword on the wall. Next to the living room, there is a bathroom, but it doesn't have a shower. There are no pipes for running water in my village. For fresh water, we go to the creek.

Before I go to school, it's my job to get water and bring it back to the house. Early in the morning, about five or six o'clock, my cousin and I put two barrels on the back of a donkey and go down to the creek. The donkey knows the way, because he goes there every morning. My cousin fills the barrels and I take them back to the house. There I dump them into an even bigger barrel and go back to the creek, where my cousin is waiting. We do this three times. The creek is only five minutes from my house if the donkey doesn't get into trouble. Sometimes he goes off the path to chase other donkeys or to eat corn in the fields, and I have to pull him back with a rope. One time I got very tired and tried to ride on the donkey's back, but he kicked me off. When the donkey gets into trouble, fetching water can take a long time.

illustration 2.5

Wash day in Oman

I am called Sameera. My family lives in a big, four-storied house in Oman. We have lots of land where we grow all kinds of fruit, such as peaches, plums, figs, bananas, apples, oranges, and grapes. My father and brother work in the fields. My mother weaves and cooks and takes care of my new sister. My job is to wash the clothes. I have four sisters who help me and my mother. I have five brothers, too. They help my father in the field.

Our family was the first in our village to get a washing machine. Everyone came to see it. That was a few years ago, when I was seven or eight.

Even though we have a washing machine, I sometimes go to the river to wash clothes in a metal tub. The weather is warm in Oman all year long, so there is no problem washing clothes even in winter. Every Friday I go with my uncle's daughters and friends. We talk and talk as we wash the clothes for hours and hours. We talk about everything — about school, and our families, and boys. Everybody says, "Why are you going to the river to wash clothes? You have a washing machine!" But my cousins and I still like to wash the clothes by hand. This is the only way we can get together to talk.

illustration 2.6

Hopscotch and jump rope

My name is Camilia, and I live in Beirut. My family lives in a large apartment building, on the 5th floor. My Baba helped to build our apartment building. He is an engineer. Mama takes care of me and my brother and sister. When I come home from school each day, I rush into the kitchen to see what Mama is cooking for dinner. The house always smells delicious when I come home, and even before we open our apartment door, my sister and I can guess what Mama is cooking by the smell . After we eat dinner, Mama makes us sit down and do our homework at the kitchen table. None of us is allowed to watch TV until we have all finished our homework, so sometimes I help my brother and sister with their assignments so we can finish early. On other days, Mama lets me help her wash dishes and clean up the kitchen while everyone else finishes their homework.

Our favorite thing to do after school is to run down to the street and play games with our friends. We always ask permission to go outside from Baba because he usually says "yes". Mama almost always says "no," even if nightfall is still a long way off. On our street, girls gather to play hopscotch and jump rope. We make up silly rhymes to sing while we jump, like: *"Ice cream, whip cream, milk and berries. Ice cream, whip cream, milk and berries."* For another game, we all stand in a circle with one girl in the middle. We walk around her in one direction, and she closes her eyes and spins in the other direction.

We say to her, *"Selwa, Selwa why are you weeping?"*
She says, *"I weep for a friend with my toys to share."*
We say, *"Choose a friend, but choose with care!"*
She spins around and points her finger saying, *"Ugly – Ugly – Ugly – Fair!"*

The person she is pointing to when she says "fair" steps into the middle and becomes Selwa, and then we play again.

We have to get home each day before dark or Baba gets very mad. Once we come inside, we bathe, put on our pajamas, and go to bed. On the weekend I help Mama with the chores, especially in my room, where I change the sheets on my bed, put away all my clean clothes, and water the plants.

illustration 2.7

Spices and airplanes

My name is Naadir, and I'm from Jordan. I have two brothers and two sisters. I'm in the middle. My family owns a shop in Amman, the capital city. The shop sells coffee, tea, and spices from all over the world. My family lives in an apartment above the shop.

When I was a kid, I studied a lot and got good grades. Of course I helped my mother and father, too, but sometimes they excused me from shopkeeping so that I could keep reading and writing. When I wasn't studying, I liked to play soccer. Sometimes I visited my aunt's house near the airport. I liked to watch the airplanes taking off and landing for hours at a time.

When my father was away on business, my older brother had to be the head of the household. He handled the paperwork and bookkeeping for our family store.

My other brother was a repairman. When there was anything to be fixed in our apartment, he fixed it. When there was nothing to be fixed, he would sometimes break something just to repair it. For example, if the TV screen was a little fuzzy, he would open it up and play around until it was really broken. Then he would fix it again.

My older sister mainly helped my mother around the house. Most of the women in my neighborhood worked at home. If my mother and sister didn't know how to cook a certain dish, they could ask the neighbors. Sometimes all the women in the neighborhood would cook different meals and exchange them. Our neighbors were very close friends, almost like family.

My other sister was good in school, like me. She went to the university and became a doctor. Now she works in a hospital in Amman. If anyone in our neighborhood gets hurt or sick, they go see my sister. Last year, for example, my

Spices and airplanes *continued*

brother tried to fix the refrigerator in our apartment. When he pulled it out from the wall, it tipped over and fell on his foot. Luckily, my sister was visiting. She put ice on his foot to bring the swelling down. Then she put a bandage around his big toe. "There," she said, "Now I've repaired the repairman!" My brother laughed and promised he would be more careful.

Now I'm a writer living in the United States. I like to write stories about my family. When my mother sees one of my stories in a book or magazine, she shows it to all the people in the neighborhood. My family often sends me packages of coffee, tea, and spices from around the world. When I open one of the packages, the wonderful smells remind me of our little shop in Jordan. Sometimes I miss Amman, but I also love my new home in Dearborn, Michigan. And I still like to go to the airport, just to watch the airplanes taking off and landing for hours at a time.

Cultural notes

1. Just like Americans, Arabs live in different ways depending on their region, occupation, ethnicity, education level, religious background, and gender. The stories in this lesson reveal substantial differences between urban and rural life-styles, between male and female activities. These differences are an effective tool for helping students think about diversity in their own culture and others. Ask your students to explain how Naadir's life and Camilia's life are different from the lives of Aadil and Sameera. In what ways are they the same? How are Aadil's chores different from Sameera's chores? You might want to start a discussion about country and city life in America, comparing it to rural and urban contexts in the Arab world. You could also ask the students to describe the chores they do at home. Do brothers and sisters do the same chores, or are they different?

Special gifts

Objectives

1. To learn about family life in Saudi Arabia

2. To learn about wanting, giving, and receiving

3. To practice story-telling and writing

Materials

1. *Amina and Muhammad's Special Visitor*, by Diane Turnage Burgoyne

2. Blackboard or chart paper and marker

3. Writing paper and pencils

Procedures

1. Read *Amina and Muhammad's Special Visitor*.

2. Discuss the baby camel that Hasan wanted more than anything. Ask the students if there is something that they want more than anything.

3. After Hasan found the baby camel, why couldn't he keep it? Ask the students if they have ever found something that they had to return to its rightful owner. Ask if they have ever lost something that they loved, and hoped that someone would find it and give it back.

4. How did Hasan get the camel after all? Why did Hasan's father change his mind? Ask the students if their parents have ever changed their minds in this way. Then ask the students if they have ever given something that they loved to someone else who wanted or needed it even more.

5. On the blackboard or chart paper, write the initials **SWBS** (see attached information about the SWBS chart). Ask the students to fill in the chart for Uncle Hasan's story. The finished chart might look like this:

Somebody: Hasan

Wanted: A camel

But: He didn't have enough money to buy one, and his father would not let him keep the one he had found

So: Hasan's father saw how much Hasan wanted the camel, and bought it for him as a surprise gift

6. Now have the students tell or write their own stories based on the SWBS pattern. First they should describe the "somebody" of the story, then what this somebody wanted, and so on. If desired, students may outline their ideas in an SWBS chart and then "flesh out" the ideas to make a story.

unit two

2

family

Special visitors

Objectives

1. To learn about hospitality and visiting between households

2. To discuss favorite relatives who live far away

3. To practice drawing and writing

Materials

1. *Amina and Muhammad's Special Visitor*, by Diane Turnage Burgoyne

2. *Sitti's Secrets*, by Naomi Shihab Nye

3. Drawing paper and crayons

Procedures

1. Read *Amina and Muhammad's Special Visitor*.

2. Discuss the hospitality of Amina and Muhammad's family. How was Uncle Hasan welcomed by the household? What special preparations did the family make? Ask the students what their own families do when they are having a special visitor.

3. Discuss Uncle Hasan. Why was he special? Ask the students about their own favorite visitors. This might be a relative or a friend who only visits on special occasions.

4. Read *Sitti's Secrets*.

5. Discuss Mona's grandmother (*Sitti*). Why was she special? Ask the students about their own grandparents or other special relatives. How far away do they live? How often do the students go to visit them? Ask the students what they like best about visiting a family member far away.

6. Have the students draw a picture of their favorite relative. If possible, the picture should show why this is the student's favorite. The student should leave room at the bottom to write the person's name.

Cultural notes

1. Arabs take great pride in the virtue of hospitality. In the Middle East, calling a person "generous" (*kariim*) is the highest compliment one can bestow. "The generous person," says an old proverb, "is beloved of God." Calling someone "stingy" (*bakhiil*) is a grave insult, since "the stingy person is despised by God." Arabs enjoy welcoming people into their homes; they do not consider it an inconvenience or a chore, and they treat all guests (invited or unexpected) with the same courtesy. Spiced coffee and tea are offered soon after a visitor arrives. Among families of modest means, expenditures for tea and sugar can eat up over half their annual income, but sweet tea is the *least* one can offer friends and visitors. Invited guests are served meat dishes as a sign of affection. Not serving an invited guest meat would be disgraceful, and even an unexpected guest, who dropped by for a quick visit, will be offered the best foods available in the refrigerator, garden, or pantry. In fact, it is hard just to "drop by" and leave, since the people you are visiting will invite you to share a meal with them, and they will usually insist that you stay. Such generosity is pleasing not only to God; it also enhances the social status of the host and his entire household.

unit three

3

home
neighborhood
community

home neighborhood community

Things in a room

Objectives

1. To describe a favorite room and the objects usually found there

2. To have the students draw their favorite room

3. To compare the rooms of Arab and American homes

Materials

1. *The Napping House*, by Audrey Wood

2. Blackboard or chart paper and marker

3. Drawing paper

4. Crayons

Procedures

1. Read *The Napping House*. Allow the students to examine each illustration.

2. Discuss the bedroom in the story. Ask the students to name all the *living things* in the room [flea, mouse, cat, dog, child, granny]. Then ask how many *objects* in the room they can remember. Make a list on the blackboard or chart paper, including:

bed	cat's bed	mirror
pillow	chair	window
sheets	sneakers	drapes
nightstand	slippers	shade
pitcher	rugs	walls

3. Ask students to name their favorite room in their own house or apartment. Discuss why this is their favorite room, and have them name some objects usually found there.

Procedures *continued*

4. Read **Arwa's favorite room** and **Hamsa's favorite room**, below. Illustrations 3.1 and 3.2 should be reproduced and handed out to the class. Make two lists on the blackboard or chart paper of the things in Arwa's and Hamsa's rooms, including:

Arwa's Room	Hamsa's Room
rug	carpet
pictures of her grandfather	pictures of soccer players and actors
pillows	beds
chairs	bookshelves and books
radio	curtains
cabinet with teapot	nightstand
television	lamp

Discuss the similarities and differences between the two rooms (see **Cultural notes**).

5. Hand out drawing paper, and have the students draw a picture of their favorite room. The picture should include the student's favorite objects usually found in that room.

6. Discuss the similarities and differences between Arwa's and Hamsa's favorite rooms and the rooms drawn by the students.

Arwa's favorite room

My name is Arwa. I'm from Yemen, where I live in a huge house. It has to be big because two families live there: my father's family (including me) and my uncle's family. My uncle has four daughters. They're my cousins, but we act more like sisters.

In our house, the women and girls have a floor all to themselves. And there is one room on that floor that I like more than any other room in the house. It's just a small room, a kind of sitting room. It has no windows because it's surrounded by five bedrooms. Each of my cousins has a bedroom, and I have one too, but my favorite room is the one in the middle where we all get together. We do everything in that room. If I have to study, I could go into my bedroom and sit at my desk, but I'd rather come out and sit with my cousins. They might be studying too, or having a snack, or just talking and laughing.

In the middle of the floor there's an oval rug with a picture of a goose on it. There are chairs, but usually we just sit on pillows around a coffee table. Off to one side is a cabinet with important things in it; things we want to save. They're

---

illustration 3.1

Arwa's favorite room *continued*

mostly old things, like a teapot that belonged to my great aunt, and an antique mirror, and pictures of my grandfather. There are a few things of mine too, like report cards and certificates from school.

Sometimes when I'm sitting in that room all alone, I'll look up at the pictures on the cabinet, and I feel as if my grandfather is watching over me. If I'm reading or studying, he seems proud of me, and it makes me try even harder.

When my friends come to visit, I invite them to the sitting room. I cook something for them and we listen to music or watch TV. The only problem is, my village doesn't have electricity during the day, so we can watch television only at night.

One night my friends and I were watching TV, when my four cousins came home. Instead of staying in their own rooms, each of my cousins stretched out on a pillow and started watching TV with us. Pretty soon the room was very crowded. My youngest cousin had her head on my shoulder. We were all feeling very sleepy.

"Why do we always end up in *this* room?" I asked out loud. My youngest cousin sat up. We all looked at each other. And then we knew the answer: your own room is private, and that's good. But the sitting room is someplace friends and cousins could be together. We had decorated it, and now we shared it. That makes it my favorite room.

illustration 3.2

Hamsa's favorite room

I'm called Hamsa. Now I live in the United States, but I grew up in a big city in Lebanon. The houses there were so close together, we could just lean out the window and talk to our neighbors. For privacy, we had to close the curtains.

My favorite room in our old house was the bedroom I shared with my brother and sister. It had two large beds, with a nightstand and a little red carpet in between. I used to come home from school, slip off my shoes, and sit on that little red carpet. It was very cozy there.

On one side of the room, there were pictures of soccer players. Those were my brother's heroes. On the other side were pictures of actors and singers. Those were my sister's heroes. As for me, I liked to look at books.

One whole wall in our room was lined with books. We had books in three languages: Arabic, French, and English. On the top shelf was the Quran, the holy book of Islam. We also had poetry, history, novels, short stories, and plays. While my brother was practicing soccer and my sister was watching television, I would sit on my little red carpet and read. Sometimes there would be books all over the room, on the bed, on the floor, and my mother would come in and make me put them all back on the shelf. She taught me to dust the bookshelf every few days, and to handle each book with care.

Hamsa's favorite room *continued*

Next to the bookshelf was a huge window with two sets of curtains, one Arab and one Swedish. The Arab curtains were pink with an old-fashioned flower design. When they were closed, the sun could still come through. The Swedish curtains, on the other hand, were thick and heavy. When they were closed, the room got very dark.

At night, even with both sets of curtains closed, we could hear our neighbors talking. Sometimes they would laugh or sing, and it was hard to go to sleep. But usually they made just a little murmur on the breeze. I used to lie there, my sister breathing softly next to me, and listen to our neighbors in the dark.

Then, before I knew it, the curtains would fly open and the morning sun would come streaming into my favorite room.

Cultural notes

1. The contrast between Arwa's and Hamsa's rooms illustrates the great range of cultural variation in the Middle East. Arwa lives in a traditional house in a Yemeni village. Her close relatives (uncles and cousins) live with her in the house, and her neighbors are probably close kin as well. The girls have their own special room, but overall there is little personal or private space in Arwa's house. She and her cousins share things, and they like to be together whenever possible. In Arwa's favorite room, people sit on the floor. They sit close to each other on cushions and pillows. In rural Yemen, chairs and sofas are for decoration. Most people think they are uncomfortable, and they use them only on formal occasions.

    Hamsa grew up in a Lebanese city. Her house is more like American homes. She lives with her immediate family (parents and siblings); no uncles or cousins share the house with them, and their neighbors are probably not related either. For this reason, Hamsa talks more about privacy. Even in her own favorite room, things are divided between her, her sister, and her brother. Compared to Arwa, Hamsa and her siblings have more material possessions they can call exclusively their own. This is a common difference between urban and rural families. Also, the special objects in Arwa's room (pictures of ancestors, an old teapot, an antique mirror) reflect the importance of tradition in her life. Hamsa's room, which is decorated with photos of soccer stars, international celebrities, and books in English, French, and Arabic, reflects the more cosmopolitan life-style common in urban areas.

Rooms in a home

Objectives

1. To compare Arab and American homes

2. To draw a "blueprint" of the main floor in the student's home

3. To reflect on how and why houses are divided into rooms with specific purposes

Materials

1. *Amina and Muhammad's Special Visitor*, by Diane Turnage Burgoyne

2. Overhead projector and transparency, or photocopy/mimeograph machine

3. Graph paper

4. Pencils

5. Ruler or straight edge

Procedures

1. Read *Amina and Muhammad's Special Visitor* to page 29. Allow the students to examine each illustration.

2. Discuss the house in which Amina and Muhammad live. It is described as "a large concrete block house" (p. 1). Ask the students what their own homes are made of.

3. When Amina and Muhammad first arrive home (pp. 5-6), they open a gate, hurry across a courtyard, and find their mother in the *majlis*, or main sitting room. Ask the students how they enter their own homes. Do they open a gate? Do they cross a yard? Is there a porch? A hallway? A lobby? A staircase? An elevator?

4. The ground floor plan of Amina and Muhammad's home (p. 51) should be reproduced in a transparency or handout. Ask the students what they notice about the furniture in each of the three sitting rooms [the seats are lined against the walls, a traditional Arab arrangement].

5. Ask the students about the main room in their own homes. Are there separate rooms for men and women, as in Amina and Muhammad's house? Is there a special room where guests are entertained? What does the main room look like? What does it have in it? Show the class the illustration on pp. 24-25. Ask the students to describe the similarities and differences between the Arab *majlis* and the main room in most American homes.

Procedures *continued*

6. Hand out graph paper and instruct the students to draw a floor plan for the main floor of their own homes. If time allows, the students should make a rough draft in class, then take their drawings home, where they may walk the rooms and check their drawings for accuracy. Ask the students to include furniture and other interior decorations if possible.

7. Final versions of the floor plans, including seating patterns and interior decoration, may be discussed in class presentations.

Cultural notes

1. Wood is not as plentiful in the Middle East as it is in the United States. As a result, many traditional Arab homes are made of adobe, a mixture of mud and straw; or they are made of stone. The concrete block house in which Amina and Muhammad live is a modern solution to an old problem. In fact, the idea of living in a building made of wood might seem strange to Amina and Muhammad. Wood can burn; termites can eat it; and strong winds can blow it away. For people who have lived all their lives in stone and cement houses, wooden homes, which creak in the wind and squeak underneath our feet, appear flimsy and unsafe.

2. Middle Eastern houses are different not only in the materials they are made of, but also in the way rooms are arranged and put to use. The layout of a Bedouin tent was described in an earlier lesson (see Unit 2, **I live in a family**, **Cultural note #2**). Stone and adobe houses are different in their external appearance, but inside they share many features with the tent. Most importantly, they are organized in ways that allow the family to show hospitality to guests while maintaining, if need be, a discrete separation of the sexes. Very often, men and women have separate areas of the house in which they entertain guests of their own gender, and certain parts of the house are not open to unrelated male visitors. In the countryside, people have very little furniture in their houses. Instead, they have mattresses and pillows that can easily be moved around. Because of this flexibility, a single room can be used for many purposes: in the morning it is a breakfast area; in the afternoon it is a workshop; in the early evening it is a parlor for guests; and late at night it becomes a place to sleep. Thus, a house of only four rooms can accommodate activities that, in America, would take nine or ten separately furnished rooms. In America — and in modern, urban homes throughout the Middle East — people often limit rooms to one use only: the TV room is for watching TV; the dining room is for eating meals; the bedroom is for sleeping; the kitchen is for cooking; the study is for doing paperwork. For many Arabs, this way of dividing space seems arbitrary and overly rigid. The activity should define the room, they say; the room should not define the activities that can take place in it.

Homes in a neighborhood

Objectives

1. To discuss the neighborhood of your school

2. To identify the components of a neighborhood

3. To discuss rural and urban Arab neighborhoods

4. To compare Arab and American neighborhoods

Materials

1. Blackboard or chart paper and marker

2. Map of your school's neighborhood (optional)

3. Overhead projector and transparency, or photocopy/mimeograph machine

4. *Amina and Muhammad's Special Visitor*, by Diane Turnage Burgoyne (optional)

Procedures

1. On the blackboard or chart paper, sketch a map of your school's neighborhood. Include as much detail as needed to situate the school in relation to other landmarks, such as parks, shopping centers, a hospital, a police station, or a student's home.

2. Discuss the components of the neighborhood, distinguishing public from private property and institutions. Emphasize the ways in which neighbors must share public spaces, such as streets and parks, and the services provided by public institutions, such as schools and fire departments.

3. Reproduce the attached map of Drees' neighborhood (illustration 3.3) as a handout or transparency. Identify the school, mosque, and other public

institutions as places that bring neighbors together. Identify the domestic and private spaces in his street such as the alley his father's house shares with his relatives and the alley which is shared my Manaal's family.

4. Reproduce the attached map of Lateefa's neighborhood (illustration 3.4) as a handout or transparency. Identify the school, mosque, and other public institutions as places that bring neighbors together. Note how the homes are spread out more across the landscape to make room for fields and orchards.

illustration 3.3

Procedures *continued*

5. Reproduce the attached map of Ismaeel's neighborhood (illustration 3.5) as a handout or transparency. Identify the school, church, mosque, and other public institutions as places that bring neighbors together. This neighborhood is in Dearborn, Michigan — a crowded, industrial city — so it has much less private space. Compare and contrast the two Arab neighborhoods with the Arab American one. What are the things they all have in common? (A mosque, school, homes, bakeries, butchers, a small shop.) Identify the elements which are unique to each

   neighborhood. (Lateefa's neighborhood has many fields, a graveyard, and public guest house. Drees' neighborhood has a fabric store, a photographer's studio, a public bath. Ismaeel's neighborhood has a factory, a church, an apartment complex in which many families live.)

6. Compare these Arab and Arab American neighborhoods to the neighborhood of your school. Discuss the similarities and differences between Arab and American neighborhoods.

illustration 3.4

Lateefa's Neighborhood

illustration 3.5

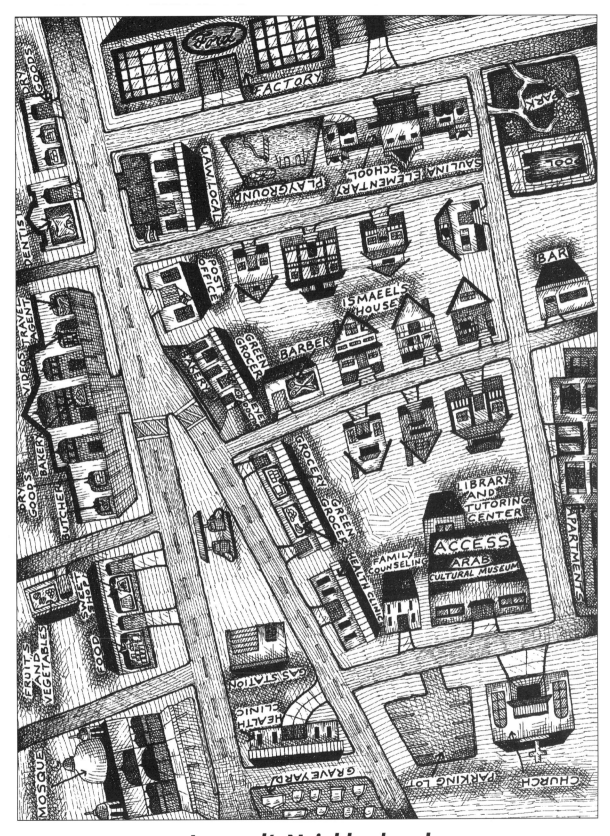

Ismaeel's Neighborhood

unit three
3

home
neighborhood
community

Cultural notes

1. The Arab neighborhoods displayed in this lesson are real places. Swaysa, where Lateefa lives, is a rural village in Jordan; Drees lives in Casablanca, a Moroccan city; and Ismaeel's neighborhood is located in Dearborn, Michigan, home of the Ford Motor Company. Despite differences in size, these three neighborhoods share several traits in common. They all have a mosque, where Muslims gather to pray, and a market, where families can buy food and clothing. These are considered public places, where people can mix freely. Each neighborhood also has its private places, where only family, friends, and guests are welcome. Strangers are not allowed to wander through these areas.

2. An important feature of Arab neighborhoods is the great value placed on maintaining private spaces. In a village like Swaysa, where everyone is related to everyone else, there is no difference between the neighborhood and the family. As a result, the entire community is considered a private space in relation to outsiders. Even in Swaysa's public places, like the mosque or the municipality building, everyone has a familiar face. Visitors to the village are usually invited guests, and they are easily distinguished from locals. Lateefa's neighbors are all close kin. Teachers at the Swaysa primary school are the only "strangers" who come and go freely, and even they spend most of their time on school property, which is considered public space.

3. In an urban neighborhood, the size of public space increases. Mosques and markets are bigger, and it is not unusual for local people to mix with strangers on the main streets. Compared to Swaysa, a city like Casablanca is crowded and noisy. But even in its most densely populated areas, people protect their private spaces. Notice how the houses in Drees' neighborhood are tucked away from the hubbub of the marketplace. A stone wall and narrow, twisting streets let outsiders know that this is a residential area, a *haara*. Drees' *haara* is like a miniature version of Swaysa; it is filled with neighbors who are also close kin. If strangers wander in from the main street, they will be stopped and asked to explain why they are in the neighborhood. Most of the streets leading into Drees' *haara* are dead ends, and many residential areas in Casablanca have a main gate which is locked at night. So, in the move from village to city, public spaces become larger and more genuinely public, while private spaces are more consciously secluded and carefully defined.

4. Ismaeel lives in a working-class, Arab American neighborhood in Dearborn. On the surface, it looks completely different from Jordanian and Moroccan neighborhoods. The houses are built in orderly rows, and the streets are ruler-straight. Space is organized in ways that guarantee easy access to the neighborhood and a smooth flow of traffic. Homes are private, but the streets and even the sidewalks in front of them belong to the public.

Cultural notes *continued*

Ismaeel's neighborhood became Arab in the 1960s. Before that, it was occupied by European immigrants — Poles, Italians, Romanians, and Slavs — who came to work in the giant Rouge Plant, which is owned by Ford Motor Company. Today, the neighborhood is over 90% Arab, and most of its residents work in industry-related jobs. A neighborhood of this sort is very rare in the Arab world, where there is very little heavy manufacturing. The grid-like quality of the streets is the product of "urban planning." In Dearborn, neighborhoods are built according to standards set by the city government. In most of the Arab world, neighborhoods expand without any central planning. As families grow larger, new homes are built and the spaces between them gradually become roads. These walkways, needless to say, are hardly ever straight, and the city is not responsible for maintaining them because they are not public.

There are several ways, however, in which Ismaeel's neighborhood is just like Arab neighborhoods in the old country. It centers on a mosque, where neighbors gather to pray, and it has a thriving marketplace. Many of the homes in the neighborhood are owned by close relatives and people who came to America from the same villages in Lebanon, Palestine, and Yemen. The streets are filled with cousins, and strangers stand out in the crowd. Also, many of the older people wear the traditional clothing described in earlier lessons; store signs and billboards are in Arabic and English; and both languages are spoken in the street. Privacy is still important to Ismaeel and his neighbors, but public spaces receive a level of attention and care that is unusual in the Arab world. Parks and pools are neatly maintained by the city, and entire families are encouraged to use them. In most of the Arab world, public spaces are dominated by men. Women and children spend most of their time in private space, where they feel more at home. In Ismaeel's neighborhood, the traditional public spaces — the mosque and the market — are still thought of as men's areas, and the swimming pool is used mostly by boys. Many of the neighborhood families consider public bathing immodest for girls.

Ismaeel's neighborhood also has a public space of a new kind: the Arab Community Center. This is a social service agency that helps newly-arrived immigrants adapt to life in America; it also contains a museum that explains Arab history and culture to the Americans who visit Ismaeel's neighborhood to shop and eat in the Middle Eastern restaurants. The Arab Community Center also helps Arab Americans preserve their heritage in the New World. Ismaeel helped organize the center in 1973, and he still works there today.

Neighbors in a town

Objectives

1. To introduce the occupational roles of an Arab community

2. To expand awareness of occupational roles in American communities

3. To practice writing

Materials

1. World map

2. Blackboard or chart paper and marker

3. Tree of helpers in an Arab community (see below)

4. Writing paper and pencil

5. Construction paper

6. Scissors

7. Magazine pictures

8. Paste

9. Crayons

10. String

11. Coat hangers or dowels

Procedures

1. Locate Egypt and the Nile on a world map.

2. Read **Ali's special job**, below, and show students illustration 3.6.

3. Discuss the community helpers in the story. On the blackboard or chart paper, draw a "tree" like the one attached (see illustration 3.7) showing the institutions and occupational roles of Ali's community. Ask the students if they can think of other helpers that might be found in each workplace, and have them fill in the helpers in the "small adobe house."

4. Have the students write a story about what they see on the way home from school. If possible, the students should take the assignment home and take notes on what they see before they start writing. Ask them to include as many community helpers as they can in the story. If they are not sure what to call someone's work role, they should ask their teacher or parents. Finally, have the students include their parents' work roles in the story.

5. When the stories are finished, ask the students to draw a tree for the various community helpers they observed.

Procedures *continued*

6. Alternatively, the students may cooperate to construct a mobile representing community helpers. Break the class into small groups. Each group should be assigned a "branch" of the community, such as the hospital or the fire house, and each student should choose a helper within that branch, such as a nurse or a fire chief. A picture of the helper may be drawn or cut out of a magazine and pasted onto construction paper. The picture should be about the size of a post card, with the helper's name written on the back.

7. Punch a small hole at the top of each picture. Have the students in each group suspend their pictures at varying lengths from a coat hanger or dowel. If desired, all the hangers or dowels may then be suspended from one long dowel to make a "super-mobile" representing the entire community.

Ali's special job

Ali lives in Tanta, a medium-sized town in Egypt. He goes to school in the morning and helps his family on the farm in the afternoon. On his way home from school, Ali sees many things: a hospital, a fire house, a university, and a mosque; the waterfront, a ferry boat, a bakery, and a bank; a bus stop, a coffee shop, and a small adobe house.

In all of these places, but especially in the middle of town, Ali sees community helpers. At his school, there are teachers, custodians, and a principal. At the hospital, there are doctors and nurses; at the fire house, there are fire fighters and a chief. Each of these people does a special job to help the town of Tanta.

Further on, Ali crosses the campus of the university. Students and professors are on their way to class, groundskeepers sweep the tree-lined paths, and an ice cream vendor rings his bell across the mall. Near the science building, a fruit seller parks his stand piled high with bananas, grapes, mangoes, figs, and tangerines. Sometimes Ali stops to buy a bag of figs. If the day is bright, there are so many people buying fruit, the vendor can hardly keep up with his customers. The most beautiful building Ali sees on his way home is the mosque. A mosque is a Muslim place of worship, similar to a church or a synagogue. The priest of the mosque is called the *imam*. The caretaker is called the *muezzin* (moo AH zin). Five times a day, the *muezzin* does his own special job, calling the people to pray.

Beyond the mosque is the waterfront. Sailors and dockworkers load and unload the cargo from up and down the Nile, the greatest river in Africa. At one dock, people wait to ride across on a ferry boat. Ali sometimes stops to watch the captains steer out into the rolling water—the same water lapping quietly at his feet.

illustration 3.6

Ali's special job *continued*

Along the waterfront is a little bakery where cakes are made around the clock. The baker knows Ali well. Almost every afternoon, Ali stops in to buy a stack of pita bread for his family. The baker always has Ali's bread ready, wrapped in newspaper and still warm from the oven. Ali pays the cashier, tears off a piece of pita for a snack, and tucks the rest away in his bookbag.

Next door to the bakery is a bank. Inside, the bank has a long counter with little windows. At each little window is a bank teller. All day long, the tellers help people cash checks and deposit money. If Ali is running late, however, the bank is already closed, and he sees the manager locking up the doors.

Ali checks the money in his pocket. He needs twenty *piastres* to catch the bus that will take him the rest of the way home. He hurries on by the bank and boards the bus at the edge of town.

On the bus, the driver is doing his special job of driving, picking up passengers, collecting money, and driving some more. Ali hands the driver twenty *piastres* and sinks into his favorite seat, where he can see the coffee shops along the road. Tanta has many coffee shops, but there is one in particular that Ali likes to see, just on the outskirts of town. Here the customers are always playing backgammon, and a boy like Ali is wiping down the tables. The men smoke slowly from a tall water pipe. Ali wonders what it might be like to bring the coffee out, or even to play backgammon with the men.

Soon the bus is barreling along the dusty road, passing fields and orchards and irrigation ditches. Sometimes, as he comes close to home, Ali sees his father in the fields, checking the system of sprinklers and canals. Then the bus pulls over near a little adobe house. Ali hops down from the bus and rushes in with his bread. All the members of his family are there: his sister is cooking, his mother is spinning, and his father is fixing a plow. Ali kisses each one on both cheeks and lays his bread down, knowing that he too has a special job to do.

Ali's tree of helpers

illustration 3.7

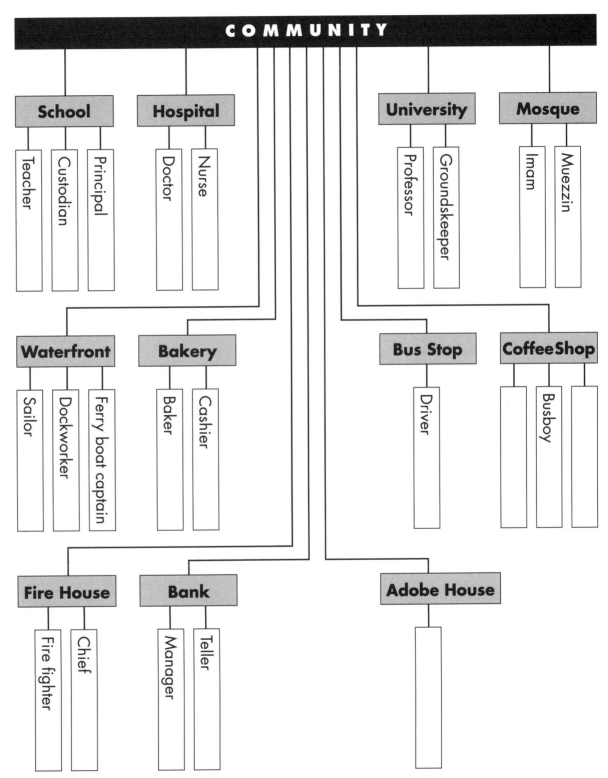

COMMUNITY

School
- Teacher
- Custodian
- Principal

Hospital
- Doctor
- Nurse

University
- Professor
- Groundskeeper

Mosque
- Imam
- Muezzin

Waterfront
- Sailor
- Dockworker
- Ferry boat captain

Bakery
- Baker
- Cashier

Bus Stop
- Driver

CoffeeShop
- Busboy

Fire House
- Fire fighter
- Chief

Bank
- Manager
- Teller

Adobe House

Towns on a road

Objectives

1. To appreciate various modes of transportation in Arab and American communities

2. To solve simple word problems involving time and distance

3. To calculate the time and distance each student takes to get home from school

4. To calculate the average time and distance for the class as a whole

Materials

1. *This Is the Way We Go to School*, by Edith Baer

2. Blackboard or chart paper and marker

Procedures

1. Read *This Is the Way We Go to School*. Ask the students how they come to school. Make a list of the different kinds of transportation on the blackboard or chart paper. How many different kinds does each student use? How many different kinds are used by the class as a whole?

2. Read **Late for lunch**, below, and show students illustrations 3.8 – 3.9. Discuss the various means of transportation used by Muhammad. How many different kinds did he use altogether? Which ones are used by students in the class? Which ones are not?

3. Have the students solve the following word problems with reference to the story:

   a. How many miles did Muhammad travel by donkey? [about 2]

   b. How many by bus? [6]

   c. How many by bicycle? [1]

   d. How many by rowboat? [1.5]

   e. How many miles did Muhammad travel altogether to get to his father's boat? [10.5]

   f. How many miles did he travel roundtrip (to his father's boat and back home)? [21]

   g. If the donkey walks at a rate of four miles per hour, about how long did it take Muhammad to get from his house to the bus stop? [one-half hour]

   h. If the bus has an average speed of 30 miles per hour, about how long was Muhammad on the bus? [one-fifth of an hour, or 12 minutes]

Procedures *continued*

4. As homework, have each student record exactly how long it takes to get home from school. Mileage can be estimated from the odometer if the student goes by car or bus. Students who walk can count the number of steps they take, or the number of blocks covered between school and home, or have a parent drive the route and determine the distance from the odometer. On the blackboard or chart paper, record the time and distance for each student.

5. If desired, calculate the average time and distance for the whole class. Have each student report whether his or her time and distance are above or below average for the class.

Late for lunch

Muhammad is eleven years old. He lives in Aden, a city on the sea, in the country of Yemen. Muhammad's father works on a fishing boat. One morning the boat was docked just off the coast, and Muhammad had to get there fast.

"It's getting late!" said his mother. "Muhammad, you must take this lunch to your father. He'll be getting very hungry!" Muhammad didn't mind. He liked to go to the ship. He was always very careful on the way, even when he was in a hurry.

So Muhammad took the lunch pail and strapped it to a donkey's back. He rode the donkey about two miles to the nearest bus depot. Once he saw the bus coming, he unstrapped the pail, and tried to send the donkey home.

Usually the donkey turned and headed home all by himself. But that day the beast wouldn't move. Muhammad tried to push and shove him down the path, but the old donkey was very stubborn. Muhammad didn't know what to do. The bus was waiting, and the driver was becoming impatient.

Then Muhammad had an idea. He opened his father's lunch pail and took out a handful of hot peppers (*fleefla*-s) from his father's favorite dish, *samak galaaba* (fish stir fry). The pail was full of fish, rice, onions, and peppers, and Muhammad was sure his father wouldn't notice that a few peppers were missing.

"If I give you some lunch, will you go straight home?" Muhammad asked the donkey. The donkey didn't answer, but just stared at the big green *fleefla*-s Muhammad held in his hand.

"Here, take it," Muhammad said, and the donkey gobbled up his snack and snorted and sneezed and shook his head. Then, as if he understood everything that Muhammad had said, the donkey turned and headed down the road.

3

home
neighborhood
community

Late for lunch
continued

"Hurry up, hop in," said the bus driver. Muhammad climbed into the bus and took a seat, holding the lunch pail in his lap.

The bus bounced along six miles of dusty road. Soon the air was cooler and the fields were greener. Muhammad shaded his eyes against the sun's glare. He was waiting to see the deep blue ocean. As the bus pulled over to the side of the road, there it was: his father's boat, like a little wooden toy on the horizon. Muhammad jumped off the bus and started to walk the rest of the way to the port. He had gone just a few steps when his friend Jameel came riding along on a bicycle.

illustration 3.8

"Hey, Muhammad! Do you want a ride?" asked Jameel. Muhammad hesitated. There was a steep hill down to the port, and the streets were very crowded at lunch time. If Jameel wasn't careful, they might have an accident. Besides, Muhammad usually liked to walk down the hill. The breeze was fresh and salty, and he could look out at the ocean, his father's boat, and the marketplace below. He looked at his watch.

"Gee, thanks," he said, "but I think I'll walk."

"Oh, come on," said Jameel. "If you don't ride with me, your dad's lunch will be late."

"All right," said Muhammad, "but be careful, okay?"

"No problem! I ride down this road every day."

So Muhammad sat on the back of the bike and Jameel started pedaling. Soon they were coasting down the long hill. At the bottom Muhammad could see cars, trucks, bikes, goats, and pedestrians all milling around in a big traffic jam. As Jameel steered the bike into the middle of the throng, a huge truck came rattling

illustration 3.9

Late for lunch *continued*

through the intersection. Muhammad felt hot wind against his cheek as the truck barreled by, nearly running Jameel off the road. "I'll never do this again," thought Muhammad. "We could have been hit!" But soon the two boys pulled up to the shorefront, safe and sound.

"Thanks for the ride," said Muhammad.

"No problem," said Jameel. "That saved you a long walk. Did you know it's a mile from the bus stop to the shore? You ought to get a bike!"

"I'll think about it," said Muhammad, still a little nervous.

With the lunch pail in his hand, Muhammad walked out on the pier and untied a little rowboat. This was the part of the trip he liked best. He climbed down into the boat, set the pail at his feet, and started rowing out to his father's fishing boat. Every few minutes he passed a little marker bobbing on the water. Each marker indicated a distance of one-quarter mile from the shore. Muhammad passed six markers before he pulled alongside his father's fishing boat.

The fishing boat was much bigger than Muhammad's little rowboat. To get on deck, Muhammad had to climb up a rope ladder. He was always afraid he would drop the lunch pail into the ocean before he made it to the top.

But he didn't drop it. Instead, he climbed right over the rail and hopped on deck, where his father was waiting.

"*Baba*—your lunch," said Muhammad.

"Thank you, Muhammad," his father said. "Right on time, as usual. Would you like to share this *samak galaaba* with me? I think your mother packed a little extra."

Late for lunch *continued*

His father opened the lunch pail and began looking for green peppers, which were his favorite part of the meal. Then Muhammad remembered the donkey's snack.

"No thank you, *Baba*," he blurted out, "I got a little hungry on the way, so I already ate some of the extra *fleefla*."

"So I see. Well, it's a long trip out to the boat. I wouldn't want you to go away hungry." His father patted Muhammad on the shoulder.

Soon Muhammad turned to go, feeling a little rumble in his stomach. He was too proud to admit that he had really given the *fleefla* to the donkey. Just then his father called him back.

"Son," he said, "This is an awfully big meal just for me. I wouldn't want to throw any of it away. Take this *jibna* (cheese) and *khubz* (bread). Maybe our old donkey would like it for his lunch."

Roads to a market

Objectives

1. To discuss how **language**, **religion**, and **trade** unite people from different countries

2. To re-create an Arab *suuq* (marketplace) in the classroom

3. To compare the Arab *suuq* with the Western department store

Materials

1. World map

2. *An Arab Family*, by Roderic Dutton (optional)

3. *Islam*, by Isma'il R. Al Faruqi (optional)

4. *Morocco*, by Martin Hintz (optional)

5. Play money (e.g., poker chips or dollar bills from a board game)

6. Magazines to be cut up

7. Scissors

Procedures

1. Ask the students to find North Africa and the Middle East on the world map. (For a simplified map of the Arab world, see p. 28 in *An Arab Family*.) Cover the names of various countries and see if the students can name them. The Arab world consists of the following countries:

Mauritania	Libya	Lebanon	Qatar
Western Sahara	Sudan	Syria	United Arab Emirates
Morocco	Egypt	Iraq	Oman
Algeria	Saudi Arabia	Kuwait	Yemen
Tunisia	Jordan	Bahrain	Palestine

2. Suggest to the class that this whole region is like one big community. How could this be, when Arabs live in so many different countries with different governments? There are three main reasons:

a) Arabs speak a common language, **Arabic**.

b) The majority of Arabs follow the same religion, **Islam**.

c) Arabs in different communities, and even in different countries, **buy and trade** with each other, as they have for many centuries.

Procedures *continued*

3. Emphasize that, wherever they come from, Arabs are able to communicate with each other through the Arabic language. This makes the Arab world a single **language community**. Remind students of the greetings they learned in Unit 1, **I have a language**. Point out that these greetings are used and can be understood in all Arab countries.

4. The Arab world is also unified through religious beliefs and practices. Many Arabs are Christians, but the large majority are Muslims. Wherever Muslims live in the world, they must face the holy city of Mecca when they pray. (For a photograph of Muslims at prayer, see p. 6 in *Islam*.) Explain to the class that this practice brings Muslims together, wherever they are and whatever they are doing, at the same times each day.

5. On the world map, point out Mecca in western Saudi Arabia. All able-bodied Muslims are expected to make a pilgrimage to Mecca at least once in their lives. This pilgrimage, or *hajj*, is an experience shared by Muslims all over the world. (See the photograph of pilgrim tents in *Islam*, p. 31). Along with prayer, then, pilgrimage to Mecca helps to unite the Arab world as a **religious community**.

6. Finally, ask the students if they have ever "swapped" toys or baseball cards or candy with a friend. If you had something you didn't want, but your friend did, you might have exchanged it for something your friend had. This is the simplest form of **trade**. Even when we buy something in a shop, we are trading. We are exchanging money for something we need. (This is adapted from *Trade*, published by Butterfly Books.)

7. A **market** is a place where people get together to trade. Grocery stores, shopping malls, and garage sales are all examples of markets. For centuries, people in the Arab world have gathered in open-air markets, similar to the farmer's markets in some American towns (see illustration 3.10). In major cities, like Damascus and Cairo, there are covered markets that are many centuries old. (See attached illustration. For photographs of traditional Arab markets, see *Morocco*, especially pp. 6, 8, 10, 61-62, 75, 77, 112.) A market brings together people of different occupations to buy and sell their goods and services. A big market attracts traders from other towns and even from other countries. In this way, markets help to unite the Arab world as a **trading community**.

illustration 3.10

Procedures *continued*

8. The students can re-create an Arab market in the classroom. First assign each
    student one of the following nine occupations:

Farmer	Leatherworker	Weaver
Musician	Carpenter	Potter
Bookbinder	Goldsmith	Baker

Students of the same occupation may either team up or compete with each other to
trade their products on the market. For the purposes of this exercise, here are the
goods produced by each occupation:

Farmers	**VEGETABLES**
Bakers	**BREAD**
Bookbinders	**BOOKS**
Weavers	**SWEATERS**
Carpenters	**FURNITURE**
Goldsmiths	**JEWELRY**
Leatherworkers	**LEATHER SHOES**
Potters	**POTS, BOWLS, DISHES**
Musicians	**MUSICAL INSTRUMENTS**

Procedures *continued*

9. To "produce" their goods, the students must hunt through magazines for pictures of the product they have been assigned. In selecting their pictures, the students should remember that quality as well as quantity is important: fresh vegetables, for example, may bring a higher price than canned or frozen ones! Give the students a fixed amount of time to cut out as many good pictures as they can.

10. Next, each student must be assigned a good that he or she needs. Write the names of the goods on scraps of paper, mix them thoroughly, and have each student draw one (it must be a good other than the one he or she produces).

11. Money has been in circulation in the Middle East for many centuries. Distribute a small amount of play money to each student. To get what they want on the market, the students must decide whether to spend their money or to trade their own goods directly for other goods.

12. Before the market opens, have each merchant (or team of merchants) make a sign to advertise the products on sale. The signs may be simple or elaborate, but they should appeal as much as possible to potential customers. The back of the sign should read

    "Sorry, we're closed." Arrange the desks or tables in the room to create separate "shops."

13. Declare the market open. Each merchant must decide whether to open for business immediately or to remain closed while shopping for what he or she needs. Of course, while shopping, a merchant may miss the opportunity to sell to someone at his or her shop.

14. In each transaction, the merchant is free to set the price for his or her goods, and the customer is free to bargain for a better price. If the merchant needs a certain product that the customer lacks, the customer may first try to obtain that product from another merchant.

15. After a fixed amount of time, declare the market closed. Everyone should return to his or her shop and count the earnings. Team members must divide the team's earnings equally. Have each merchant announce what was "made" on the market, plus what is left over from his or her original holdings.

16. Discuss the results. Did anyone get "rich"? Was anyone left without being able to sell his or her products? Was everyone able to obtain the products he or she needed? What would each merchant do differently next time to improve business? How could the market in general be improved?

17. Ask the students to compare their own Arab *suuq* to an American supermarket or department store. What are some of the differences and similarities? Emphasize the way that both Arab and American markets bring people together from many different occupations and regions, creating a single economic community.

Cultural notes

1. All cities in the Arab world have markets, called *suuq*s. The *suuq* is the center of urban life. Unlike the suburban shopping mall in America, the *suuq* is situated in the heart of the city, often in the same place it has been for centuries. Many of the shop keepers who do business in the *suuq* are from merchant families who have lived and worked in the *suuq* for generations; others are just starting out. Most shops and stores in the *suuq*, both old and new, are family businesses.

   The *suuq* is divided into streets and alleys, lined by shops selling the same item. One street has rug shops, another has spice shops, another street has fabric stores. Jewelry, meat, vegetables, blankets, household supplies: each is sold in its own traditional area of the *suuq*. Department stores, which sell a variety of products under one roof, are still not common in the Middle East. Americans want to do their shopping quickly and conveniently, but Arabs approach this task with a more relaxed attitude. Shopping, in the Middle East, is a social experience. You sit and talk with the shop keeper — you have probably known him for years! — you drink tea, haggle over prices, make a purchase (or hold out for better terms), then start the process all over again in another shop. Supermarkets, fixed prices, and cash registers are inevitably creeping into the marketplace, but most Arabs would like to keep business transactions as personal and friendly as possible.

   In some parts of the Arab world, such as Yemen, it is the men who do most of the shopping, while women stay at home. The *suuq* is filled with coffee shops, where men can sit, visit, exchange news, and compare prices with friends before returning home. In Jordan, rural families rise at 2:00 in the morning, load their trucks with grapes or figs, then drive to the central market in Amman, where they sell their produce at the going rate. To most rural people, Bedouin and village farmers alike, going to the city means going to the *suuq*; buying and selling are thought to be enjoyable, sometimes exciting experiences. The *suuq* has all the sparkle and glitzy allure of our own shopping malls; in fact, the American shopping mall is modeled on the Middle Eastern "bazaar," another name for the *suuq*.

REVIEW LESSON

Camp, village, and city

Objectives

1. To explore variation in rural and urban settings in Arab and Western countries

2. To review readings from Units 1, 2, and 3

3. To write a report comparing two or more communities

Materials

1. Chart paper and marker

2. *The Day of Ahmed's Secret*, by Florence Parry Heide and Judith Heide Gilliland

3. *Nadia the Willful*, by Sue Alexander

4. *Sami and the Time of the Troubles*, by Florence Parry Heide and Judith Heide Gilliland

5. *Amina and Muhammad's Special Visitor*, by Diane Turnage Burgoyne

6. *Sitti's Secrets*, by Naomi Shihab Nye

7. *An Arab Family*, by Roderic Dutton (optional)

8. *A Family in Egypt*, by Olivia Bennett (optional)

9. *A Family in Morocco*, by Judy Steward (optional)

10. World map

11. Arab stories from Units 1-3.

Procedures

1. Construct a chart like the one below, including as many of the listed books and Arab stories provided in Units 1-3 as possible. Add titles of other books or stories that seem appropriate.

2. Some of the stories will be familiar from earlier lessons. Those that are not should be read either orally or individually over several days.

3. When the entire class has read all the stories on the list, have the students fill in the chart. This may be done in a group discussion or as an individual assignment.

4. Discuss the countries in which the stories take place. Find each country on the world map.

5. Discuss the differences between three types of community: camps, villages, and cities (see **Cultural notes** on urbanites, peasants, and bedouin in previous units).

6. Have the students write a report comparing two or more of the communities on the chart. For example, the student might choose to compare *camps* and *villages* by using the examples of Nadia's camp (in *Nadia the Willful*) and Ezzat's village (in *A Family in Egypt*). Alternatively, the student might choose to compare two examples of the same kind of community: two cities, such as Cairo and Beirut, or two villages, such as those portrayed in *An Arab Family* and *A Family in Egypt*. In writing their essays, the students should consider both similarities and differences in homes, possessions, occupations, food, clothing, family life, and transportation.

7. Discuss the similarities and differences between the examples in the essays and the students' own communities.

	Location	Type of community	Occupations/ Social roles	Means of transportation
The Day of Ahmed's Secret	Cairo, Egypt	city	delivery boy	donkey cart
Nadia the Willful	Arabian Desert	camp		
Sami and the Time of the Troubles	Beirut, Lebanon	city		
Amina and Muhammad's Special Visitor	Saudi Arabia	city		
Sitti's Secrets	West Bank	village		
An Arab Family	Oman	village		
A Family in Egypt	Egypt	village		
A Family in Morocco	Tangier, Morocco	city		

(complete the chart)

unit four

4

plants
and animals

plants and animals

Ecology

Objectives

1. To introduce the idea of *ecology*, the pattern of relations among plants, animals, people, and the physical environment

2. To represent ecological relations in the form of a flow chart

3. To perform a short play illustrating ecological relations

Materials

1. Mimeograph or photocopy machine

2. Pencils or crayons

3. Drawing paper

Procedures

1. Illustration 4.1 should be photocopied and handed out to the class.

2. Introduce the idea of ecology as represented in the flow chart. Discuss the illustrated relations between soil, water, plants, animals, and people.

3. Help the students to fill in the blanks in the chart. How does the sun, for example, affect water, plants, animals, and people? [Under the sun's radiation, water evaporates and forms clouds, delivering rain to plants and animals. Through photosynthesis,

plants make food from the sun's rays in combination with rain and nutrients from the soil. Directly or indirectly, all animals and people depend on the vegetable proteins and other food produced in photosynthesis. Under sunlight, furthermore, people make vitamin D in their skin. This vitamin is essential for building and maintaining bones and teeth. Too much sun, however, can cause sunburn or even skin cancer.]

Procedures *continued*

4. Remind the class of the community helpers introduced in Unit 3. Discuss the idea that some of the most important aspects of a human being's ecology are *other human beings.*

   This is especially true when the members of a community specialize in certain jobs or social roles. The farmer, truck driver, shopkeeper, doctor, nurse, police officer, fire fighter, banker, teacher, and student all need each other, because they form a kind of human ecology: they could not survive without each other.

5. Read **How the fox got back his tail**, below. If desired, assign the students roles and read the play out loud or perform it in costume.

6. After they have read the play, have the students draw a flow chart (or hand out to them Illustration 4.2) of the relations among the characters [old woman, fox, goats, olive trees, laborer, cobbler]. Ask the students to think about relations that are not represented in the play. For example, what materials does the cobbler use to make shoes? [To produce leather, animal hides must be soaked in *tannins*, chemical compounds from plants that give leather its strength and resistance to moisture. Cloth shoes are often made of canvas, originally derived from the hemp plant (which also gives us rope). Thread is usually made from cotton, which comes from the cotton plant.]

illustration 4.1

RAINFALL

THE RED SEA

TOWNS AND VILLAGES

TERRACED FIELDS

SOLAR ENERGY

DESERT

DRYLANDS

OLIVE ORCHARD

GRAZING LAND

A SHORT PLAY

How the Fox Got Back His Tail

(Adapted from *Arab Folktales*, translated and edited by Inea Bushnaq, pp. 220-21)

Characters

Woman goatherd	Goats
Zayd, the woman's son	Olive trees #1, 2, & 3
Nasreen, the woman's daughter	Gardener
Fox	Cobbler

Props

(Most of these can be made from cardboard or construction paper.)

Milk pan	Milk pail
Embers	Green twigs
Fox tail	Old slippers
Cleaver	Hoe

Scene: *a small clay bakehouse, where a woman goatherd is heating milk over embers. Goats are grazing at stage left, and olive trees are standing at stage right.*

Woman: This goat milk will be delicious for dinner tonight.

The woman stirs the milk, then exits stage left. A few seconds later, a fox enters from stage right and sneaks into the bakehouse. He snoops about, then discovers the milk.

Fox: Oh, I'm *sooo* hungry...What's this? Goat milk! My *faaavorite*...

The fox begins lapping up the milk, and quickly drains the pan.

Fox [*licking his chops*]: What a nice surprise! I'll have to remember to stop by here again...

The fox exits stage right. A few seconds later, the woman returns to the bakehouse with her two children and finds the pan licked clean.

Woman: What's this? All my delicious goat milk is gone! Zayd, did you drink it?

Zayd: No, *umma*.

Woman: Nasreen, did you?

Nasreen: No, *umma*, not me.

Woman: Well, well, well. Perhaps I'll just stay up tonight and see who—or *what*—has been sipping at our supper! Now run along to bed, children—I'm afraid we'll have no milk tonight.

Zayd: May I stay up with you? You might need protection!

Nasreen: Yes, *umma*, may we please? It could be dangerous!

Woman: No, no, no. The only one who needs protection around here is the thief who drank my goat milk! Now out of the bakehouse and into your beds!

How the fox got back his tail *continued*

Zayd: Yes, *umma.*

Nasreen: Yes, *umma.*

The children exit the bakehouse and curl up on mats at stage left. The woman takes a pail out to the goats and fills it with milk. Returning to the bakehouse, she dumps the milk into a pan and begins warming it over the ashes. She then takes out a cleaver and hides behind a table in the corner. Before long, the fox returns and begins snooping around the bakehouse.

Fox: Well, well, well...more goat milk! On top of my lovely supper, this will make a *maaarvelous* midnight snack.

Just as the fox begins to dip his chin into the pan, the woman leaps out from behind the table and cuts off his tail with her cleaver. The woman snatches up the tail and sees that her thief is a fox.

Woman: Ah ha! Old fox! I should have known!

Fox: Oww! Oww! Owwwww! My *taaail!*

Woman [*waving the tail in the air*]: That will teach you! What kind of a creature sneaks about and steals the supper of women and children?

Fox: A hungry one, I assure you, madam, a *huuungry* one. We all need to eat!

Woman: Well now that you've had your supper, you can pay for it...[*holds out tail*] with *this*!

Fox: Oh please, please, please, not my tail! Please give it back. I use my tail for many things, you know—for balancing my body when I walk along a narrow path, for waving at my friends...How can I be a fox without a tail?

Woman: And how can I be a goatherd without my milk? All right, I'll make you a deal—first give me back the milk you stole, then you can have your tail.

Fox: Oh dear, oh dear, oh dear...okay. Okay, I'll get you some milk.

The fox slinks out of the bakehouse and approaches the goats at stage left. The woman puts her cleaver away, takes the fox's tail, and lies down to sleep with her children.

Fox: Dear she-goat, may I have some milk to give to the woman goatherd so she'll give back my tail?

She-goat: But my milk is very precious— I feed it to my kids. I can make more milk only if I have grass and twigs to nibble. Bring me some green twigs from the olive tree and I'll give you a little milk.

Fox: Oh dear, oh dear, oh dear....okay. Okay, I'll get you some twigs.

The fox crosses to stage right and approaches the olive grove.

Fox: Lovely olive trees, please give me green twigs for the goats so they'll give me milk to give to the woman goatherd so she'll give back my tail.

Olive tree #1: But our twigs hold our *leaves*...and our leaves make our *food.*

Fox: Make your food?

Olive tree #2: Well of course we don't chew and swallow our food as you poor animals do. Our leaves make food out of air and sunlight.

Olive tree #3: We also drink water and vitamins through our roots.

Olive tree #1: Hmmm....that gives me an idea. Bring us a gardener who will hoe round our roots.

Olive tree #2: Yes, yes! A gardener!

How the fox got back his tail *continued*

Olive tree #3: Bring us a gardener! Then we'll give you some twigs.

Fox: Oh dear, oh dear, oh dear...okay. Okay, I'll get you a gardener.

The fox calls to the gardener off stage.

Fox: Oh Uncle! Please stop for a moment. I must ask you a favor.

The gardener enters stage left.

Gardener: What is it, old fox?

Fox: Please, Uncle Gardener, will you come hoe round the roots of the olive trees so they'll give me green twigs for the goats so they'll give me milk to give to the woman goatherd so she'll give back my tail?

Gardener: Hmmm....shoes. I need shoes first. Then I'll do your hoeing.

Fox: Oh dear, oh dear, oh dear...okay. Okay, I'll get you shoes.

The fox crosses to stage right and calls to the cobbler off stage.

Fox: Oh Uncle! Uncle Cobbler!

Cobbler: Yes, son?

The cobbler enters stage right.

Fox: Uncle, please give me some shoes for the gardener so he'll hoe round the roots of the olive trees so they'll give me twigs to feed the goats so they'll give me milk for the woman goatherd so she'll let me have my tail back.

Cobbler: Whoa, slow down, son. I'm not sure I understand.

Fox: Well, I've lost my tail, you see, and the only way to get it back is to get milk from the she-goat, but she won't give me milk without some green shoes...I mean trees...I mean hoes...I

mean...oh dear, oh dear, oh dear, I'm very confused!

Cobbler: That's okay, son. I understand you want some shoes. Well, I can't give you a brand new pair, but will this old pair of slippers do?

The cobbler offers the slippers.

Fox [*taking the slippers*]: Oh yes, oh yes, oh yes, thank you, Uncle Cobbler!

The fox runs to the gardener, who is leaning on a hoe.

Fox: Here, here, here, Uncle Gardener, here are your shoes!

Gardener [*taking the slippers*]: Ah, slippers! I need a pair slippers. Thank you, old fox.

The gardener puts on the slippers and begins to hoe around the olive tree roots.

Fox: Lovely olive trees, here is your gardener! May I please have some twigs?

Olive tree #1 [with eyes closed in pleasure]: Mmmm...that feels good. My roots can *breeeathe* again.

Olive tree #2: Do mine too!

Olive tree #3: Did you know we use our roots for many things: to draw water and food from the soil, to keep ourselves upright in the wind, to...

Fox: That's wonderful, really, but I must get my tail back! May I *pleeease* have some twigs now?

Olive tree #1 [*opening eyes*]: Well of course, why didn't you say so? Just pluck them from my branches.

Fox: Oh thank you, thank you, thank you!

The fox plucks a bunch of twigs and rushes to the goats.

illustration 4.2

Fox: Oh she-goat, dear she-goat, I have lovely twigs for you...

She-goat: Hmmm...those look *gooood*. All right, you may have some milk.

Fox: Oh thank you, Sister Goat, you have gotten me back my tail.

The woman goatherd and her children wake up, rub their eyes, and enter the bakehouse. Just then, the fox rushes in with a pail of fresh goat milk.

Fox: Oh goatherd! I've brought you my milk.

How the fox got back his tail *continued*

Woman: You mean you've brought me *my* milk—the milk you stole from me.

Fox: Yes, yes, yes...now may I please have my tail back?

Woman [*offering the tail*]: Here, old fox. May it always remind you that to receive, you must give.

Fox: Thank you, my goatherd friend. [*Re-attaching the tail*] Ahhh...that's better.

The woman begins to warm the milk over the ashes.

Fox: Say...that's an *awwwful* lot of milk. Might I trouble you for just a taste...

Woman [waving her cleaver above her head]: Out! Out! Oooout!

The fox runs out of the bakehouse and exits stage right.

~ THE END ~

Cultural notes

1. You will have noticed that the characters in this play sometimes call each other kin terms — uncle, brother, sister, aunt — even when they are not related. This is a very common practice in the Arab world. It is considered disrespectful, for instance, for a younger person to call an older person by their first name. They will use the term "uncle" or "aunt" instead. The older person will call the younger person "uncle" or "aunt" as well! It is also common for people of the same generation and social status to call each other "my brother" or "my sister." The term *seedi*, which means "my grandfather" or "my lord," is used when talking to older men; *sitti*, or "my grandmother" or "my lady," is used when talking to older women. They, in turn, will use the same terms to address young people. This custom shows how important family relationships are in the Arab world. To behave appropriately with friends and acquaintances, you should treat them as if they were kin.

The food pyramid

Objectives

1. To introduce the food pyramid, a guide to proper nutrition

2. To consider some Arab and American examples of each food group

3. To explore how the daily fare of an Arab family and your students' families fit into the pyramid

Materials

1. Chart paper and marker

2. Magazines with pictures of food

Procedures

1. Reproduce the food pyramid (Illustration 4.3) in the form of a large chart. Discuss the pyramid with the class, introducing the food groups and the number of servings recommended per day.

2. Divide the class into six teams and have each team sit together in a group. Assign each team one of the six food groups.

3. Have the members of each team cut out magazine pictures of foods in their food group. Instruct the students to look for pictures of simple foods rather than complex dishes with many ingredients.

4. Review the selected pictures for each group and make sure that each one clearly depicts the appropriate food group.

5. Write the names of the six food groups on the blackboard and help each team place the pictures it found under the appropriate heading.

   Breads and Cereals
   Vegetables
   Fruits
   Dairy Products
   Meats, Beans, and Nuts
   Fats, Oils, and Sweets

6. Read **Everything we eat on Friday is especially good** to the class.

7. Discuss the foods mentioned in the story and help the students identify the appropriate food group for each one. For example, labne is made of yogurt, it belongs with dairy products. Zaatar is made of thyme, sesame seeds, and other spices and is eaten with olive oil. It falls under three separate categories; Vegetables, Meats, Beans and Nuts, and Fats, Oils and Sweets. Note how Maha's diet is distributed across the pyramid.

Procedures *continued*

8. Ask the students to write down everything they ate yesterday. Pick a few students whose lists look fairly complete and ask them to place their own diet on the pyramid. Other students can help them or they can take turns placing one another's diets on the pyramid.

Discuss with them the strengths and weaknesses of their daily diet.

illustration 4.3

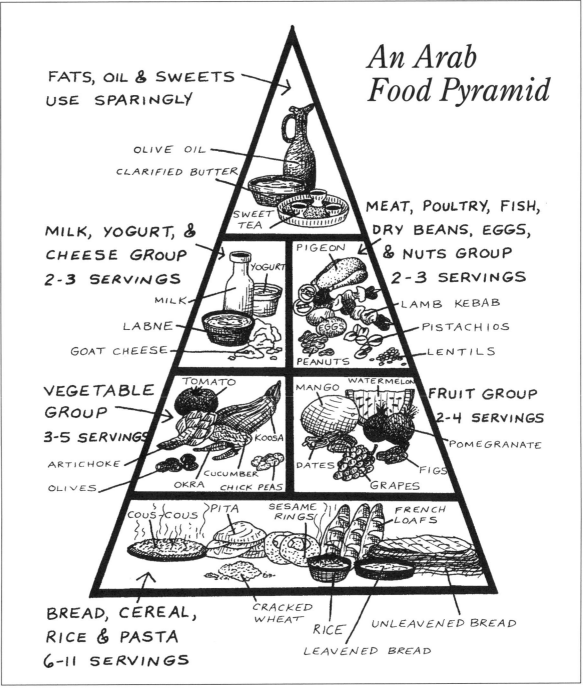

An Arab Food Pyramid

FATS, OIL & SWEETS USE SPARINGLY

OLIVE OIL
CLARIFIED BUTTER
SWEET TEA

MILK, YOGURT, & CHEESE GROUP 2-3 SERVINGS
YOGURT
MILK
LABNE
GOAT CHEESE

MEAT, POULTRY, FISH, DRY BEANS, EGGS, & NUTS GROUP 2-3 SERVINGS
PIGEON
LAMB KEBAB
PISTACHIOS
EGGS
LENTILS
PEANUTS

VEGETABLE GROUP 3-5 SERVINGS
TOMATO
KOOSA
ARTICHOKE
OLIVES
OKRA
CUCUMBER
CHICK PEAS

FRUIT GROUP 2-4 SERVINGS
MANGO WATERMELON
POMEGRANATE
DATES
FIGS
GRAPES

BREAD, CEREAL, RICE & PASTA 6-11 SERVINGS
COUS-COUS
PITA
SESAME RINGS
FRENCH LOAFS
CRACKED WHEAT
RICE
LEAVENED BREAD
UNLEAVENED BREAD

Everything we eat on Friday is especially good

My name is Maha and I live in the city of Nazareth. Nazareth is in the country of Israel. My family, and most of the people who live in our city, are Palestinians. My father is a school teacher and my mother is a nurse in the local hospital. Today is Friday. My brothers and sisters and I love Friday because we have no school. Friday is the day that our father and uncles go to the mosque to pray, so it is the most important day of our week. Friday is also my favorite day because Muma stays home from work and cooks us a delicious lunch. Everything we eat on Friday is especially good.

Today, for example, we woke up a little late and went to sit outside in the garden. Muma brought coffee for my father, and the rest of us had little glasses of hot, sweet tea. Sometimes I think my eyes cannot open in the morning without my cup of tea. Only Muma makes it the way I like — nice and strong and sweet (but not too sweet or too strong like our neighbors make it.) On most school days, we will eat a little bread and cheese and maybe some bread dipped in olive oil and zaatar (a mix of thyme, sesame seeds, and spices). But on Friday Muma also cooks eggs, brings out our very best olives, and makes sure we have fresh labne (a thick, rich yogurt spread). She usually slices tomatoes and cucumbers and makes sure we have some of that as well. On Fridays we sit and take our time over breakfast. No one is in a hurry.

Today, a farmer from a nearby village came by in his truck selling watermelons. My aunt Nura went down and spent half an hour arguing with him over the price. This entertained us all during breakfast. We knew they must be very good watermelons because she spent so much time haggling. She and the farmer are old friends. He knows that she won't buy melons from anyone but him. They love to argue over the price. After twenty minutes of shouting and laughing, we knew they were getting close to an agreement. Suddenly, Aunt Nura threw a great big watermelon on the ground, one of the prettiest, roundest, sweetest ones. It split open and the pink fruit and seeds flew everywhere. Aunt Nura told the farmer that his high prices and his arguing make her head, and her wallet, feel like that smashed watermelon. Baba laughed so hard he had to go inside the house. Finally, Nura and the farmer compromised, and Nura called us to help her bring the melons into the house. She bought 10! We were very excited. Muma slit one open for us right then, and we ate it with our breakfast.

After Baba got back from the mosque, we sat down for our big meal of the day: lunch. Muma made Sultaan Ibraheem, a dish of grilled fish, rice, taheena sauce, and salaata. Most people fry the fish, but Muma works in the hospital, and she says it is better to grill or steam it. One of my favorite foods is fish with taheena sauce. The taheena is made with ground sesame seeds, kind of like American peanut butter. It is great with fish and rice. Whenever Muma cooks rice like today, she also makes a special salaata, a vegetable sauce with everything chopped up really fine and a little hot pepper thrown in. I have seen on TV that Americans eat salsa. I think that if I ever went to America, your salsa would remind me of home and of Muma's salaata. We mix the salaata in with the rice. On Fridays, Muma also made a big salad with lots of fresh vegetables in it. She baked some fresh pita bread until it was dry, then

Everything we eat on Friday is especially good *continued*

she crumbled it up in the salad. This is called fattoosh.

Of course, we also had bread. I don't remember ever eating a meal in our house without bread.

After lunch I ran outside and played with my brothers and sisters. We came back in around 5:00 o'clock and asked for a snack. Muma boiled a pot of tea for us and brought out a big bowl of watermelon. In return, we gave Muma a surprise gift: some fresh grapes from our garden. They weren't quite ripe yet, but Muma smiled and sat down with us and popped them into her mouth one by one.

For dinner, we had the same thing we always do. Muma was tired from her day of cooking and visiting the neighbors. Every night for dinner, at this time of year, we have tea, bread with olive oil and zaatar, goat cheese, tomatoes and cucumbers dribbled with oil, and a little leftover fruit. How can it be that the same foods that wake me up in the morning can put me to sleep at night? We usually eat dinner while watching television. Tonight, I am writing this story to keep myself from falling asleep. Yesterday, I fell asleep watching TV and almost spilled my tea. Baba carried me to bed. Tonight, I have already finished my tea, and Baba is looking at me every couple of minutes to see if I am still awake. My brother Ibraheem is already fast asleep. Sometimes, when I fall asleep first, Ibraheem tickles my feet to tease me. I would do the same to him right now if I hadn't eaten so much zaatar. It is putting me to sleep. Good night.

Cultural notes

1. In the Arab world, people eat from the same food groups as North Americans. What differs is the *way* foods are prepared and the *proportions* of each food group in the overall diet. Unless they are very wealthy, people in the Middle East (as well as other regions of the Third World) tend to eat very little meat. Meat is expensive compared to vegetables and cereal grains, which are consumed every day. Americans are known the world over for their (bad) habit of eating meat with every meal, a dietary custom that contributes to our cardiovascular problems. In the Arab world, meat is associated with holidays and the visits of special guests, who are given meat as a sign of respect. In arid climates, where grazing is limited, farm animals are too valuable to slaughter; it is more economical to consume animal protein in the form of dairy products such as milk, yogurt, cheeses, and butter. As a result, Arab cuisines are rich in dairy products. Other non-meat sources of oil and protein, especially olives, are also prominent in the diet.

2. It is rare to find sugar in Arab dishes which are not prepared specifically as a desert. In fact, people throughout the Middle East receive most of their refined sugar in tea or coffee, which they drink in astonishing amounts, even by American standards. Hot drinks are almost always heavily sugared.

3. Perhaps the most popular item of the traditional Arab diet is bread, which makes up the bulk of most meals. Bread fills the stomach, leaving more of other foods to be shared, but it derives additional importance from the fact that it can be used as a utensil, to pick up food or sop up soups and broths. Before the age of European influence — and even today — most Arabs used bread to eat with instead of forks, spoons, and knives. Since most of the breads eaten in the Middle East are thin flatbreads (like *pita* bread), people can easily tear off a small piece of bread, wrap it around a morsel of food, then pop the bite into their mouths. When the meal is done, there is hardly any silverware to wash!

4. Bread is also a symbol of hospitality. According to an old Arab custom, once two people have eaten bread and salt together, they are considered friends who must protect each other. "They have bread and salt between them," is a common way of describing the bond of friendship.

5. You have already been introduced to some favorite Middle Eastern dishes in earlier lessons. You might want to refer to these again to refresh your memory.

Herbs and spices

Objectives

1. To point out that tea and spices, like many other things we use every day, come from *plants*

2. To discuss the importance of the tea and the spice trade in world history

3. To make decaffeinated tea in the classroom

Materials

1. Pepper
2. Cinnamon
3. Cloves
4. Cardamom
5. Ginger
6. Mint
7. Coffee beans
8. Tea leaves (decaffeinated)
9. Small unmarked jars or other glass containers for spices
10. Blackboard or chart paper and marker
11. World map
12. Small stove or hot plate
13. Teapot and cups

Procedures

1. Label the containers of pepper, cinnamon, cloves, cardamom, ginger, mint, coffee, and tea with the numbers 1 through 8.

2. Before the class arrives, write the eight names on the blackboard or chart paper and cover each name with a removable flap of construction paper. The flaps should be numbered 1 through 8, corresponding to the numbers on the jars.

3. Have the students pass the coffee, tea, and spices around the room. On the basis of smell and appearance only (no tasting), the students should guess what is in each jar. As a memory aid, have the students note down their guesses from 1 to 8.

4. When all eight jars have been passed around, hold up the first one and ask the students to guess its contents. Record the various guesses next to flap number 1, then have the students

Procedures *continued*

vote on which guess they think is correct. Once the vote is taken, remove the flap to reveal the name. Follow the same procedure for containers 2 through 8.

5. Invite the students to tell what they know about each spice: how it smells and tastes, what dishes or drinks are made with it, where it comes from. Although we buy coffee, tea, and spices at the grocery store, they come originally from *plants*:

   Pepper (*filfil*) is produced from the red berries of a woody vine.

   Cinnamon (*girfa*) comes from the dried inner bark of a tree.

   Cloves (*granfal*) are made from the dried flower buds of a tree.

   Cardamom *(haal)* is made from the seeds of a plant.

   Ginger (*zinjabeel*) is made from the rhizomes (rootstalks) of an herb.

   Mint (*na'na'*) is an oil present in the leaves of a plant.

   Coffee (*gahwa*) is brewed from the roasted seeds (or "beans") of a small tree.

   Tea (*shay*) comes from the dried leaves of a shrub.

   All eight of these plants are *tropical* — and all but coffee, in fact, are native to what used to be called the "East Indies" (India and the countries of South East Asia).

6. Point out Southeast Asia, India, the Middle East, and Europe on the world map. Explain how Arab merchants once acted as "middlemen" between East and West, buying spices in India and Southeast Asia and bringing them back for sale to Europeans (see **Cultural notes**).

7. Point out Yemen on the world map. Coffee originated here and spread throughout the Middle East. Later it was introduced in Europe and the Americas. Though the beverage is now consumed all over the world, coffee has a special place in Arab culture (see **Cultural notes**).

8. If desired, the students can help make tea in the classroom. To make tea the Arab way, add lots of sugar to boiling water, then turn down the heat while the sugar dissolves. Add about 1 1/2 tablespoons of (decaffeinated) tea leaves. Mint, cardamom, cinnamon, fresh thyme or sage may be added to individual cups. (If desired, make several batches of tea with various spices before class and have the students identify the spices by the smell and taste of the teas.)

9. While waiting for water to boil, read **Drinking Tea in Libya**, below, to the class. You might want to simplify some of the vocabulary. Discuss the various rituals involved in preparing the tea. If you like, act out the tea-drinking ritual with the students, with yourself as host and the children as guests.

Drinking Tea in Libya

by Emrys Peters
(an anthropologist who lived in Libya)

During a session of tea-drinking, which lasts an hour or so, many frills are added to the simple techniques of boiling water, mixing sugar with tea, and drinking it.

The proceedings begin with a brief argument about who is to make the tea. This decided, little tea glasses and a small enamel teapot are placed on a tray in front of the tea-maker. Embers are brought in on a piece of metal and put near the tray. The water is boiled in a tin can. All these items are standard, and no others would serve the purpose.

As soon as the tea-maker has put the water on to boil, the assembled men fall to conversing. They converse with conspicuous zest; not to do so would be improper. As the water comes to a boil, the tea-maker pours some into the small teapot, adding a handful of tea and two or three handfuls of sugar. The conversation, meanwhile, continues unabated. After the mixture has been boiled to a thick syrup-like brew, the tea-maker fussily washes a few glasses, arranges them in a row, and then, from a great height, pours some tea into the little glasses, mixes it, and pours it back into the pot again. He then replaces the lid of the teapot by slapping it shut with quite unnecessary vigor, as if angry with it. Three or four such mixings usually suffice. He then pours off a small amount of tea into a glass, again holding the pot high above it, tastes it, pours the remainder back into the pot, and, without comment, returns the pot to the smoldering embers, his every move watched closely by those sitting around him.

Tea is finally poured into all the glasses and handed around. Each man brings the glass to his mouth by a circuitous route, before quaffing the tea noisily. Three rounds of tea are offered. Each round is prepared with the same flourishes. When the third round is complete, the men rise as if propelled and depart abruptly.

Cultural notes

1. For centuries, Arab traders acted as "middlemen" between East and West. Among the most important trade goods were spices from Asia. On the coasts of India and Sri Lanka, the Arabs bought pepper and cinnamon. Ginger, cloves, and nutmeg were purchased from Chinese merchants in Southeast Asia. The spices were shipped and carried overland to the ports of the Mediterranean, where they were sold to Europeans.

2. The most important commodity in the spice trade was *pepper*. In an era without refrigeration, pepper was especially prized because it was the only way to make decaying or heavily salted meat palatable. Pepper was so precious in medieval and early modern Europe that it sometimes served as money. Even the European discovery of the Americas may be seen as a "by-product" of the European search for pepper!

3. *Coffee* is a symbol of hospitality throughout the Middle East. People drink it at social gatherings and routinely offer it to guests and visitors. Coffee as we know it today first appeared in Arabia in the late 1400s. Drinking coffee (as opposed to chewing coffee beans) is a Yemeni invention. By the mid-1500s, coffee-drinking was widespread in the Middle East. Coffeehouses went up in cities and towns. In the countryside, each Bedouin tent became a coffeehouse of its own. The new habit was popular, but it was opposed initially by religious leaders and politicians. Coffee was considered by some to be like wine, which is forbidden to Muslims. Its reputation was further sullied by its association with controversial Sufi Muslim brotherhoods (the so-called "dervishes") who used it to induce trance-like states and to enhance mystical awareness. Local rulers also suspected that coffeehouses were meeting places for dissidents and political schemers, as well as "dens of iniquity" where all the vices of the day (gambling, prostitution, music, dancing, and a general laziness) could be pursued. The campaign against coffee failed, however, and even the groups that had opposed the new drink came to have coffeehouses of their own.

In the early 1600s, the Dutch brought coffee seeds from the Yemeni port city of Mocha, the center of the Arabian coffee trade, to Europe. The drink caught on quickly, and by 1675 there were over 3000 coffeehouses in London alone. Soon the Dutch had established their own coffee plantations in Sri Lanka and the East Indies. In 1723, a single coffee tree was transported to the Caribbean by the French. From this tree sprang the huge coffee industries of coastal South America and Brazil, where most of the world's coffee is now grown. Though the beverage is now consumed all over the world, coffee has a special place in Arab culture. Coffeehouses are not just businesses; they also serve as informal, neighborhood men's clubs where a wide range of activities take place. Friends come together to talk politics, to read poetry and discuss literature, to perform and listen to music, to play cards,

Cultural notes *continued*

backgammon, and other games, or simply to watch television. In the home, coffee is always served to guests. To refuse a cup is considered impolite, and the failure to offer one is an even greater insult. Coffee is drunk in small, heavily-sugared doses throughout the day.

4. *Tea*, a drink made from the dried leaves of a shrub, came originally from China. In the Middle East today, tea is as popular as coffee, and tea-drinking has been strongly influenced by the traditions that grew up around coffee. Both are *social* beverages. They reflect the Arab values of hospitality and good company.

   Emrys Peters' account of tea-drinking in Libya makes these points very well. The ritual he describes might seem highly social and strangely elaborate to most Americans, who rarely turn the preparation of tea into "performance art." The American approach to tea-making is shaped, instead, by our individualistic, fast-paced lifestyles. When Americans make a pot of tea, they seldom add sugar in advance. Instead, they offer people cream, sugar, and lemons to prepare their own cup individually. The same is true for coffee. In most of the Arab world, the pot is spiced and sweetened to the taste of the household in general. Special pots are made for people with diabetes or for those with picky tastes. Americans like a "serve yourself" approach to tea and coffee drinking; in Arab families, it is appropriate for the host to serve guests, for juniors to serve elders, and for women to serve men. Also, Americans like to drink their coffee and tea "on the run," while doing other things. In the Arab world — and in England — tea-drinking is an *occasion*, a daily ritual which brings competing activities to a close. Above all else, it is an experience to be shared with friends and family.

5. In the Arab world, herbs and spices are used to cure aches and pains as well as add flavor to foods. When people have cramps or an upset stomach, for instance, they can drink tea spiced with sage (*marameeya*) for relief. Or they can brew sage by itself, and drink it until they feel better. Likewise, mint (*na'na'*) is prescribes as a traditional cure for headaches, cold, and flu. A rich cinnamon (*girfa*) tea is often prepared for women after childbirth, "to clean out the system." Licorice (*yanasoon*) tea is said to cure insomnia. And cardamom (*haal*) ground up in coffee is widely believed to clear the bloodstream and open the mind.

Trees

Objectives

1. To explore the ecological and economic significance of trees

2. To introduce two important trees of the Arab world: the date palm and the olive tree

Materials

1. Mimeograph or photocopy machine

2. Blackboard or chart paper

3. *Amina and Muhammad's Special Visitor*, by Diane Turnage Burgoyne (optional)

4. *An Arab Family*, by Roderic Dutton (optional)

5. Whole, unpitted black olives, enough for each student to taste one.

illustration 4.4

OLIVE TREE

TREE NEEDS:
- HOT, DRY WEATHER
- ROCKY, ARID SOIL
- LOTS OF SUN
- PRUNING
- SEASONAL, MODERATE RAINFALL
- GOOD NUTRIENTS AND FERTILIZER

PARTS OF TREE

OLIVE

LEAF

FLOWER

TRUNK

OLIVE PIT

USES OF TREE

PITS & BRANCHES (ANIMAL FEED)

OLIVE SOAP

WOOD CARVING

FIREWOOD

OLIVE OIL

OLIVES

unit four

4

plants
and animals

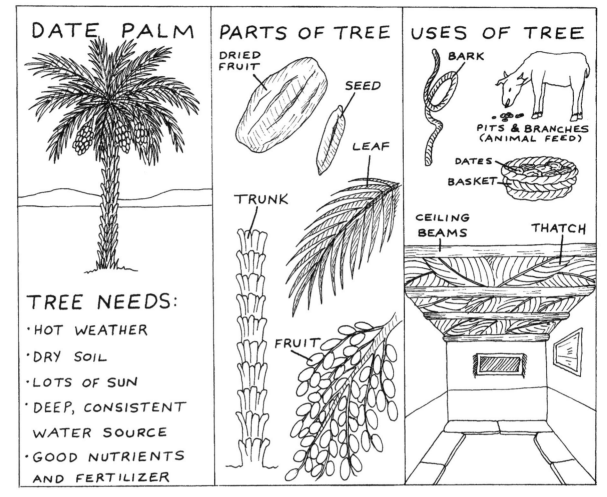

DATE PALM

TREE NEEDS:
- HOT WEATHER
- DRY SOIL
- LOTS OF SUN
- DEEP, CONSISTENT WATER SOURCE
- GOOD NUTRIENTS AND FERTILIZER

PARTS OF TREE

DRIED FRUIT

SEED

LEAF

TRUNK

FRUIT

USES OF TREE

BARK

PITS & BRANCHES (ANIMAL FEED)

DATES

BASKET

CEILING BEAMS

THATCH

illustration 4.5

Materials *continued*

6. Olive oil and a small dish ("extra virgin" is preferred because of its more distinctive odor)

7. Dates, enough for each student to taste one.

Procedures _____

1. Mimeograph or photocopy Illustrations 4.4 and 4.5 and hand them out to the class.

2. Ask the students to name as many kinds of trees as they can. Record their responses on the blackboard or chart paper. Next, see if they can name at least one product from each tree. Some examples:

ash	baseball bats	**oak**	furniture
cedar	pencils	**orange**	orange juice
cocoa	chocolate	**pine**	antiseptics
eucalyptus	writing paper	**rubber**	tires
maple	syrup	**willow**	aspirin (now man-made)

Procedures *continued*

3. Ask if any of the students have heard of a tree called the *date palm*. This is one of the most important trees in the Arab world.

4. Distribute the Date Palm chart to each student. Emphasize the ways in which the tree is connected to its physical environment and with the economy of the Arab world (*Amina and Muhammad's Special Visitor* features an interesting discussion of date farming, p. 57). Point out the many uses to which Arabs put different parts of the date palm (the bark for making ropes, the leaves for weaving baskets, the dates themselves for fruit.) Pass dates out to the classroom, if available, so each student can feel and taste one (*warning: do not swallow the pits!*). Explain that these are the fruit and primary product of the tree. Is this tree grown in your state? Based on the environmental needs of the tree listed in the chart, discuss why the tree would survive well in the Middle East and how it would do in your (similar or different?) environment. For example, the date palm needs plenty of sunshine and cannot produce fruit if it freezes. Does it freeze over and snow in your state?

5. Distribute the Olive Tree Chart to each student. Describe the many products and by-products of the tree. In America, do we put trees to so many different uses? If olives are available, pass them around for the class to see and/or taste (*warning: do not swallow the pits!*). Explain that these are the fruits of the olive tree.

6. Pour a small amount of olive oil for the class to see. This oil, pressed from the fruits of the tree, has been used in Mediterranean and Middle Eastern cuisine for thousands of years. The oil is also used to make *soap*. Soap, in fact, was probably invented by the ancient Egyptians (see **Cultural notes**).

Cultural notes

1. The olive tree, one of the most important food sources in the Middle East, has been cultivated in the region since ancient times. It grows well in rocky, barren soils, and it can withstand high temperatures and lack of rain. The first cultivated varieties of the tree probably appeared in Syria or North Africa. The olive tree is valued for its fruit and, just as importantly, for the natural oil the fruit provides. It is kept orchard-style and can grow to a height of 25 feet or more; a well-preserved orchard can produce fruit for well over a century. The olive tree has several by-products that are useful to people and domesticated animals. Its leaves are fed to sheep and goats; its dead branches are a source of precious firewood; its shade provides a place for people to sit outdoors in the hot, sunny climates of the Middle East; its roots hold onto topsoil during winter floods. Olive oil, the most valuable of all olive products, is extracted from fresh olives, which ripen in October and November, by crushing them in a press. The oil is then stored in pottery jars, tin cans, and glass bottles and used all year long for cooking, as fuel for lamps, as soap, as a moisturizer for skin and hair. The olives themselves can also be eaten solo or as an ingredient in larger dishes; usually, they are preserved in brine, which explains their very salty taste.

2. The date palm is another important tree with many useful by-products. Indigenous to North Africa and the Arabian Peninsula, this tree is a common sight in desert oasis towns, where it is essential to the survival of the community. Its sweet fruit, the date, is dried and eaten singly (sometimes dipped in olive oil or a thick yogurt spread) and used in a variety of cooked dishes as well. A healthy tree will produce fruit for two hundred years. Date pits are fed to animals and burned as fuel; the palm fronds are woven into baskets or used to construct thatch-like roofs for houses; the bark is used to make ropes; the wood is used to make farm tools and beams and rafters for the ceilings of houses. In the past, the tree itself, which grows one hundred feet tall, could be used as a lookout from which to spot approaching caravans and other visitors.

Farms

Objectives

1. To emphasize the fundamental importance of agriculture in our everyday lives

2. To learn about wheat, the main source of bread, cereal, and pasta

3. To discuss the history of farming, which began in the Middle East about 10,000 years ago

Materials

1. Pita or other whole wheat bread

2. Wheat cereal (e.g., Wheaties)

3. Couscous (A North African pasta, couscous can be found in many grocery stores alongside whole grain or specialty rices. It is also widely available in health food stores.)

4. Spaghetti or other pasta

5. Small bowls

6. *Libya*, by Marlene Targ Brill (optional)

7. *Morocco*, by Martin Hintz (optional)

8. *A Family in Morocco*, by Judy Stewart (optional)

9. *Syria*, by Margaret Beaton (optional)

10. World map

Procedures

1. Pass out small bowls of bread, cereal, couscous, and/or pasta for the students to examine and taste.

2. Ask the class what bread, cereal, and pasta are made of. The answer is *wheat*, the most important cultivated grain and probably the first plant to be domesticated.

3. Ask the students what they think wheat looks like before it is harvested and turned into food. Does it look more like a tree, a bush, or a grass? The answer is, a grass — not like the green grass on a lawn, but more like the tall yellow grass one might see in a field. (See *Libya*, p. 17, for pictures of wheat fields, and *Morocco*, p. 77, for a picture of harvested grain.) But domesticated wheat is different from wild wheat and other grasses because it has been bred by farmers over many centuries. If we tried to make bread from wild wheat, the bread would be very coarse and fibrous, and might give us a stomach ache.

Procedures *continued*

Domesticated wheat, by contrast, has more plump, tender seeds and softer husks, allowing us to make bread that is both delicious and easy to digest. (For a picture of a Moroccan girl kneading bread dough, see *A Family in Morocco*, p. 6.)

4. Ask the students what they would do without agriculture. If any grocery stores were left in business, there would be very little to buy in them. Not just bread and cereal and pasta, but most fruits and vegetables, even cookies and candy, would all just disappear. Without grain to feed the farm animals, there would be no meat or milk to buy either. How could we feed ourselves? There would still be some game animals, such as deer, and some wild plant foods, such as nuts and berries. Although it would be difficult to feed the whole world, or even a whole city, in this way, a few people might be able to hunt and gather enough wild foods to survive. In fact, before there was agriculture, all human beings lived as *hunters and gatherers* of wild foods. Back then, however—over 10,000 years ago—

there were more wild foods and far fewer people in the world, so hunting and gathering could feed everyone. Now we need agriculture for almost everything we do.

5. Before reading **The first farm** (below), point out Syria on the world map. Ask the students if they can find the Euphrates, the river near Baalia's home. For a photograph of the Euphrates as it looks today, see *Syria*, p. 15. For a picture of small round huts similar to the ones in Baalia's village, see *Syria*, p. 17.

6. After reading the story, discuss it with the class. How did Baalia's grandmother live when she was a little girl? How was this different from Baalia's own way of life? How might life change even more for Baalia's children and grandchildren?

7. How is wild grain different from domesticated grain? How is a wild dog (such as a wolf) different from a domesticated dog? Ask the students what they think the last line of the story means.

*How did agriculture begin? No one knows exactly,
but the story below gives an imaginary account.*

The first farm

About 10,000 years ago, there was a young woman called Baalia. Baalia lived in the land now known as Syria, but long before there were any presidents or kings. In fact, Baalia lived so long ago that there were no cars, or books, or cities, or even farms. Baalia's village was just ten or twelve circular huts, a short walk from the Euphrates River.

Next door to Baalia lived her grandmother. "When I was a little girl," her grandmother would say, "there were no huts. We did not sit in one place, rooted in the ground like a tree, but roamed throughout the year. We slept beneath the stars, and spent our days hunting gazelles and gathering pistachios and wheat."

Baalia's grandmother had in fact seen many changes during her lifetime. Only lately had Baalia's people settled down in houses along the river. Here they enjoyed fresh water and plenty of fish, but certain things—like wheat—were hard to find. If they wanted bread or roasted cereal, then they had to bring wheat from far away.

One day Baalia's cousins came to visit, carrying many bundles of wheat. They had come from the hills to the north, where wild wheat grew in great abundance. Baalia loved wheat. She would spend hours sifting the little seeds, grinding the kernels into flour, rolling the flour into dough, and baking the dough to make bread.

What kind of bread was it? It was dark and tough, with lots of fiber. Wild wheat is a grass—a tall, tough grass—and the seeds are covered with little jackets called husks. These husks protect the delicate kernels from frost and blazing sun—*and* from people like Baalia, who want to make bread. Baalia had to sift and sift to separate the kernels from the husks, and sometimes the tough, dry husks still got into the bread. Yet Baalia loved wheat. She didn't mind working hard to turn it into bread.

When her cousins arrived, Baalia ran over to greet them and to help them with their load. "Wheat!" she cried, "What wonderful wheat!"

"Be careful," said her oldest cousin, "It's very ripe, and the seeds are scattering far and wide."

Baalia and her cousins carefully carried bundle after bundle to the threshing floor. Back and forth into the hut, wheat seeds dribbled along the path. "Even if we lose some to the birds," Baalia thought, "there will be plenty of grain for the storage pit, and soon I'll make the most delicious bread my cousins have ever tasted!" Just then, however, as she was picking up another bundle, Baalia turned around quickly and ran headlong into her oldest cousin. Hundreds of tiny wheat seeds flew up in a cloud and then rained down upon the rich black earth.

"Baalia!" cried her cousin, "This wheat has come all the way from the Anatolian hills! Did we carry it for six days just so you could spill the seeds all over the ground?"

Baalia was very embarrassed. She threw the bundle on the ground and ran into the hut, sobbing.

*   *   *   *   *

The first farm *continued*

A few days later, Baalia came home from the river with a large jug of water on her head. Just outside her hut, she set the jug down and noticed dozens of little green sprouts against the rich black earth. She kneeled and examined the sprouts closely. Then she took one gently between her thumb and index finger.

"Why, this is *wheat!*" she thought to

weather was dry, she would bring a little water up from the river and sprinkle it over their roots. Soon everyone in her village took notice.

"Have you seen it?" they would say, "Wheat is growing on Baalia's doorstep!"

Some people did not approve of the wheat. According to tradition, wheat was to be found only in the hills, not down here in the river valley. For Baalia to be watering

illustration 4.6

herself. "Wheat...right outside my door." Her eyes wandered along the path to the hut, then back to the patch of sprouts. Suddenly she realized she was kneeling in the very spot where she had run headlong into her cousin, spilling wheat seeds all over the ground.

Over the next few weeks, Baalia watched the little green sprouts develop into healthy young stalks. When the

wheat right outside her door was a very strange thing. Some thought the gods would be angry. Others whispered that Baalia was a witch.

Just as the wheat was fully ripe, the elders of the village held a meeting. They had to decide what to do about Baalia.

"We should send her away!" one old man said. "Banish her from the village. And she can take her precious wheat stalks with her!"

The first farm *continued*

"I agree," said another. "Have you seen the way her wheat is growing? There is some dark power at work here!"

Some people supported Baalia and tried to speak in her defense, but their voices were drowned out by her accusers. One old man claimed that anyone who defended Baalia was probably a witch as well, and ought to be banished from the village along with her. Things looked bad for Baalia. Village opinion was turning against her. One elder after another called for her to be banished or worse.

Just then, there was a sharp *tap, tap, tap* from the back of the room. Everyone turned to see, and a hush fell over the crowd.

"You know me," said an old woman, tapping her cane. "I am Baalia's grandmother, and I have lived longer than anyone in this room. The first half of my life, I roamed the Anatolian hills and slept beneath the stars. Now I sleep inside a stone hut on a riverbank. Things change. In the hills we had plenty of wheat. Here, there was none... until now. *Things change.* Perhaps, now that we are rooted here like a tree, we need to bring the things we once loved in the hills and make them into things we can love again, right here on the riverbank."

Before the elders could give any response, the door of the hut swung open and everyone gasped. There in the doorway stood Baalia, holding a huge stack of bread in her arms.

"Bread for the elders!" she cried. "Bread for the whole village!"

She quickly passed out loaf after loaf of the finest flat bread she'd ever baked — baked, of course, from the flour of her own wheat plants. Before long, all the elders

illustration 4.7

The first farm *continued*

were chewing happily. It was the best bread they'd ever tasted.

So Baalia was not banished after all. In fact, by planting her own seeds the next year, Baalia became the world's first farmer. Soon everyone in her village was tending a little garden of wheat. In later centuries, people would grow vast fields of wheat and many other crops, enough to feed great cities and empires. By that time, the plants had become *domesticated*. Compared to the wild varieties of wheat, each stalk now had more rows of seeds, with plumper kernels and softer husks.

And, you might say, *people* had become domesticated too; they could no longer live without agriculture.

Cultural notes

1. Agriculture probably began in the Middle East, between the Tigris and Euphrates Rivers, in what is now Syria and Iraq. The story above is set in Syria, where archaeologists have discovered some of the earliest evidence for plant cultivation. It appears that, about 9,000 years ago, people gave up their nomadic wandering and settled in small villages while continuing to practice intensive gathering of wild wheat and other plants. Only later, as populations increased, did they begin to domesticate plants and animals. From the Fertile Crescent, agriculture spread throughout the Middle East and the rest of Eurasia.

2. Wheat is still vital to agriculture in the Arab world. We have already noted that Arabs use bread in their diets much more than North Americans do. They also use cracked wheat and bulgur in many of their recipes, thus taking advantage of a wider range of wheat products than are commonly used in North America. The stalks and husks of the wheat are left for livestock to graze on after harvesting and threshing; so wheat, like other Middle Eastern agricultural products, is put to a variety of uses.

Gardens

Objectives

1. To introduce some basic techniques of gardening

2. To appreciate gardening as a source of food and a source of pleasure

3. To read a story about gardening and growing up in the Middle East

4. To compare Arab and American gardens

Materials

1. Blackboard or chart paper and marker

2. Zucchini or other yellow squash (optional)

3. *Koosa* (a Middle Eastern squash), if available

4. Seeds (tomato or other, optional)

5. A small glass or glass jar and some fresh water for sprouting seeds (optional)

Procedures

1. Ask the students if any of them have a vegetable garden at home. What kinds of vegetables do they (or their parents) grow? List these on the blackboard or chart paper.

2. If squash is available, pass it around for the students to examine. This will help them to understand the references to squash in the story. If *koosa* is available, compare it with American forms of squash. *Koosa*, in both shape and color, combines the two types of squash most commonly found in American grocery stores. Its color is a much paler green than the zucchini and more monotoned, like yellow squash. Its shape is long and straight like a zucchini, but plumper like a yellow squash. Arabs prefer to pick them very small and tender.

3. Read **Garden of dreams**, below.

4. Discuss the story. Ask the students if they ever find themselves daydreaming as Khadeeja did. How were Khadeeja's dreams similar to squash on the vine?

5. Ask the students if they can name all the crops mentioned in the story [squash, grapes, wheat, figs, green beans, tomatoes, okra, and herbs]. Compare these crops with the ones grown in the students' own state or neighborhood. How many crops appear on both lists? Which ones are grown on Khadeeja's farm, but not in the students' neighborhood? Which ones are grown in the neighborhood, but not on Khadeeja's farm?

6. If desired, the students may soak seeds until they sprout or grow tomato plants on the windowsill of the classroom.

Garden of dreams

In a little country, on a tiny farm, there was an even smaller garden. The country belonged to a noble king; the farm belonged to a handsome farmer; and the garden belonged to Layla, the farmer's hard-working wife. Because Layla worked so hard — cooking meals, sewing clothes —she needed help from her daughter, Khadeeja, in tending the little garden.

When Khadeeja was a young girl, she used to help her mother in the garden every day. She had loved to fill great round baskets with the vegetables she'd helped her mother grow. But now Khadeeja was going to school, and she was losing interest in gardening. In fact, she hardly helped her mother anymore at all. If you want to know the truth, she spent most of her time daydreaming.

That year Layla planted squash. Now one thing to remember about squash is this: if it gets too big, it gets tough. For sweet and tender squash, you have to watch it carefully and pick it before it's too late.

"Bye, *umma*," said Khadeeja one morning, "I'm off to school."

"Oh Khadeeja!" her mother replied, "On your way home, please check the squash."

"Sure," said Khadeeja, and never gave it a second thought.

That afternoon, Khadeeja came breezing in the door, thinking of her future career as a movie star. Her mother called out from the kitchen, "Did you check the squash?"

"The squash?" said Khadeeja. "Oh yes, the *squash*. It's...not ready yet." Khadeeja didn't want to admit that she'd forgotten to stop in the garden. "Oh well," she thought to herself, "I'll check the squash tomorrow. How much can it grow in just one day?"

But the next day she walked right past the garden again, dreaming of her wedding to a handsome prince. "Or perhaps an American movie star," Khadeeja thought to herself.

"How's the squash?" her mother called, as Khadeeja came in the door.

"Still too small," said Khadeeja. She could have run back to the garden, but she was too busy thinking of how beautiful she would look as a bride. "Besides, I can always check the squash tomorrow," she said to herself.

The next day she came home to find her mother standing in the doorway.

"Well, where's the squash?" her mother asked.

"Still on the vine," said Khadeeja. "Squash grows slowly this year."

"Hmmm," said her mother. "That's odd. We've had plenty of rain—I thought it would be ready by now."

Over the next few days, Khadeeja tried her best to remember the squash on her way home. One day she was walking with a friend, and they were talking so much she forgot to check. Another day there was a brilliant white cloud that looked exactly like a cruise ship sailing across the sky. Khadeeja was staring at the cloud, thinking of how she might sail away to Europe or India or Japan, and she walked right past the garden. Each time she considered going back, but she told herself she'd be walking that way tomorrow, and might as well save herself the trip. "How much can it grow in just one day?"

After a week or two, Khadeeja's mother began to worry about her squash. "I can't understand it," Layla said to herself. "The squash has never taken this long to grow. And I've been wanting to cook squash for so many days now." She decided to go out to the garden herself.

That afternoon, Khadeeja came strolling home at her usual time. Her mother's voice stopped her dead in her tracks.

"Oh, Khadeeja! *Khadeeja*!"

"Yes, *umma*," Khadeeja replied. "What are you doing in the garden?"

"Just checking the squash," said Layla.

"Oh," said Khadeeja, a little timidly. "Is it...ready yet?"

"Well...come see for yourself."

Khadeeja hesitated a moment, then started across the garden to where her mother was standing.

"Come along," said Layla, "It's right over here." Khadeeja came alongside her mother and peered down between the broad green leaves. Then Khadeeja's eyes went wide. There on the ground was a squash, but not just any squash—a huge squash, a *gigantic* squash, a squash as big as a melon. Up and down the garden, in fact, all Khadeeja could see were squash, dozens of them, each one bigger than the last, and each one tougher than shoe leather.

"Lazy creature!" cried her mother, wagging her finger in the air. "Ungrateful daughter! I told you to check the squash! Now it's as big as a house!" Layla pulled a gigantic squash off the vine and began waving it at her daughter. "Look at this squash! This is not the way we eat squash! What will your brothers and sisters have for dinner?"

Khadeeja was so embarrassed, she took off across the garden, looking for a place to hide. At the edge of the garden, she tried to climb under the grape arbor, but her mother soon found her.

"I see you, you lazy creature! Growing up wild! No respect for your elders!"

Khadeeja slipped out of the arbor and dashed into her father's wheat field. Soon she was swallowed up by a sea of wheat, tall and golden brown. When she heard her mother coming, she tried to hide by ducking down between the rows. But her mother, waving the gigantic squash, cut a path right through the wheat to where Khadeeja was hiding.

"Come out here now!" her mother cried. "I'll cook you no supper tonight, ungrateful creature!"

Khadeeja escaped again and scrambled up a fig tree. Her mother came to the bottom of the tree and pointed the gigantic squash in the air.

illustration 4.8

Garden of dreams *continued*

"Okay," said Layla, a little out of breath. "You just stay up there. Don't come home until you've found your own dinner."

Clinging to a slender branch, Khadeeja watched her mother toss the squash to the nearby goats and march back to the house. The sun was setting and the air was turning cool. Feeling quite sorry for herself, Khadeeja climbed down and went back to her mother's little garden. In the fading light, she picked green beans, tomatoes, okra, and herbs. She even found two or three squash that were still small and tender, and she placed them delicately on the top of the pile. When her great round basket was brimming over, she carried the vegetables up to the house and slipped quietly into the kitchen.

An hour later, she presented the whole family with the most delicious meal they'd ever had.

*   *   *   *   *

"I'm sorry, *umma*," Khadeeja said. She and her mother were alone now, relaxing around the television.

"Oh my daughter," said Layla, now quite full and content, "I remember what it was like at your age. So many possibilities, so many dreams." Then Layla leaned forward and looked her daughter in the eye. "But Khadeeja," she said, "your dreams are like squash. They must be harvested at just the right moment. If they are too small, you must let them grow a little longer. But if they're too large, they will lose their sweetness and no one will want them—not even you."

"Yes, *umma*," said Khadeeja, lowering her eyes. "I understand."

Layla took her daughter in her arms and rocked her gently. "Just remember," Layla said, "even if you become a movie star, you'll still have to *check the squash*."

"I'll remember," said Khadeeja, and she buried her face in the folds of her mother's robe. It felt so warm and cozy, Khadeeja thought she'd stay that way forever. After a while, though, she couldn't help peeking at the TV screen. There, in the blue light of another world, a jet plane was soaring overhead.

illustration 4.9

Cultural notes

1. In the Middle East, it is common for households to keep a small garden. Squash, green beans, tomatoes, okra, and other vegetables are grown for the family's personal use. On a farm, such garden vegetables are grown in addition to larger crops, such as wheat and figs, which are usually intended for sale at market. Household gardens supply families with fresh vegetables for most of the year. Open-air markets also make extremely fresh produce available to people in urban areas; as a result, the diet of most Arabs contains more fresh fruit and vegetable than do most Western diets. Because fresh produce is tastier than frozen or canned goods, this means that most Arabs enjoy a healthy, flavorful diet. People are very proud of their household gardens. Because they appreciate freshness and enjoy eating home-grown produce, Arab families tend to eat a lot of whatever vegetable is in season and then eat no more of it until the next year. In America, because our climate varies so much from one region to another, we have grown accustomed to eating the same fruits and vegetables year round. For gardeners, both here and in the Middle East, there is a renewed appreciation for each fruit or vegetable as it comes into season each year.

2. Recipe for *koosa mahshi* (stuffed squash), adapted from *A Taste of Lebanon: Cooking Today the Lebanese Way*, by Mary Salloum.

8 small zucchini *or* vegetable marrow (5-6" long)	1/4 tsp. pepper
3/4 cup rice (washed and drained)	1/2 tsp. cinnamon
1 cup finely ground beef or lamb	2 Tbsp. butter
1-1/2 tsp. salt	2 Tbsp. dried mint
1 5-1/2 oz. can tomato paste	water
Preheat oven to 400.	

    Cut off the stem of zucchini or marrow. Hollow out with an apple corer, table knife, or zucchini corer, making sure to leave 1/4" of skin all around. Set aside.

    Mix together the remaining ingredients, except for tomato paste and water. Stuff the zucchini or marrow with the filling, leaving a half inch of space at the top. Lay them side by side in small roasting pan. Mix 1 cup of water with the tomato paste. Pour it over the stuffed vegetables. Add additional water to cover the zucchini. Cover and bake for 1 hour, or until the rice is fully cooked. Serve with fresh yogurt and salad.

unit four
4
plants and animals

Horses and camels

Objectives

1. To learn about horses and camels, the most famous animals of the Middle East

2. To learn about pastoralism, a traditional way of life based on herding

3. To read and discuss a just-so story about the relations between animals and humans

Materials

1. World map

2. *The Arabian Desert*, by John Carter (optional)

3. *Egypt*, by Wilbur Cross (optional)

4. *Arab Horses*, by Butterfly Books (optional)

5. *Khaled and Aida*, a traditional Arab tale published by Butterfly Books (optional)

6. *Camels*, by Butterfly Books (optional)

Procedures

1. On the blackboard or chart paper, draw two large columns labeled "Horses" and "Camels." First ask the students what they know about horses. Prompt them with questions such as:

    How tall is a horse?

    How many legs do horses have?

    What covers a horse's neck?

    How do horses help people?

    How fast can horses run?

    What part of the world do horses come from?

2. If the students are unsure where horses originated, explain that they once lived wild in great herds on the grasslands of Eurasia, including parts of the Middle East. (Point out the Middle East on the world map.) Many centuries ago, some of these wild

horses were tamed by tribespeople and kept for breeding. Arabian horses became famous throughout the world for their beauty and speed. (This is illustrated in *Arab Horses*, a picture book for younger readers.)

3. *Khaled and Aida* illustrates how Arab tribespeople once used horses in hunting and warfare. If desired, this book may be read and discussed. Emphasize that the story takes place a long time ago, and that the Bedouin (desert nomads) no longer live in the traditional ways depicted here.

4. Next ask the students what they know about camels. For each observation made about horses, try to elicit a comparable one about camels. For example, if horses are tall, are camels even taller? (Photographs of camels may be found in *The Arabian Desert*,

Procedures *continued*

pp. 74-79, and in *Egypt*, p. 94. *Camels* is a picture book for younger readers.) Write the students' observations in the "Camels" column on the blackboard or chart paper.

5. Read **Why camels spit and bellow**. Explain that this is a "just-so" story, an imaginary tale meant to explain how things came to be: in this case, how horses were created and camels acquired the habit of spitting and bellowing.

6. At the end of the story, ask the students what kind of animal Sabra became. Why did the humans love Sabra when she was a camel? Why did they love her even more when she was changed into a horse? What kept the camels from understanding the relationship between Sabra and the humans?

7. Discuss the camels in the story. Ask the students what they learned about camels and add these observations to the chart. For example, the story mentions the following points:

    a. There are several kinds of camels: pack camels, riding camels, and she-camels

    b. Camels are used to carry loads and cross the open sands

    c. Camel's milk is an important part of the Bedouin diet

    d. Camel's hair is used to make clothing, such as the shaykh's jacket

8. Discuss the horse in the story. Ask the students what they learned about horses and why humans keep them. If the students offer new observations, add these to the "Horses" column on the chart.

9. Ask students to write their own just-so stories. Possible topics include: why camels have humps; why horses have manes; why humans ride horses (or camels); why humans keep horses (or camels); and so on.

Why camels spit and bellow

Long ago, when the Arabian Desert had seen neither a pipeline nor a pickup truck, the only way to cross the sands was by camel. Camels were the prized possessions of the people known as *Bedouin*. Moving from water hole to water hole, the Bedouin relied on camels to carry their houses (which were tents), their clothes (which were long, flowing robes), and their food (which was camel's milk).

The Bedouin loved their camels. They gave them names, sang songs about them, and could tell tales about each member of the herd. For the Bedouin, no two camels were alike. Each had a special face, a special job to do, and a special personality. Some camels were slow and strong and could carry great loads. Faster ones were kept just for riding. And most beloved of all were the she-camels, because they were the bearers of delicious milk.

And so it was that in one herd, belonging to a great shaykh, there lived a she-camel called Sabra. Sabra was an old camel with many sons and daughters. Because she was well-traveled and wise, Sabra was respected by the people of the tribe, including the great shaykh himself. Whenever they had a problem, the people would come to Sabra for advice. They would sit with her at night and tell her their secrets.

This made the other camels very jealous. "We agreed to serve humans," they muttered among themselves. "We did not agree to love them as Sabra does." The most respected camels in the herd went to the Lord of Creation to complain about Sabra, in hopes that she would be punished for her vanity. They prepared a long list of complaints against her, and they recited them, one by one, to the Lord of Creation, who listened in the wind.

"Sabra gives the humans milk," a young she-camel said, "but because she loves them, her milk is sweet, and they pamper her."

illustration 4.10

Why camels spit and bellow *continued*

"Sabra gives them hair," said a camel with a bushy coat, "but because she loves them, her hair is glimmering and soft, and their shaykh will wear clothes of no other material."

"Sabra carries their loads across the open sands," a pack camel said, "but because she loves them, she carries more than any camel should bear."

"Sabra carries messages between their far-flung camps," said a riding camel, "but because she loves them, she never stumbles."

The Lord of Creation listened in the wind, and he knew that Sabra had done nothing wrong. He would not punish Sabra; he would reward her.

"This is my judgement," he said to the gathering of camels. "I will change the taste of Sabra's milk and staunch its flow. I will make her hair short and slick — except on her neck and tail — so that no shaykh will wear it for his robes. I will straighten her back and shorten her legs, so she cannot carry heavy loads. I will make her thirsty, so she cannot cross the open sands, and turn the pads of her feet into bone. This is what Sabra deserves for loving humans as well as serving them."

When the camels returned to their camp, they saw the humans gathered around a strange and beautiful beast. It was smaller than a camel, but it ran much faster. Its hair was short and slick and black as night, but it shined like polished steel. The animal dashed and pranced and snorted, and the people cheered in amazement. Soon, the animal grew thirsty and its feet, which were as hard as bone, grew sore. The humans warily approached the creature, stroked its sides and played with the hair on its neck and tail. Silence fell over the crowd.

Suddenly, the shaykh spoke in a loud voice. "People of my camp," he said, "we began this day in sadness, when we woke

illustration 4.11

Why camels spit and bellow *continued*

to discover that Sabra, the noblest of camels, had disappeared. But the Lord of Creation has given us a better beast in her place. Nobler and more beautiful than the noblest and most beautiful of camels. Let this be our new custom. This animal will never carry heavy loads. It will drink as we drink. It will be fed the best grain. Its hair will be brushed like the hair of our sons and daughters. We will make shoes of iron for its tender feet, and we will not take milk from its young."

Then the camels realized that this strange and beautiful beast was Sabra! The Lord of Creation had changed her, but now the humans loved her even more. The camels were filled with envy. "Why has the Lord of Creation done this?" they asked each other. But no one knew the answer. All they could do was spit and bellow. And camels spit and bellow to this very day.

illustration 4.12

Cultural notes

1. The camel is immediately associated with the Middle East. Few people realize, however, that another domesticated animal, the horse, is also indigenous to this region. Horses were domesticated about 4,000 years ago, and they have played an important role in human history ever since. Horses changed the way we hunt, fight, travel, and farm. Most modern varieties of horse — and *all* thoroughbred race horses — descend from genetic stock which horse-breeders describe as "Arabian," "Oriental," or "Libyan." This stock originated in North Africa and is distinguishable from the "Mongolian" breeds of the Eurasian steppes and the "Celtic pony" breeds of northwest Europe. The Middle Eastern horse is known for speed, intelligence, and beauty. The pure-bred Arabian horse is the modern breed closest in appearance to the ancient North African ancestor. It has flared nostrils, like those of a camel, which help it breathe the hot desert air; and its hooves are flatter and wider than those of other horses, which helps it gallop at great speed over rocky or sandy soil.

2. In the Arab world, horses have traditionally been used for hunting, racing, and warfare. They were considered too precious to be used as pack or plow animals; that work was left to donkeys, mules, and camels. The horse was the ultimate prestige symbol; it allowed men to move very quickly in battle — much faster than the fastest camel — and it helped hunters pursue animals, such as lions or gazelles, which were known for their lightening speed. Only wealthy people could afford to keep horses. Unlike camels, which can survive on very little water, horses must be watered frequently. Unlike sheep and goats, which survive easily on natural grasses and shrubs, domesticated horses are more delicate and must have their diets supplemented with barley and oats. Their coats must be groomed; special care is given to their hooves, which must be protected with special shoes; and expert riding requires expensive saddles, stirrups, reins, and other paraphernalia. For these reasons, Arabian horses have often been associated with wealthy and powerful people: aristocrats, warriors, merchants, and royalty.

3. A sample report on camels is included in the review lesson for Unit 4. Please refer to it for background information on camels. Make sure your students understand the difference between a highly specialized animal like the horse, and a more generally useful one like the camel. In the Middle East, horses are used almost exclusively for transportation; the camel, by contrast, has a variety of uses: its stamina makes it good for long-distance transport across dry terrain; its dung can be used as fuel and fertilizer; its hair and hide can be used to make tents, clothes, ropes, saddlebags, saddleblankets, rugs, and bedding; its milk can be drunk or used to make cheese, butter, and yogurt; its meat can be cooked. And so on. To help your students comprehend these differences, you might want to compare horses and cows, since the latter are more familiar to North American children. What do we use horses and cows for? Do we eat horses? Do we drink horse milk? Do we eat cows? Do we drink cow milk? If cows are so useful, why do we keep horses at all?

Goats and sheep

Objectives

1. To compare the ways in which Arabs and Americans use animal resources

2. To learn about goats and sheep, the most important herd animals in the Middle East

3. To read a story about modern Bedouin and their changing ways of life

4. To solve word problems based on information in the story

Materials

1. Blackboard or chart paper and marker

Procedures

1. Ask the students to list some four-legged animals they have seen on a farm or in a petting zoo. Examples might be cows, pigs, or sheep. Use three or four of these as column headings on the blackboard or chart paper.

2. Now ask the students how many products they can think of from each of the listed animals. To help organize the answers, construct three rows labeled **Food**, **Clothing**, and **Other**. The finished chart might look like this:

	Cows	**Pigs**	**Sheep**
Food	roast beef hamburger milk cheese butter	ham pork chops bacon pork rinds lard	lamb yogurt clarified butter milk cheese
Clothing	leather shoes leather belts leather bags	shoes belts	wool sweaters wool caps wool mittens
Other	leather furniture	toothpaste (from lard)	rope

3. Read **Jaafar's solution** (below) and discuss the story. Who are the Bedouin, and where do they live? How is life changing for Jaafar's family? When his father was trying to solve arithmetic problems, why did Jaafar hesitate to tell the solution?

Procedures *continued*

4. Make a chart like the one above, but this time for goats and sheep. Ask the students how many products Jaafar's family got from goats, on the one hand, and sheep, on the other. The chart might look like this:

	Goats	Sheep
Food	milk yogurt	lamb *mansaf*
Clothing		wool clothes wool mattresses
Other	hair tents	

5. Other products from goats and sheep are discussed in **Cultural notes**. If appropriate, these products may be added to the chart.

6. Discuss the similarities and differences between the two charts. On the basis of these similarities and differences, the students should compare how Bedouin and Americans use animal resources.

7. Have the students solve the following word problems with reference to the story. (*No calculators, please!*) JD are Jordanian Dinars.

    a. How many fines did Jaafar's father have to pay last spring? [6 or 7]

    b. About how much did he have to pay in fines? [JD30-JD35]

    c. How many goats did Jaafar's family own? [18] How many sheep? [10]

    d. About how much was each goat worth? [JD50] Each sheep? [JD60]

    e. If Jaafar's father sells half of the goats, about how much would he get? [JD450]

    f. If Jaafar's father sells half of the sheep, about how much would he get? [JD300]

    g. About how much would Jaafar's father get if he sells half of the goats *and* half of the sheep? [JD750]

    h. How much did each seedling cost? [JD14]

    i. If Jaafar's father sells half of the goats and half of the sheep, how many seedlings could he buy? [53]

    j. If Jaafar's father buys only 45 seedlings, how much money would be left over for Hiyyam's wedding? [JD120]

    k. If Jaafar's father buys 45 seedlings, and his investment is tripled when he takes his olives to market, what is the total amount would he bring home? [JD1,890. This is called his *gross* income.]

    l. How much of that total would be profit? [JD1,260. This is called his *net* income.]

illustration 4.13

Jaafar's solution

My name is Jaafar. I spend the summer in a tent made of goat-hair in the country of Jordan. My people are called *Bedouin*.

A long time ago, most Bedouin lived in the desert. They moved from place to place with the seasons, herding their animals from one watering hole to another. Though my family and I are Bedouin, we don't live in the old way. Most of the year, we stay in a village where our family has a nice house and I go to school. In the summer though, I live in a tent in the countryside where we still keep goats and sheep. Nowadays, even in the countryside, we have to stay on our own land. If we wander into someone else's garden or start grazing on someone else's land, we have to pay a fine of five dinars. My father hates paying fines.

Last spring the goats kept trespassing on our neighbors' land and nibbling on their olive trees. After paying six or seven fines, my father came home and made a startling announcement.

"The price of olives has gone way up," he declared. "If we grow olives, we could be rich!"

"What are you saying?" said my mother. "We are not farmers. Where would we get these trees you are talking about?"

"We could sell the goats to buy the seedlings," said my father. "The goats are no good anyway; they eat everything in sight. If I have to pay another fine, I swear I'll sell all the goats tomorrow!"

"But we need the goats!" cried my big sister, Hiyyam. "If we have no goats, how will we make *mansaf* for my wedding?"

Mansaf is a special yogurt dish we make from goat's milk. A wedding is not a wedding without *mansaf*. In America, it would be like Thanksgiving without turkey or Halloween without candy.

My father could see that Hiyyam had a point. "Well, let's think about this," he said. "If we make enough money in the olive business, we could *buy* the *mansaf* for the wedding..."

My sister stared in horror at my father. Store-bought *mansaf* could never be as good as homemade. Before Hiyyam could say anything, my mother jumped in.

Jaafar's solution *continued*

"God forbid!" she cried. "How can we sell the goats? The very tent you're sitting in is made of goat-hair! We will keep our goats and make our own *mansaf*, as we've always done! If we must sell something, it should be the sheep. The sheep are a nuisance, and I'm tired of spinning so much wool and weaving things for the tent. With all the money you say we'll be making, we can just buy the extra things we need in town."

Now my sister stared at my mother. "But *umma*! What about my wedding! If we have no sheep, we'll have no lamb for the feast. And we need their wool to stuff my mattresses!"

According to Bedouin custom, you see, a bride usually receives plump mattresses as part of her wedding gift. Without wool, there could be no mattresses, and without lamb, there could be no feast.

My mother could see that Hiyyam had a point. An awkward silence filled the tent.

No one knew what to do. Meanwhile, I had already thought of a solution. Now that everyone was stumped, I cleared my throat to speak. Even though I was the youngest in the room, my father and mother and sister all turned to listen.

"May I make a suggestion?" I asked politely. "Right now we have eighteen goats and ten sheep. If we sell half of the goats and half of the sheep, would we have enough money to buy the seedlings?"

"Hmmm ... interesting suggestion, Jaafar," said my father. "Let me see. Each goat is worth about 50 dinars. Each sheep could bring about 60. To plant olive trees, we need a lot of seedlings, and they cost about 14 dinars each." My father tried to calculate the figures in his head, but he got confused and had to start over. Finally he picked up a stick and drew the numbers on the ground.

Meanwhile, I had already figured it out. If I spoke too soon, though, it would look

illustration 4.14

Jaafar's solution *continued*

like I was showing off. My father was very sensitive about that kind of thing. So I held my tongue and waited patiently for him to finish.

Suddenly he looked up from the floor. "I've got it!" he declared, pointing the stick into the air. "If we sell half the goats and half the sheep, we'll be able to buy 45 seedlings, and still have money left over for Hiyyam's wedding."

"Oh *abu*!" exclaimed my sister. "Thank you! A thousand, thousand thanks!"

"What a relief," said my mother.

"Do you know what this means?" asked my father, beaming. "Next year, when we bring the olives to market, we can *triple* our investment!"

"How much would that be?" asked Hiyyam.

"Well, let's see," said my father, and soon he was squatting again, drawing numbers in the loose earth. Of course, I already knew the answer, but I didn't say a word. That's the way it is with us; as long as I live in my father's house, I have to show respect.

Someday, though, I plan to move out. Maybe I'll become a school teacher or start a business in the city. And the first thing I'll do, once I have a little money of my own, is buy a present for my father. I've already got the perfect gift in mind: a *calculator*.

illustration 4.15

Cultural notes

1. The modern-day goat is descended from the wild, Bezoar goat, which is still found throughout the Middle East, in Turkey, Iraq, Iran, Afghanistan, and Pakistan. Wild goats were domesticated at least 9,000 years ago; they are one of the first animals to be domesticated by humans. They can live in dry climates and subsist on meager vegetation. Unlike sheep, which are commonly thought to be "stupid," goats are known for their intelligence and adaptive skills. They can be raised very cheaply — if forage exists in the local environment, they will inevitably find it — a fact which makes them the most popular variety of livestock in the world today. In the Middle East, goats are kept for their hair (which can be woven into tents and beautiful rugs), hides (which provide leather), flesh (which can be cooked and eaten), and milk (which can be drunk or stored in the form of cheese, yogurt, or butter). In the past, goat bones were used to make awls and needles; their horns were used to make bugles and fluid containers.

2. Goats are hardy — when need be, they can live off tree bark, paper, dried-out plants, even human waste — and they breed quickly. All this makes goats a reliable source of "drought insurance." More valuable livestock (camels, sheep, horses) cannot live on the goat's highly diversified diet, and they are less likely to survive extended periods of drought. If a core herd of goats lives through the drought, a family can gradually recoup its losses. If a family owns only sheep or camels, however, their situation will be much more desperate. In fact, as soon as the drought breaks, they will be forced to buy goats as a short-term solution to their dietary and financial problems. For these reasons, it is wise to keep a healthy mix of livestock; or, if you are poor, to keep *only* goats.

3. Sheep were domesticated in the Middle East, probably alongside goats, about 9,000 years ago. Although they provide all the by-products associated with goats, sheep are kept primarily for their wool; this product makes them much more valuable than goats, which can only produce coarse hair. On average, sheep require greater care and better vegetation than do goats, but the value of wool on the market makes this higher investment worthwhile. It is widely believed that the meat of sheep ("mutton") is finer than goat meat, and this is another reason to keep them. As a family's financial situation improves, they will tend to buy more sheep than goats. This pattern can be seen on a world scale as well: when sheep and goats are kept largely for subsistence and local trade, goats prevail; when sheep and goats are raised commercially for international trade, sheep are by far the more popular species.

Review lesson on plants and animals

Objectives

1. To explore the overall environment of the Arab World

2. To review readings from Unit 4 and discuss the Middle East's many plants and animals

3. To research and write a detailed report about one plant or animal discussed in Unit 4

Materials

1. Chart paper and marker

2. World map

3. Arab stories and cultural notes from Unit 4

4. Pen and paper for each student

5. Library reference books on date palms, olive trees, wheat, camels, horses, sheep, goats, squash, coffee, tea, or any other plant or animal mentioned in Unit 4

Procedures

1. Construct a chart like the one below, including as many of the listed plants and animals discussed in Unit 4 as possible. Be sure also to include any fruits or vegetables listed in the Pyramid of Arab Foods (illustration 4.3).

2. Some of the plants and animals will be familiar from Unit 4, others many need to be introduced to the class (such as okra and pomegranates).

3. Using the information provided throughout Unit 4, have the students fill in the blanks in the chart below. This may be done in a group discussion or as an individual assignment.

4. Much of the information required for filling in the chart is not provided in Unit 4 lesson plans. Assign, or have

the student select, a plant or animal discussed in Unit 4. Provide each student with reference materials for writing a brief essay on the plant or animal of their choice. Make sure that as many of the plants and animals as possible are assigned to students.

5. Read **Camels** (below) to the class. This report was written by Benjamin Shryock, of Statesboro, Georgia, when he was in the 4th grade. Encourage your students to write similar reports based on the information provided in Unit 4 and available reference materials. Make sure that the relationship between people and the plants or animals discussed is included in the essays. In what ways do humans care for the plants and animals? What resources are they given in return for their labor?

Procedures *continued*

6. A very important animal in the Arab world which has not been discussed in this unit is the donkey. Encourage some of your students to write their report on donkeys, or mules. An illustration of a donkey is included in this lesson.

6. After the assignment has been completed — it may take several days of in-class work or may be assigned as homework — have the students read and discuss their reports. Add all newly acquired information to the below chart.

7. Discuss the similarities and differences between the examples in the essays and the plants and animals found in the students' own communities.

Plants	Caretaking and Environmental Needs	Products and By-products	Land of Origin or Indigenous Region
Olive tree	arid soil plenty of sun	olive oil wood for carving	Syria or North Africa
Date Palm	hot temperatures steady water source	ropes dates	Arabian Peninsula North Africa
Wheat	water, fertile soil	flour bread pasta	Mesopotamia
Coffee			

[Add other plants to the list.]

Animals	Caretaking and Environmental Needs	Products and By-products	Land of Origin or Indigenous Region
Sheep	plenty of green food	wool meat	Middle East and South Asia
Camels	arid climates	labor milk	India Arabian Peninsula
Goats			
Horses			
Donkeys			
Mules			
Dogs			
Hunting falcons			

[Add other animals to the list.]

illustration 4.16

A+

Nice Report!

Camels

by Benjamin Paul Shryock

In this report I will be writing about Dromedary camels that live in the desert of Africa and the Mideast. The camel family is bigger than you think. Not all camels live in the desert. Did you know that some members of the camel family live in South America? They are the Alpaca, Guanaco, Vicuna and Llama. Some of them live where it is cold and snowy in Asia. These camels have two humps on their backs. Some people have even shipped camels to Australia. There are 50,000 of them there. The Dromedary camel has only one hump on his back.

Camels are special because they live in the desert. Everyone knows that camels have humps, but they are not filled with water. The hump is really filled with fat used for energy. A camel's long neck and long legs help him to raise his head as high as 12 feet in the air. On a flat desert he can see for miles. To protect their eyes during a sand storm the camels have long eyelashes and three eyelids. One eyelid acts like a windshield wiper and is so thin that the camel can see through it. When sand is blowing a camel can close its nose. Camels have huge feet shaped like big plates that help them walk on the sand. Because camels lose water very slowly, they can lose four times as much water as a man. They can drink as much as 35 gallons of water in less than six minutes! Camels will eat almost anything.

People and camels need each other in order to survive in the desert. If camels and people did not need each other they would probably never be together. Camels depend on people to give them food and clean water from deep wells. Did you know that when it rains in the desert, camels will run away because there is plenty of water? Camels have nasty tempers. They can hold a grudge for years. A camel has a painful bite and a dangerous kick. Arabs love their horses, but they never get close to their camels. In the desert, the camel is the only animal that can do hard work. He can carry a load of his own weight for 25 miles a day.

Camels are valuable to Arabs. Tents of Arab tribes are woven from the hair that camels shed from their skin, and ivory can be made from their dried bones. Camel's milk is thick and rich, and Arabs drink and make cheese out of it. The desert people also eat young camels. Today, Arabs drive around in Toyota pickup trucks, but sometimes they carry their camels in the back.

The End

Sources of information:

1. The World Book Encyclopedia
2. Mammals, A Golden Nature Guide
3. Childcraft: About Animals
4. Zoobooks, Camels
5. Conversations with my brother, who has lived with the Arab people of Yemen.

holidays and celebrations

What are holidays?

Objectives

1. To identify some important American holidays

2. To discuss the special activities and observances associated with these days

3. To learn three categories of holidays: **religious**, **national**, and **personal**

4. To practice categorizing information in the form of simple charts and diagrams

5. To introduce three important Muslim holidays: **Ramadan**, **Eed Al-Fitr**, and **Eed Al-Adha**

Materials

1. Blackboard or chart paper and marker

2. Construction paper

3. Crayons or other markers

Procedures

1. Ask the students to name the most important holidays they celebrate. It will help to write the months on the blackboard or chart paper and to list the holidays according to the calendar. Although the students are unlikely to name all the holidays listed below, a complete calendar might look like this:

January	New Year's Day Martin Luther King Day Eed Al-Fitr (see **Cultural notes**)	**July**	Independence Day (Fourth of July)
February	Valentine's Day President's Day	**August**	
March	Eed Al-Adha (see **Cultural notes**) Saint Patrick's Day	**September**	Labor Day Rosh Hashanah Yom Kippur
April	Passover Easter	**October**	Halloween
May	Mother's Day Memorial Day	**November**	Thanksgiving
June	Father's Day	**December**	Hanukkah Christmas Kwaanza Ramadan (see **Cultural notes**)

2. Choose one or two of the most important holidays on the list and have the students describe what they do on that day. If desired, the responses may be organized according to categories such as **What we wear**, **What we eat**, **Where we go**, **What we hear**, **What we see**, and **What we do**. A simple chart might look like this:

	What we wear	**What we eat**	**What we do**
July Fourth	shorts t-shirts bathing suits sandals	barbecued chicken hot dogs corn-on-the-cob potato salad watermelon, etc.	fly the flag sing patriotic songs watch fireworks
Halloween	costumes of ghosts witches super heroes monsters, etc.	chocolate bars candy corn apples	carve pumpkins scare people go trick-or-treating bob for apples

Procedures *continued*

3. Ask the students if they know the difference between a **religious** and a **national** holiday. See if they can name an example of both. If the students name Christmas and the Fourth of July, for example, ask them who celebrates Christmas [Christians all over the world] and who celebrates the Fourth [Americans of all religions]. This may be illustrated with a Venn diagram on the blackboard or chart paper. Ask the students to fill in examples of (a) people who celebrate Christmas but not July Fourth, (b) people who celebrate July Fourth but not Christmas, and (c) people who celebrate both Christmas and July Fourth.

4. When the distinction between religious and national holidays is clearly understood, introduce the idea of a **personal** holiday or celebration. Ask the class what kind of celebration is a birthday, a wedding, or an anniversary. Is it a religious holiday, like Christmas or Hanukkah? If not, why not? Is it a national holiday, like July Fourth or Thanksgiving? If not, why not? Explain that all holidays bring people together. The difference is that **religious holidays** bring together *people of many different countries*, **national holidays** bring together *people of just one country*, and **personal holidays** bring together *the family and friends of just one person* (or a married couple).

5. As a classroom or homework assignment, ask the students to make a chart classifying each of the holidays on the calendar as a religious, national, or personal holiday (have them include their own birthdays and the birthdays of their close family members). Students will probably disagree about the status of some holidays. Many people consider Thanksgiving a religious holiday. Other holidays, such as Halloween, Valentine's Day, and St. Patrick's Day, used to be religious holidays but now are largely secular. Even Christmas does not seem as explicitly religious as it once did. Many non-Christians in North America and around the world celebrate Christmas as a kind of "winter festival." If necessary, ask students to explain why they categorized the holidays in different ways. A finished chart might look like this:

Religious	**National**	**Personal**
Ramadan	New Year's Day	My birthday
Eed Al-Fitr	Martin Luther King Day	My mother's birthday
Passover	Valentine's Day	My father's birthday
Easter	St. Patrick's Day	My sister's birthday
Eed Al-Adha	Mother's Day	
Rosh Hashanah	Memorial Day	
Yom Kippur	Father's Day	
Hanukkah	Independence Day	
Christmas	Labor Day	
Kwaanza	Halloween	
	Thanksgiving	

Procedures *continued*

6. If desired, the students may draw a picture of how their favorite holiday is celebrated.

7. If your students mention Islamic holidays — and in some parts of the United States, this is a good possibility — let them explain the holidays to their classmates. If no one mentions Islamic holidays — another strong possibility, even when their are Muslim boys and girls in your class — then briefly do so yourself, using the material provided in **Cultural notes**. More detail on these topics will be provided in the next few lessons. Explain to students that these are religious holidays, like Christmas and Hannukah, celebrated by millions of people around the world.

Cultural notes

1. Islam is the fastest-growing religion in America. Many school districts also include its holidays along with the more familiar Jewish and Christian ones. The dates of Islamic holidays are not determined by the solar calendar we use in the West. Instead, Muslims follow a lunar calendar which is based on the phases of the moon. The Islamic calendar moves ahead of the Gregorian (solar-adjusted) calendar at a rate of ten days each year. In 1999, Ramadan should start on or near December 9. In 2000, it will begin roughly ten days earlier, on November 29. The same pattern holds for all other Islamic holidays as well. Some important Islamic holidays are:

   Ramadan. A month of fasting, set aside to celebrate God's revelation of the Quran (the holy book of Islam) to the Prophet Muhammad. (For more details, see the upcoming lesson on **Ramadan and Eed Al-Fitr**).

   Eed Al-Fitr. A feast which marks the end of Ramadan (see the upcoming lesson on **Ramadan and Eed Al-Fitr**).

   Eed Al-Adha (sounds like **odd**-*hah*). A feast commemorating Abraham's willingness to sacrifice his son in obedience to God. Eed Al-Adha is also associated with the *Hajj*, or pilgrimage to Mecca (see the upcoming lesson on **Eed Al-Adha and the Hajj**).

2. In 1999, the holy month of Ramadan should begin on December 9, Eed Al-Fitr should fall on January 8, 2000, and Eed Al-Adha should fall on March 16, 2000. To determine the exact date on which the holiday will fall this year, call the Office of Islamic Affairs at the Royal Embassy of Saudi Arabia, (202) 342-3800. If desired, you can request that the Embassy send your class an Islamic calendar as well.

Three great religions

Objectives

1. To introduce three major religions that originated in the Middle East: **Judaism**, **Christianity**, and **Islam**

2. To learn more about Islam and its followers (who are called Muslims)

3. To draw a Venn diagram illustrating differences between **Muslims** and **Arabs**

4. To learn more about the Islamic calendar

Materials

1. *Islam*, by Isma'il R. Al Faruqi (or a comparable picture book on Islam)

2. Blackboard or chart paper and marker

3. World map

4. Calendar chart from previous lesson

5. *Egypt*, by Wilbur Cross (or any comparable picture book on Egypt)

6. Construction paper (optional)

7. Ruler (optional)

8. Crayons or other markers (optional)

Procedures

1. Explain to the class that people around the world follow different religions. Each religion has its own way of worshipping and celebrating. Christians go to churches and Jews go to synagogues. Buddhists often have a small personal shrine in their home, while Native Americans may worship outdoors.

2. Some religions, such as Hinduism in India or Shinto in Japan, have many gods or other supernatural beings. These are called *polytheistic* religions. Belief in only one God, by contrast, is called *monotheism*. Among the major world religions, there are just three monotheistic faiths: Judaism, Christianity, and Islam.

3. In the United States, most students are at least passingly familiar with Judaism

and Christianity. Islam, however, is only vaguely understood. Explain to the class that Islam is a major world religion, with nearly one billion followers. These followers are called *Muslims*. For aspects of Islamic belief and practice, see **Cultural notes**.

4. Muslims and Arabs are often assumed to be the same people, but this is not the case. *Arabs* are people who speak Arabic as their native language. By this definition, most Arabs are Muslims, but millions of others are Christians or Jews. For many, the idea of an "Arab Jew" might seem to be a contradiction in terms, yet the hard line that is drawn between Jewish and Arab identities today was not always so sharply drawn in the past. In Israel and the Arab states, there are roughly

a million Jews who speak Arabic as their native tongue. For the most part, these are "Sephardic" or "Oriental" Jews, and their social customs and ways of life closely resemble those of Arab Muslims (as well as Turks, Persians, and other Middle Eastern Muslim peoples). Many Westerners are also surprised to learn that the Arab world is nearly 10% Christian. Some countries, like Lebanon, Syria, Egypt, Jordan, Palestine, and Iraq, have large Arab Christian communities. These Christians are not "converts" from Islam; they are descendants of the Christian communities that existed in the Middle East before the rise of Islam (see **Cultural notes**).

5. Most of the world's Muslims, fully 80%, are *non*-Arabs who live outside the Middle East. Americans are sometimes astonished to learn that the four countries with the largest Muslim populations are Indonesia, Pakistan, Bangladesh, and India — all in South or Southeast Asia (for a simple map of the Islamic world, see *Islam*, p. 2).

6. To illustrate these points, draw a Venn diagram on the blackboard or chart paper. First draw a circle to represent the category of *Arabs* (in the sense of native speakers of Arabic). This circle contains roughly 200 million people. Then draw a large rectangle overlapping most of the circle but extending well beyond it. This rectangle represents the category of *Muslims* worldwide, and it contains roughly one billion people.

7. Now ask the students how they would label the *intersection* of the circle and the rectangle [Arab Muslims]. In what part of the world do most Arab Muslims live? [In the Middle East and North Africa.] On the world map, point out the Middle East and North Africa.

8. Next, ask the students how they would label the area of the rectangle *beyond* the circle [non-Arab Muslims]. Where do most non-Arab Muslims live? [In South and Southeast Asia, but also in the former Soviet Union, Eastern Europe, Turkey, and sub-Saharan Africa.] Point out the major Islamic countries outside the Arab world.

9. Finally, ask the students how they would label the part of the circle not intersected by the rectangle. [This area represents Arabic speakers who are not Muslims.] About one million of these Arabic speakers are Jews and another fourteen million are Christians. If desired, draw two more large rectangles that partially overlap the non-Muslim section of the circle. These rectangles represent the categories of *Jews* and *Christians* worldwide. Ask the students how they would label each of the two *intersections* with the circle [Arabic-speaking Jews and Arabic-speaking Christians, respectively]. Then ask how they would label the area of each rectangle *beyond* the circle [non-Arab Jews and non-Arab Christians, respectively]. If desired, discuss the geographic distribution of people in each of these categories.

Procedures *continued*

10. How is Islam different from Judaism and Christianity? The Muslim house of worship is called a *mosque* [for pictures of mosques, see *Islam*, pp. 15, 63, 79]. Ask the students if they can name the Jewish and Christian equivalents of the mosque [the *synagogue* and the *church*]. The holy day for Muslims is Friday (the day of collective prayer); for Jews it is Saturday (the Sabbath, or "day of rest"); and for Christians it is Sunday (the day of Christ's resurrection).

11. Explain that Muslims celebrate their own religious holidays, as do Jews and Christians. On the calendar chart from the last lesson, point out the major Jewish holidays (Passover, Rosh Hashanah, Yom Kippur, Hanukkah), the major Christian holidays (Easter, Christmas), and the major Islamic holidays (**Ramadan**, **Eed Al-Fitr**, and **Eed Al-Adha**). For the significance of these Muslim holidays, refer to upcoming lesson plans.

12. Explain that Muslims, like Jews and Christians, have their own calendar. It is called the *Hijra* or Hegira calendar, and it begins in AD 622, the year when Muhammad established the first Muslim community in Medina. The Christian year 1000 corresponds to year 391 of the Hijra calendar. AD 1500 corresponds to AH 906; AD 1995 corresponds to AH 1416; and when the year 2000 arrives, it will be AH 1421 in the Muslim world.

13. The Hijra calendar is unusual because, unlike the Gregorian calendar used in the West (and, nowadays, throughout the world), the Islamic calendar is based on a lunar month, not a solar one. The traditional Jewish calendar is lunar as well. A lunar year contains only 354 days, as opposed to 365 in a solar year, so the Islamic calendar moves faster than the Gregorian calendar at a rate of 10-11 days per year. If the fast of Ramadan begins on, say, March 15 this year, then it will begin on March 5 in the following year. This means that, in contrast to Christian holidays and even Jewish ones (which are solar-adjusted so they fall within the same 28 day period each year), Muslim holidays are not *seasonal* at all. Christmas always comes in Winter; Easter always falls in the Spring. Ramadan, however, can arrive in Winter for several years, in Autumn for several years, then in Summer and Spring, over the course of a long, thirty year cycle.

14. If desired, you can pose several math problems for your students based on the difference between lunar and solar calendars. If a boy was born on June 20, 1985, his lunar birthday in 1986 would fall on June 10 (because a lunar calendar runs approximately 10-11 days faster than a solar one). When the boy turned five, in 1990, what was the distance between his "sun birthday," June 20, and his "moon birthday"? Since the boy is aging about 10-11 days faster per year according to the lunar calendar, how long will it be before he is a year older in "moon years" than he is in "sun years"? If the boy lives to be 100 years old in sun years, how old will he be in moon years? [To make these problems easier, you might want to ignore the occurrence of leap years.]

Cultural notes

1. Although Judaism, Christianity, and Islam are often portrayed as distinct traditions, they are closely related historically and retain many beliefs and practices in common. All worship the same deity, known as "Allah" in Arabic, "Yahweh" in Hebrew, and "God" in English. All three religions share the traditions of the Old Testament, including Adam and Eve, Noah's Ark, the Ten Commandments, and many other sacred traditions. Both Moses and Jesus, furthermore, are recognized by Muslims as Islamic prophets. According to Islam, Mohammed is the last in a long line of prophets stretching back to Adam. All three religions encourage people to pray daily, to fast on certain occasions, to give alms and tithes to the poor, and to profess their faith in public and before God.

2. Jesus and his disciples, it should be emphasized, were all Jews by birth and religious practice. Their native tongue was Aramaic, a Semitic language closely related to Hebrew and Arabic. Christianity spread first among the Aramaic-speakers of Palestine. Today, there are nearly fourteen million Christian Arabs, many of whom speak a modern derivative of Aramaic called Syriac (as well as Arabic) and consider themselves direct descendants of the original Christian believers. For more information, see *The Arab Christian: A History in the Middle East*, by Kenneth Cragg (Louisville, KY: Westminster/John Knox Press, 1991).

3. About 600 years after Jesus, another great man lived in the Middle East. His name was Muhammad, and he was the prophet of *Islam*. In Arabic, the word *islaam* means "submission" or "surrender," and the message Muhammad taught was *Islam*, or "submission to the will of God." Muhammad lived in Mecca, on the Arabian peninsula, in what is now Saudi Arabia. Like Moses, Muhammad was a law-giver and religious leader. He was visited by the angel Gabriel, who revealed to him the word of God. The written record of the divine message Muhammad received is called the *Qur'an* (or *Koran*), the holy book of Islam. People who accept Muhammad's teachings are called Muslims, or "those who submit to the will of God." They must respect the "five pillars" of Islam: (1) they must profess that "There is no god but God and Muhammad is the messenger of God"; (2) they must pray five times daily; (3) each year, they must give at least 2.5% of their wealth to charity; (4) they must fast from sunrise to sunset during the month of Ramadan; and (5) if they are capable, they must make a pilgrimage to Mecca at least once in their lifetime.

4. To determine the exact date on which the Islamic holidays will fall this year, call the Office of Islamic Affairs at the Royal Embassy of Saudi Arabia in Washington, D.C., (202) 342-3800. The Embassy will also send you, upon request, a free Hijra calendar (and other information about Islam).

Ramadan & Eed Al-Fitr

Objectives

1. To learn about the most important Muslim holidays, Ramadan and Eed Al-Fitr

2. To discuss the significance of fasting

3. To raise donations by giving up snacks for a week, and giving alms to a favorite charity

Materials

1. Blackboard or chart paper and marker

2. Addresses of charitable organizations

3. Check or money order

Procedures

1. Ask the students if they have ever been hungry or thirsty for a long time. Perhaps they were on a long trip and could not stop to eat; perhaps they were playing outside in the sun with nothing to drink. Invite them to tell their own stories of hunger or thirst.

2. Now remind the class that there are many people in the world who go hungry all the time. Poor people live, not just in poor countries, but in the United States and other rich societies. Ask the students if they have ever seen homeless people in their own town or neighborhood. Explain that homeless and hungry people sometimes need help from more fortunate people. If everyone with extra food or money gave a little to those who have none, there might be enough for all.

3. This is one idea behind the festival of Ramadan, the most sacred Muslim holiday. Explain to the class that for one full month, Muslims are required to **fast**—to go without food or drink

—from sunrise to sunset (see **Cultural notes**). By fasting, Muslims purify themselves and practice self-restraint. They also remind themselves of the plight of those who are less fortunate. At the end of this fast, Muslims also make an annual contribution to the poor. These alms are given before Eed Al-Fitr, the Islamic holiday which marks the end of Ramadan.

4. Ask the non-Muslim students if they have ever fasted as part of their own religious holidays. Jewish students may have fasted on the Day of Atonement (*Yom Kippur*).

Some Christian students may have fasted during Lent, the fifty-day period between Ash Wednesday and Easter. Explain to the class that fasting is an important part of many religious traditions. Have the class read **Memories of Ramadan in Atta, Saudi Arabia**, below. Discuss with the class the Muslim concept of fasting (see **Cultural notes**).

Procedures *continued*

Ask the students if they have ever gone without food or drink for a whole day before.

Could they function well at school if they had? Is their ever a time when their community stays up late at night and celebrates? [Perhaps New Year's Eve] Are the students allowed to join in this late night celebration?

5. Now ask the students if they can distinguish between the religious and the cultural observances of Ramadan that Saalih and his family celebrate. [Religious observances include fasting and praying. Cultural observances include shorter school hours, staying up late, watching *Al Fawazeer* and playing *al-ghazaala*.]

6. Ask the students if they would like to try fasting in a limited way. Perhaps they could give up foods they eat when they're not hungry and drinks they enjoy just for the taste. Ask the students to help you list snacks that might fall into these categories (sweets, chips and other "junk foods" and sodas) on the blackboard or chart paper.

7. Next, have the students estimate how much it costs each week for each student to supply his or herself with candy, cookies, soft drinks, and other snacks. One easy way to estimate this amount is to write down all the snacks a student has had over the last twenty-four hours, add up the cost, then multiply the total by seven. The students may be surprised at how much they (or their parents) spend each week on junk food.

8. Have the class read **Memories of Eed Al-Fitr in Beirut**. Discuss with the class the significance of Eed Al-Fitr

to Muslims (see **Cultural notes**). Now ask the students if they can distinguish between the religious and the cultural observances of Eed Al-Fitr that Naahida describes. [Religious observances include giving alms and praying. Cultural observances include, among others, a public holiday, receiving gifts of money from family and friends, buying new clothes, and visiting.] Ask your students if they are familiar with similar holidays in America. [No one American holiday will include exactly the same list of observances but many holidays such as Christmas, Thanksgiving, Passover, and others may combine many of the elements Naahida describes.]

9. Challenge the students to give up some or all of their junk food for one week, and to donate what they would have spent to a charitable cause. (Charities to help the homeless or to wipe out world hunger might be appropriate. If several classes join together in this observance, you can request that the hunger relief organization you choose apply your gift to a Muslim country such as Bangladesh, Somalia, or Sudan at the time of its religious holiday, Eed Al-Fitr.) Have the students keep a record for one week of what snacks they gave up and how much they saved.

10. At the end of the week, the students may pool the money they saved, calculate the total, and send a check or money order for this amount to the charity of their choice. If desired, have the class compose a letter to accompany the contribution.

Memories of Ramadan in Atta, Saudi Arabia

For kids, there is no time of year like Ramadan. We have so much fun during this special month, that sometimes we forget what the season is really about. Now that I am a little older, I take fasting more seriously. But I still enjoy all of the special events and celebrations that go on at this time.

My name is Saalih, and I am from the village of Atta on the Saudi Arabian border with Yemen. Each year during Ramadan there are so many special things for kids to do, that I don't know where to begin. First, of course, we must fast. This means that we cannot eat or drink anything from the break of dawn until the sun has sunk all the way into the horizon in the evening. This is hard to do if you live in a hot, dry country like Saudi Arabia. Some years, Ramadan falls in the Winter, like this year. The days are short and not too hot, so it's easier to fast. But during some years, Ramadan comes in the Summer, when it seems like the days will never end, and the sun's heat beats down on you like a hammer. Whenever the holy month comes, we have to fast. This tradition can be very hard on kids at school, so the government gives us a shorter school day (from 9:30 to 2:30). This is one reason why kids love Ramadan!

Now I'll tell you how we fast. We break the fast every night after sundown, with a big family meal. Later, we eat a light meal in the middle of the night. It's called *suhoor*. During Ramadan, even kids don't go to bed until 3:00 or 4:00 in the morning. They have to make school later so we can stay awake. They also let us off early because there is no lunch hour (who would eat?) and no gym (who could play?). It is very hard to go all day without eating, but it is even harder to avoid drinking. Even in the Winter, our country gets hot in the afternoon. If they didn't let us out of school early, we would not be able to pay attention or stay awake anyway.

After school we go home and try not to think about food or water. Usually, I just feel thirsty. My mother encourages us to sleep at this time of day. She is usually busy cooking for the *fatoor* (the fast-breaking meal). It is hard to work when you are hungry. Mama gets cranky in the afternoon, so we pretend we're asleep just to stay out of her way. An hour before sundown we get excited and feel like we cannot wait any longer. Mama finishes preparing the food, and my brothers and sisters and I begin to gather around the spot where we eat. Every night during Ramadan, we have different people over to eat with us, or we go and eat at the house of friends or family. When the men come in to join us, we get really excited. But everyone stays quiet so we can hear the call to prayer, which my uncle announces over the loudspeaker of the village mosque. The call to prayer means that the sun is officially down and the fast can be broken. We still have to be patient though. All the men and boys eat a few dates and drink a bit of water. This is how the Prophet Muhammad broke his fast, so we do the same. Then we line up in another room of the house and pray with the men. After we have prayed, we return to the room where all the food is spread out and begin eating. We always start with a thick, nourishing soup. Mama says it calms our stomach and keeps us from overeating. We are usually so hungry by then that we think the soup tastes like the best food on earth. After the soup we eat a large meal. Because it is a holiday and we have guests over, there is always much more food than we can eat. We eat *samosas* (vegetable and meat pies), *asiid* (a large dumpling in broth), *kibsa* (boiled meat on piles of rice), salads, sweets, and all kinds of Saudi and Yemeni delicacies. Usually we get to drink a Pepsi or orange soda, too. If there is no pop available, we make ourselves happy with spiced tea.

Kids like to eat in their own part of the room, so they can watch TV while they eat. There are all sorts of special TV programs during Ramadan. We especially like the quiz shows. Adults have shows that test your knowledge of religion or history. But for kids, there is a show called "Fawazeer". This show is challenging and very funny. It is a quiz show designed just for kids, and it tests your knowledge of everything. After this show is over, if we have an important old guest, my father will often make us sit and listen to the old man's stories. Sometimes they are exciting folktales about *jinn*

(genies), or hilarious stories about Joha (see **Unit 6**). At other times, they are "important stories" about the history of our family, or town, or something like that. We don't like to listen to these so much. When we get restless, father lets us go outside and play. Other nights, when we have no guests, my parents will read fun stories to us or we will watch special Ramadan soap operas on TV.

The nearby town is alive late into the night during Ramadan, so we like to go outside and wander around. All the banks and stores are open late, and sometimes we go into town with Baba and check out the scenery. Baba always buys us fire crackers, which we love. He also does our shopping for the upcoming Eed. Each person in our family gets several new outfits to wear for the coming year. On other nights, we go to the outskirts of our neighborhood and shoot off firecrackers. The adults always warn us to be careful. One of my uncles usually lights a big bonfire on his land, and our parents take us out there to play. We sing songs around the fire, all the regular songs, and occasionally a special Ramadan one like the one that goes "*Welcome the month of Ramadan, Welcome the holiday. Welcome the month of holy observance...*" We also have a special game we play called "Ghazaala," where we decorate a piece of wood to look like a horse and we pretend to ride around on it, playing great warriors. This is the number one game for boys. Mostly we just stay awake late at night playing games, visiting with our friends and family, and having fun. Eventually we go home and eat *suhoor* and go to bed.

All the suffering you go through fasting during the day is worth it for how much fun you have at night. But it is also nice because at the end of the month of Ramadan, there is always Eed Al-Fitr!

Memories of Eed Al-Fitr in Beirut

My name is Naahida, and I have fond memories of my beautiful country, Lebanon. Lebanon is a small country where people live close to one another, have strong relationships, and are very generous. The recent civil war in my country forced many people to seek refuge elsewhere. That is why I live in America today.

My happiest memories of Lebanon are those of Eed Al-Fitr, the holiday that comes at the end of Ramadan. It was very exciting to awaken in the morning to the sound of our local *mooahzin* (custodian of the mosque) calling out the special holiday prayer. When I looked out my window, the streets would be filled with people rushing to the mosque. As soon as we could, Mama and I would turn on the radio and listen to the prayers while we worked in the kitchen, preparing special holiday dishes for our friends and family. One of my favorite recipes was for *mulakheeya*, a delicious chicken dish. After cleaning up in the kitchen, my mother would let me put on my new dress, which she had bought me just for the holiday. I would run into the street to play with all my girlfriends, who were also

wearing new dresses. This was a special time for me and my friends because we got three days off from school.

In Beirut, where we lived, most people spent the first day of the Eed with their close family. On the second day we visited neighbors and friends, and on the third day we had a picnic or went to an expensive restaurant.

Children are anxious to visit relatives and neighbors during the holidays. One of our favorite customs is giving small amounts of money to children who visit on the holiday. I always had to ask permission from my mother before I could visit people. As soon as she said yes — she always said yes! — my bother and I would run with our friends to visit all our neighbors. We would greet them by shouting "*eed mubaarak*" (Happy Holiday!), and they would serve us juice, *mamool* (a special holiday cookie filled with dates) and then give each of us a few coins. They would also offer us Arabic coffee, which is loaded with caffeine. So you can imagine how crazy we were by the end of the day! This is our Lebanese custom. Everyone's house did things the same way.

Life was always wonderful during the

holiday. People were busy driving all over the countryside to visit their relatives and friends. We took our own car for these visits, but Lebanon had a very good bus system, and even people without cars could visit their family all over the country.

Eed Al-Fitr is a religious holiday, and we also had religious obligations to remember. The wealthy people were expected to give food, money, and clothing to the poor. This Islamic tradition is called *zakaat*. My father would make sure he had paid our family's *zakaat* before the beginning of the holiday.

Eed Al-Fitr is also a happy and joyous occasion. Many people wait for this time to announce their good news to family and friends. I remember many times when our neighbors or cousins broke the news of their engagements on this holiday. One year my father received a big promotion at work. His boss told him during Ramadan, but Baba waited and announced it to the family, and to all our friends, on Eed Al-Fitr. We were so excited and proud. It was like that every year: someone always had big news.

It was also a special day because my father would wait for my brothers and sisters who lived outside Lebanon to call us and give us their holiday greetings. First, my brother who lived in Germany would call. My brother and sister in Sweden would always call next. We were delighted to hear of their lives in these strange, faraway countries — our faces would light up when we heard their voices on the line — but then we would be sad because they were not with us. They should have stayed close to us in Beirut ... always.

After the war became too much for our family, we came to the United States. We love it here in our new country, and we continue to celebrate Eed Al-Fitr in Dearborn, Michigan. There are thousands and thousands of Arabs and Muslims here to celebrate it with us, just like back home. There are even mosques to pray in, special programs on TV, bakeries that make all the holiday sweets, and plenty of new dresses to buy. But I still remember Eed Al-Fitr in Lebanon as the happiest of times for my family. One day soon, if God is willing, we will be able to go back to Beirut and celebrate the holiday with all our relatives and friends.

Cultural notes

1. Ramadan is a holy month for Muslims. It is the month in which the Quran was revealed to the Prophet Muhammad. Muslims fast during this month to purify themselves, to learn self-restraint, and to glorify God. The Quran mentions the fasting of earlier Jewish and Christian prophets, such as Moses, Daniel, and Jesus, who put aside food and drink in hopes of bringing themselves closer to God. Around the world, Muslims who fast during Ramadan do so in the faith that their sacrifice will bring renewed spiritual strength. They believe it will make individuals more pious and societies more peaceable.

2. To fast properly, a Muslim must abstain from all food, drink, and sexual intercourse from dawn until sunset on each of the 30 days of the moon of Ramadan. People who are sick, or travelling, or otherwise not in a position to fast, are allowed to make up lost fast days later in the year. Likewise, pregnant and menstruating women are not expected to fast, but should make up lost fast days at a time when their health is not at risk. Children usually do not fast until they are old enough to understand what fasting is about.

3. Eed Al-Fitr marks the end of the Ramadan fast. In colloquial Arabic, it is called Eed Al-Sagheer, "the little feast." This diminutive title belies the significance of the holiday to Muslims. Eed Al-Fitr is one of the most important holidays of the year. All Muslims should give *zakaat*, or alms, by the eve of (or during the first day of) the holiday. For some, this *zakaat* is simply a special holiday donation. For others, it represents their annual payment of alms, which is required in Islamic law. This obligatory *zakaat* should amount to at least 2.5% of a family's annual income. Most adult males attend mosque on Eed Al-Fitr, and sermons often focus on the moral lessons of Ramadan and their application in every-day life. Families, neighbors, and entire communities take this holiday as an opportunity to make peace and celebrate good news. If, for example, two brothers have been fighting, family members or neighbors will encourage them to greet one another, resolve the conflict, and forgive one another. Likewise, families will make public their good news: wedding engagements, job promotions, new purchases or financial successes, even pregnancies. It is customary to save up good news for sharing on the holiday in order to add excitement and joy to the celebration.

4. In 1999, the holy month of Ramadan should begin on December 9, and Eed Al-Fitr should fall on January 8, 2000. To determine the exact date on which these holidays will fall in the current year, call the Office of Islamic Affairs at the Royal Embassy of Saudi Arabia, (202) 342-3800.

Eed Al-Adha

Objectives

1. To learn about Eed Al-Adha, a festival of visiting and peace-making

2. To learn about the *Hajj* (pilgrimage to Mecca), a key event in every Muslim's life

3. To stage a festival of visiting in the classroom

Materials

1. Candy, nuts, cookies, dates, or fruit to be given out to the class (If your community has an Arab or Middle Eastern bakery, you can order *mamool*, a date-filled holiday cookie.)

2. Decaffeinated sweet tea, or milk or juice

3. Trays or small platters (1 for every 5-6 students) for passing out sweets

4. Pitchers (1 for every 5-6 students) and cups (2 for every student in the class)

5. Napkins

Procedures

1. Ask the students if they know of a holiday in which people visit their families and friends, give gifts to one another, and eat a big feast including special sweets. Such a holiday, for Christian students, might be Christmas; for Jewish students, it might be Hanukkah. Muslims also celebrate such a holiday: **Eed Al-Adha**.

2. Explain to the students that Eed Al-Adha is the Islamic holiday which falls during the annual pilgrimage to Mecca, called the **Hajj**. It is every Muslim's obligation to make this *hajj* at least once in their lifetime, if they are physically and financially capable. For Muslims, the *hajj* is a deeply moving religious experience; it requires much sacrifice and self-denial.

It is also a very happy time in the life of a Muslim. The *hajj* is the high-point in his or her life as a devout Muslim. Eed Al-Adha is also called Eed Al-Kabiir ("The Great Holiday") because of its importance to the Islamic community. It commemorates Abraham's faith in God, which was so strong that he was willing to sacrifice his own son, Ismaeel, to prove his commitment to the Creator. (*Note: In Jewish and Christian tradition, the son to be sacrificed was Isaac, Ismaeel's younger brother.*) God was impressed by Abraham's faith, and allowed him to sacrifice a ram in Ismaeel's place. Each year, as part of the *hajj* ritual, Muslims gather from all over the world sacrifice a sheep or goat in

Procedures *continued*

remembrance of this event. One third of the meat is donated to the poor.

3. Ask the students if they can think of similar rituals in their own religious practice. For Christians, this might be baptism or the baptism of one's children. For Jews, it might mean Bar (and Bat) Mitzvah rituals, or making a journey to Jerusalem.

4. Not all Muslims can make the Hajj, and certainly not everyone can go every year.

   Therefore, the majority of Muslims celebrate Eed Al-Adha in their home communities.

5. Read **Memories of Eed Al-Adha** to the class. Ask the students if this story reminds them of any holidays they celebrate. Which ones? [Some answers might include: Christmas, when children receive new clothes and toys; Thanksgiving, when families comes together to share a holiday meal; or even family reunions, when relatives gather from distant parts of the country to see each other.] What customs described in Naadir's story seem different to your students? [Unless they live in rural areas, Americans almost never sacrifice the animal they will eat during the holiday. Many Americans specifically avoid visiting friends and neighbors during the holidays. In general, Americans only visit family or celebrate with very close friends on the major holidays. Also, most Americans prefer giving toys, food, and other items to children instead of money. Ask the students which they would prefer: money or toys?]

4. Divide the class into "families" of five or six students each. Arrange their desks so that each family has a "home" to receive guests in. If desired, you can include other classrooms in your celebration.

5. Each family should receive a fair division of the candy, nuts, cookies, dates, and fruit that you have provided, and a tray to serve it on. (*Note: the students should be told that this is not for their own consumption, but should be given out to their "visitors"*). Each family should also be given pitchers of decaffeinated sweet tea (or milk or juice) with cups (also to be offered to guests only.)

6. Once the students from each family have assembled. They should divide themselves up into even smaller groups. Some family members should prepare to go out visiting, while the rest should stay home and prepare to receive guests. Later, they can rotate.

7. Encourage the students to visit one another's families. Visitors should greet their hosts with the words "*eed mubaarak*" (happy holiday). "*Allah yabar-rak feek*" (God bless you) is the appropriate response. Hosts should invite their friends into their "homes" and offer them something to eat and drink. If any students have special news to share, they should be encouraged to do so on these visits. Likewise, if any two students are known for not getting along, they should be encouraged to shake hands and offer each other sweets. (The students should all be reminded that

Procedures *continued*

when they are guests it is appropriate for them to take one or two sweets. When hosts, they should also eat, but no more than one sweet to make their guests feel comfortable. If the students obey this simple rule, the sweets you have provided should last throughout the class period.)

8. After a few minutes, the students should return to their homes and trade places with family members who stayed behind. The second set of visitors should then find new families to visit. This can be repeated once or twice. (Enough sweets and beverages should be provided for each student to receive three pieces of candy and one drink per round.)

Memories of Eed Al-Adha

My name is Naadir. I live in Zarga, a big city in Jordan. Of all the holidays, my favorite is Eed Al-Adha. I like it because it's almost a whole week long. Eed Al-Fitr, my second favorite holiday, lasts only three or four days. It comes first, right after Ramadan, and it is very fun, but I think Eed Al-Adha is even *better*. Every year during the Eed (holiday) my parents buy us new clothes. We don't get new clothes at any other time during the year — except for our school uniforms — so I get really excited on the holidays. Usually my parents buy me clothes and other people, like my aunts and uncles, give me money. When relatives come for holiday visits from Kuwait or Saudi Arabia, where my father works, they always bring their nieces and nephews and cousins money. Mostly coins for the little kids, but paper money for older kids like me.

The first thing my father does on Eed Al-Adha is slaughter a sheep or goat for the family. The meat is divided up, and two thirds of it are given to my mother to prepare for the family and our many guests. The other third we take with us to the big mosque in the middle of Zarga, where they give it to poor families. I go to the mosque with my father and brothers. My mother and the other women don't go to the mosque. On holidays, the big mosque is filled with men and boys from across the city. Everyone is wearing their new clothes and it is fun to find my friends from school and show off my new shoes and pants and shirt. Because my father works in Saudi Arabia, he always brings really nice clothes that can't be found in Jordan. This makes me especially proud. The mosque is also very exciting. All the men chant "*Allahu Akbar, Allahu Akbar, La illahi ila Allah,*" over and over again. This means "God is great! God is great! There is no god but God!" I don't know how many times they chant it — hundreds and hundreds of times — and Mama says she can hear it all the way from our house. It sounds like beautiful music from heaven, she says, even though they are not singing, just chanting. Then the *Imam* (the preacher) gives a sermon that usually embarrasses me. He says that the holiday is intended to remind us of Abraham's great obedience to God. Abraham was so faithful that he was willing to sacrifice his son, Ismaeel. God was gracious and allowed the

---

Memories of Eed Al-Adha *continued*

angel Gabriel to sacrifice a lamb instead. Then the Imam says people are wrong to think the Eed is more about getting new clothes and visiting their relatives than about remembering God and making the pilgrimage to Mecca. But even at the mosque, I can't help it. I love showing off my clothes to my friends, so every year I feel sad about this. My father told me that the Imam was right and that I should be thinking about God and not my clothes, but he said I was still young. "When you get older, you will understand more about the true meaning of the holiday and care less about your clothes," he said. I hope so.

Then we go home, where Mama has made us a great breakfast. It is a special breakfast that we eat only during this time of the year. It's called *mi'rab*, and it's made from the organs of the sheep we slaughtered for the holiday. The livers and kidneys of the sheep are cooked with tomatoes and onions. They are very delicious.

After we eat, I visit people in our neighborhood with my father, saying

"*Eed Mubaarak*" (Happy Holiday!) to all of our friends and relatives. We always start with our closest family, like my aunts and uncles and my married sisters and their husbands. When we are expecting visitors, we stay home and make *qahwa saada* (black bedouin coffee) for them. This black coffee is always served on the holidays with *baklawa*, a pastry dripping with butter, nuts, and syrup. On ordinary days, we drink regular coffee and put sugar or milk in it. Only the bedouin drink the strong black coffee every day. That's what my Baba says. Anyway, we spend the whole day visiting people or having people visit us. Along with the coffee and baklawa, we give visitors, nuts, chocolates, dates with a thick yogurt spread, and lots of candy to the kids. For lunch we invite our closest family to eat *mansaf* with us. *Mansaf* is everyone's favorite, and my mother makes it perfectly (see **Unit 2**, **Family Interviews**, for a description of *mansaf*). She always puts lots of parsley, pine nuts and almonds on top. It is delicious.

This is what Eed Al-Adha is like for us.

For the whole holiday we visit each other back and forth. On the second day we visit my cousins who live in far away cities like Irbid. Sometimes we even get to stay the night with them. Our parents welcome people in our home and chat with them over coffee, the neighbors just stay for a little while because we see them every day, but our family who live far away come and stay for meals and we get to catch up on everyone's news. In every house you visit, the adults give children bits of money. No one gives you very much, but when you visit a lot of people, you get lots of money. By the third and fourth day of the *Eed*, we go into the market and buy toys. We also go to the movies. They always put on new movies and special ones for the *Eed*, so it is our favorite thing to do. We don't really go to movies at other times of the year, so we make sure we don't miss them during the *Eed*. By the last day of *Eed*, we are so full of candy and meat that we are sleepy all the time. At night, we dream of all the fantastic movies we saw during the day. I always try to save a little of my money to buy something for my mother or my sisters, but it never seems to last. By the time we go back to school, my money is already spent and my clothes no longer look so new. Next year, during Eed Al-Adha, I will try and be more grown up and think more about the true meaning of the holiday...if I am old enough.

Cultural notes

1. Eed Al-Adha means "feast of the sacrifice." It commemorates Abraham's willingness to sacrifice his son Ismaeel to God, and God's mercy in substituting a lamb for Ismaeel. You will notice that Islamic tradition differs from Jewish and Christian accounts of the sacrifice, in which it is Isaac, not his older brother Ismaeel, who is offered to God. Eed Al-Adha falls on the 10th day of the month of pilgrimage and marks the apex of the Hajj, the holy pilgrimage to Mecca. Muslims around the world celebrate this holiday by slaughtering a sheep or goat. A third of the meat is set aside for the poor. In the Arab world, Eed Al-Adha is celebrated in much the same way all holidays are: with much visiting and feasting.

2. In 2000, Eed Al-Adha should fall on March 16. To determine the exact date on which the holiday will fall this year, call the Office of Islamic Affairs at the Royal Embassy of Saudi Arabia, in Washington, D.C., (202) 342-3800.

Easter and Christmas

Objectives

1. To read about how Easter is celebrated in one Arab community

2. To compare Arab Easter customs with American ones

3. To play a Palestinian Easter game from Fassuta, Israel

4. To compare Arab Christmas customs with American ones

Materials

1. Blackboard or chart paper and marker

2. 2 eggs for each student in the class

3. The outer skins of several regular or yellow onions (one onion skin for every 2-3 eggs)

4. A large pot for boiling, filled with water

5. An electric eye for boiling the water

Procedures

1. Bring a large pot of water to a boil. Add two or three eggs for every onion skin, making sure you have enough for two eggs per student. Boil the eggs until well done; they should turn a rich brown from the onion skins. If they haven't, allow them to remain in the water as they cool. Set the eggs aside and allow them to cool. (You may want to carry out this activity at home a day ahead.)

2. Ask the students if they are familiar with Easter. Ask those who celebrate the holiday how they do so, both at home and at school. Do any of them enjoy painting eggs or participating in Easter egg hunts? If they do, ask them if they think that this is a religious, or a "secular" observance. Explain that religious holidays like Easter are celebrated in both religious ways (attending sunrise services) and secular ways (Easter egg hunts). Ask students if they can think of examples from other major Western holidays.

3. Explain to students that Christians in the Arab world celebrate Easter by performing religious rituals, just as Catholics and Protestants in the Unites States do. They attend church, participate in special masses, and read scriptures associated with the story of Christ's resurrection.

4. Read **Anton: Champion of the Egg Smashers**. Ask the class whether Anton celebrates Easter the way they celebrate it. [Anton and his family attend church (a religious practice). They buy special clothes for the holiday and eat a special holiday meal with their relatives (both secular practices).] Ask what Anton does differently. [Instead of brightly decorating and hiding eggs, Anton and his friends dye them brown and compete to smash them.] Point out that the Easter Anton celebrates and the Easter many Americans celebrate is, despite these differences, the same holiday.

Procedures *continued*

5. If desired, explain to the class that egg smashing symbolizes the resurrection of Christ. The egg shell represents the tomb Christ was sealed in; the egg itself, new life; and the breaking of the egg, the opening of the tomb and Christ's defeat over death.

6. Explain the rules of the egg smashing game to the class.

   A) Each student begins the game with two eggs. The class should be divided into two teams.

   B) The object of the game is to win as many eggs as possible from your opponents.

   C) Eggs are won in egg duels. A duel involves two students each with an egg in their writing hand (see the story for successful egg-smashing strategies). The students, without having any part of their bodies touch, knock their eggs together. If both egg shells crack, neither student wins and the teacher should take both eggs. If one egg shell remains solid and the other cracks, the student with the solid egg takes the cracked egg and places it in a basket or bowl set aside for his or her team. If neither egg shell smashes, the students should try again until one does. (Warn students not to be too aggressive. The point is to tap hard enough to break your opponent's egg without also breaking your own.)

   D) Line each team up facing the other. The first students in the line should duel. The victor claims the loser's egg. The teams should compete one pair at a time, down to the end of the line.

   E) Each student has two eggs, so everyone can have at least two chances at winning a round. After the first round, play a second. At this point, students who have lost both eggs should take their seats, but should continue to cheer for their teammates.

   F) As many rounds should be played as necessary to reduce the teams to one or two players each. The teachers should keep track, not just of how many players are left, but of how many eggs each team has collected. Final rounds are played between teams, and then if there is more than one player from one team left at the end, they can duel amongst themselves for the individual title: "Champion of the Egg Smashers."

   G) The Champion of the Egg Smashers is the last remaining person with a solid egg shell. Teams can win by having the most players left, or the most eggs at the end of class.

7. Proceed with the game. After the game has been completed, the eggs can be shelled and rinsed and then shared equally among the students.

Anton: Champion of the Egg Smashers

Once upon a time in Fassuta, a small Christian village in the north of Israel, there lived a boy named Anton. Anton was a first-born son, loved and adored by his mother and father. Unlike his playmates, Bootros, Michel, and Fileeb — who were also first-born sons — Anton had not been spoiled by the limitless affections of his parents. He was a talented boy, clever and courteous, and he excelled at everything he did. Everything, that is, except for egg smashing.

What, do you ask, is egg smashing? Listen, and you will learn.

Once a year, in the early Spring, all the Christians of Fassuta celebrated Easter. This was Anton's favorite holiday. There were so many special games to play, meals to eat, new clothes to show off. Anton dreamed of Easter all year long. Even church was fun on that day. On the night before Easter, the people of Fassuta gathered for a special midnight mass. The village priest and the elders of the church acted out a frightening and exciting play. It was taken from the Bible, and it showed what happened to Jesus after his death on the cross: how he went down to Hell and saved all the sinners. The priest walked around and around outside the church, pretending to be Jesus fighting the Devil. The elders of the church locked the doors and would not let the priest enter. He circled the church three times, bellowing and shouting at the Devil. Each time he passed the front of the church, he pounded on the door, demanding to be let in. Finally, on the third try, the elders threw open the doors, and the whole church stood and shouted for joy. "Christ has beaten death!" "He has crushed the Devil!" "He had risen from the dead!" This was the signal for the young boys — like Anton, and Bootros, and Michel, and Fileeb — to fire off their cap guns, which they had brought to church just for this occasion. As the priest marched into the church triumphantly, the boys shot their guns in celebration. Bang! Bang! Bang! The smell of sulfur mingled with the smell of incense, like Heaven mixed with Hell. Normally, Anton fell asleep during church — while Bootros kicked, and Michel made noises, and Fileeb whined — but *this*, the boys of Fassuta believed, was what church would be like in Paradise.

There was only one thing about Easter that Anton didn't like: the egg smashing game. It was a silly game that all the children of Fassuta played on Easter Sunday. They took eggs from their chicken coops and boiled them with onion skins. The eggs hardened and turned brown. Boys would stuff them into their pockets and wander around the village, challenging each other to egg smashing duels. They would tap their eggs together until one broke. Anton

Anton: Champion of the Egg Smashers *continued*

always, always lost. This year, Bootros smashed one of his eggs; Michel cracked two in a row; and Fileeb broke the only one Anton has left in his pocket.

And so ... despite the wonderful tray of *couscous* his mother made for lunch; despite the visits of his cousins from Haifa and Jerusalem; despite his new shirts and shoes; despite even the special date-filled *mamool* cookies his sister made for him, Anton's father found his first-born son crying in the corner of the courtyard.

"Why are you crying, my son" asked his father. "Easter is a happy holiday. All of your family is here with you. You were good in church this morning and acted like a big boy. You were patient and waited until the priest came into the church to fire your pistol, not like Bootros and Michel and Fileeb, shooting off caps all during the service, making babies cry and old people jump. I was very proud of you. Why would such a big and noble son want to cry on Easter Sunday?"

His father's words made Anton feel very proud. He didn't think anyone had noticed that he was being so proper and dignified in church. He cheered up for a moment, but he was still ashamed to tell his father what had upset him. Just thinking about the egg smashing game made him cry all over again.

"Now, son..." admonished Anton's father, pulling Anton close to him, "how can you cry like this? You must tell me what is wrong so I can help you. No problem is too big for you to face with your father's help."

"Baba", Anton said, "I am ashamed to tell you my problem. I am afraid that you will laugh at me and call me a coward."

His father stood up immediately and looked down at his son in distress. "No son of mine is a coward. Now you *must* tell me what this is all about."

"You know the egg game we play every year at Easter? I hate this game. Our eggs are not as strong as the other boys', and mine break first every year. No matter how hard I smack my friend's eggs. No matter how long the eggs boil. No matter what strategies I try. My eggs always crack right on the first hit. I am the laughing stock of the village. Is there no game I can ever win? Why don't our good-for-nothing chickens lay stronger eggs?"

Now Anton's father was confused. He knew about the egg smashing game. He had played it himself as a boy, and he had been very good at it. He knew that Anton's problem didn't come from the eggs.

"How do you hold the eggs, Anton, when you play this game?" asked his father. "How do you hit the other boys' eggs?"

"I hold them in my hand like this," said Anton. He picked up an egg-shaped clod of dirt and squeezed it tightly in his fist.

"Where do you point the sharp end of the egg?" his father asked.

"Toward my palm, so no one can hit it. I strike with the round part of the egg. It's much bigger," Anton replied.

"Ahhh!" chuckled Anton's father. "This is how you hope to smash eggs?" He then took the clod of dirt from Anton and, holding it just as Anton had described, he rapped it against the courtyard wall. It crumbled into a dozen pieces. "This is what happens when you smash with the fat side of the egg," he said. "If you want to win this game, you have to smash your friends' eggs with the *pointy* tip of your egg. You must try to hit the side of their egg with the tip of yours. If you use the very tip of your egg like this" he said, rapping another dirt clod against the hard stone wall, "you will never lose." And sure enough, the dirt clod did not crumble.

"Oh, Baba!" cried Anton in disbelief. "How can it be this easy?"

His father laughed and ruffled Anton's hair. "My poor boy is a first born son. He has no older brothers to teach him the secret strategies of all the village games.

Anton: Champion of the Egg Smashers *continued*

Next time you have a problem like this, come to me sooner. I will teach you all the secrets of Fassuta. I promise you that this year you will be declared Champion of the Egg Smashers!"

Anton ran immediately to the kitchen and begged his mother to boil an extra batch of the Easter eggs she had set aside for him that morning. He brought them to his father, who was drinking tea in the shade of the courtyard, and they practiced. The trick to winning, Anton realized, was really quite obvious, once you had the hang of it. He ran into the street with his pockets full of eggs and called out a challenge to Bootros, his next-door neighbor.

Bootros, the reigning Champion of the Egg Smashers, was fast and big and strong. He always laughed at Anton for being clumsy. Anton knew that if he could beat Bootros, he could beat anybody.

"Do you really think you can beat me?" teased Bootros. "I will take all your eggs in two minutes!" Bootros loved to brag.

But one by one, Anton smashed all six of Bootros' eggs. Bootros stomped his feet and ran into his house. Anton carefully placed the broken eggs in a bag and ran to Fileeb's house. He smashed Fileeb's eggs, too. Michel was next. By the end of the afternoon, Anton's sack could hold no more

eggs, and he still had two of the six eggs he started with.

One by one, the boys of Fassuta gathered on the steps of the church to compare their successes. Only Anton had more than ten eggs in his sack. It was so heavy, no one even bothered to count them. All the boys shouted with delight. There had never been such a victorious egg smasher before in all of Fassuta. Bootros, the old champion, ran over to Anton and wanted to hit him, but as Bootros neared Anton, he thought twice. If Anton could find out the secrets of egg smashing, perhaps he could figure out other village secrets as well, and share them with other first-born sons. So instead of pushing him around, Bootros grabbed Anton and, with the help of Michel and Fileeb, lifted him into the air. They paraded him up and down each alley and pathway in the village, shouting "Cheers for Anton! Champion of the Egg Smashers!" As they approached Anton's house, his mother and sisters stood in the doorway and trilled their tongues in joy. Anton's father came out, kissed his son on both cheeks, and greeted all the boys with date-filled cookies and fresh milk.

"Surely," Anton said to himself, "this is the happiest Easter ever."

Cultural Notes

1. Easter and Christmas are celebrated in the Arab world as religious holidays, much
    as they are in the West. Of course, Protestant, Catholic, and Orthodox Christians all
    have their own variations on these holidays, but the basic meaning of Christmas and
    Easter is the same among all three groups. For Arab Christians, however, Easter is
    by far the more important of the two holidays. In celebrating Easter, they
    commemorate the origins of their faith. Christmas celebrates Christ's birth, which
    despite the various miracles associated with it, remains a birth like any other human
    birth. Easter, however, celebrates Christ's rebirth and resurrection, a far more
    miraculous event.

2. In the Arab world, the secular customs which accompany Easter and Christmas
    resemble, quite closely, the customs Muslims observe during their holidays. Children
    are given new clothes and small amounts of money. Special feast dishes are prepared
    and enjoyed. Relatives and friends visit from far and wide. Special news is shared and
    rejoiced in. School and work come to a stop. And so on.

3. In the West, Christmas overshadows Easter. Because the glitzy allure of Western
    consumer culture is spreading around the world, Christmas is becoming more popular
    in the Arab world. In many Arab homes, both Christian and Muslim — remember,
    Jesus is also revered as an important prophet by Muslims — Christmas is celebrated
    nowadays by putting up elaborately decorated Christmas trees, a custom borrowed
    from Europe. Homes are decorated with cards and tinsel and wreaths. In some urban
    areas, exchanging wrapped gifts has replaced the more traditional custom of buying
    new clothes and giving children small amounts of money. Despite having adapted
    many of the superficial signs of Christmas in the West, Arab Christians still place a
    heavier emphasis on visiting friends and neighbors, performing Christmas plays,
    singing Arabic carols, and preparing holiday recipes which have been in the family
    for generations. The commercial aspect of the holiday, with its glorification of
    spending, is not yet so well developed in the Arab world.

4. An additional note about religious holidays in the Arab world: friends of different
    faiths enjoy visiting one another on their religious holidays. Arabs who live in cities
    or villages where there are both Christian and Muslim populations will visit one
    another on the holidays to offer the appropriate greetings and join in the fun. These
    visits are always returned when the holiday of the second group arrives. Often,
    Christians bring their Muslim friends sweets, fruit, and nuts to help them meet the
    hospitality burdens of the holidays. Muslims return the favor. Arabs from religiously
    diverse parts of the Middle East — e.g., Lebanon and Syria — are often very familiar
    with the celebrations of their friends from other religious backgrounds, and eagerly
    take part in them. This might seem unusual to Americans, who are constantly
    reminded that they should not impose their religious holidays on others, and have
    become less tolerant of each other's religious traditions as a result.

Weddings

(Note: This lesson may be presented over two or more days.)

Objectives

1. To learn about "rites of passage": celebrations which mark our passage through the life cycle

2. To consider wedding ceremonies as a "rite of passage" found all over the world

3. To compare wedding customs in Arab and American societies

4. To stage an Arab wedding in the classroom

Materials

1. Blackboard or chart paper and marker

2. Poster paper

3. Paints or magic markers

4. Balloons, streamers, and other party decorations

5. Wagon, audio-visual cart, or other suitable vehicle

6. Portable tape deck (optional)

7. Tapes of Arabic music (optional)

8. Bongos or other drums (optional)

9. Monopoly money

10. A small purse

11. Hard candy

12. Juice or punch

13. Party favors (optional)

Procedures

1. Ask the students if they have ever been to a wedding. Those who have should describe what it was like and what role, if any, they played in the ceremony. Invite the students to re-enact the significant parts of a wedding for the rest of the class.

2. Now ask the students what they think weddings are for. Why do people have weddings in the first place? If a wedding is a celebration, what does it celebrate? How does a wedding help the bride and groom? How does it help their families and friends?

3. Explain to the class that a wedding is one example of a rite of passage: a ritual or ceremony marking an important transition in the life cycle, such as birth, puberty, marriage, or death. Each time a member of society passes through one of these transitions, it can be a difficult adjustment, not only for the immediate participants, but for all of their family members and friends. Rites of passage announce to the community that the transition has

Procedures *continued*

taken place, and helps prepare the participants for new social roles, such as adulthood, parenthood, or widowhood.

4. As a rite of passage, then, a wedding helps the friends and relatives of a bride and groom to get to know and trust each other, and helps the bride and groom themselves to start their new life. Yet weddings in different cultures do these things in quite different ways.

5. At American weddings, guests are expected to bring gifts that help the couple set up a new household together. Gifts might include dishes, silverware, sheets, towels, appliances, and sometimes money. In the Middle East, however, guests are more likely to contribute gifts of money that can be used to cover the cost of the wedding or to help out with household items (see **Cultural notes**).

6. Suggest to the class that they stage an Arab wedding in the classroom. This will take some preparation, so it is best to plan the wedding a day or two ahead of time.

7. First, divide the class into two "families." Take volunteers or draw lots to determine who will be the bride, the groom, the bride's mother, the bride's father, and so on. Include some close friends, as well as relatives, of the bride and groom.

8. On the blackboard or chart paper, draw two family trees to represent the important kinship relations, writing each student's name next to his or her kinship role. (Explain to the class that, in Arab weddings, a brother of the bride may play the role that Americans assign to the father of the bride. Similarly, a brother of the groom may play the role Americans assign to the father of the groom or the "best man.")

9. On the day (or morning) before the wedding, the students should help to decorate the classroom. Each family should have a separate space or "house" in which to celebrate the wedding. At each "house," place two chairs on a table against a wall. This will be the place of honor for the bride in her house or the groom in his. (Note that the bride and groom are not together until the end of the ceremony.)

10. Have the students make posters and other decorations to hang around the two houses, especially above the seats for the bride and groom. The posters should express such sentiments as *alf mabrook* ("One thousand congratulations!") and *bil-rafaa wal-baneen* ("Let there be happiness and many children"). Balloons, streamers, and whatever other decorations are available should be hung on the chairs to make them the focal points of two separate celebrations. Students can color the illustration of a Jordanian bride that accompanies this lesson — pass out photocopies to the class — and then create a long banner by stringing the pictures together.

unit five

5

holidays and
celebrations

Procedures *continued*

11. A wagon, an audio-visual cart, or other suitable vehicle should be decorated to serve as a "limousine" for the groom, who will ride in a procession to the bride's "house."

12. On the day of the wedding, the students should wear their best school clothes to stress the formality of the occasion. Ideally, the bride should wear white with a traditional wedding veil, and the groom should wear a jacket.

13. Have the bride and groom take their seats in their respective "houses." In each house, the other students should visit with each other, play tapes of Arabic music, sing, dance, and play along with bongos or other drums.

14. While the bride's family continues to celebrate, the groom's family should form a procession. The groom should ride in front on the "limousine," accompanied by his father, brothers, and good friends. The groom's female relatives should follow along behind. They should all wind their way to the bride's house, where the groom should wait in the limousine while his father goes in to greet the father of the bride. The groom's mother should then enter to greet the mother of the bride. All the guests should shake hands or kiss each other on both cheeks. The groom, however, should remain outside the bride's "house," and men from the bride's family should come out to greet him.

15. When everyone has greeted and celebrated a bit, the bride's father should lead her down from her chair and out to the groom's limousine. The groom should then help the bride into the limousine and join her. If there is room, the bride's mother or best female friend should also join her. Then the entire party, made of both families, should form a procession to return to the groom's house. The principal male relatives of both families should accompany the limousine in front. The important female relatives should be next in the procession, and the other guests should follow along behind.

16. At the groom's house, the bride and groom should be led to the groom's place of honor where they both will sit. The wedding guests should resume their celebrating and dancing. The bride's mother and the groom's mother should occasionally throw hard candy into the air for their guests. Juice or punch should be served and party favors may be distributed.

17. At any point, the guests may contribute monopoly money to the bride and groom. The bride should put the money in a small purse or the groom may put it in his pockets. A streamer made of monopoly money may be draped over the bride and groom. If you want a more dramatic effect, have some guests throw their gift of money into the air above the heads of the bride and groom. The groom's relatives can then pick it up and present it to them. The couple is now ready to start their new life.

Procedures *continued*

18. When the wedding is over, discuss it with the class. What did the students learn about weddings in general? What did they learn about Arab weddings in particular? What was the most surprising thing about the Arab wedding compared to an American wedding? Consider such elements as the separate celebrations for the two families, the segregation of the sexes during the processions, and the absence of a religious or legal authority to preside over a formal ceremony (see **Cultural notes**).

Cultural notes

1. American couples often get married before they are able to buy or furnish a house. They may work together for several years before they attain the financial security needed to "build a home." In the Arab world, however, most couples do not marry until they are ready to establish themselves and bear children. In most cases, an Arab groom will already own whatever type of housing is appropriate to his background. In the city, this may mean that he has his own furnished apartment. In the countryside, it often means that he has added one or more rooms to his father's home, or built a whole new house, to accommodate himself and his bride. In any case, a young man will attempt to acquire and furnish a home before taking a bride. The bride's family, furthermore, will insist that the groom's family furnish the home in a manner appropriate to the upbringing and education of the bride. The groom may also be required to supply the bride with new clothes and gold jewelry. The amount of gold an Arab woman wears symbolizes both her marital and social status.

2. For Muslim Arabs, the actual marriage — in the sense of a legal ceremony, overseen by a religious authority figure — takes place at what Americans would call the engagement party. This event can occur a few days, or a few years, before the actual wedding day, when the bride and groom move in together. The wedding day itself is not a religious event, merely a social one. All vows and pledges were said earlier at the engagement. The gifts of money given to the bride and groom on the wedding day are meant to offset the cost of the wedding party, which is usually as lavish as the families can afford, and to help the groom pay for the gold and furnishings he has given to his bride.

3. The wedding example used in this lesson is based on real weddings as they are celebrated by families who live in the suburbs of Amman, Jordan. Among more urban families, there might be less sexual segregation, and there would probably be a good number of professional musicians and dancers involved. The city weddings, nowadays, are held in a large hotel or banquet facility, not in the homes of the bride and groom. But the custom of showering the newlywed couple with gifts of cash is found throughout the Arab world, as is the custom of buying household furnishings and gold for the bride.

folktales and stories

What are folktales?

Objectives

1. To appreciate storytelling as a traditional form of entertainment and education

2. To distinguish four types of folktale: sacred stories, legends, fairy tales, and fables

3. To read and discuss a tale about the importance of telling tales

4. To write and illustrate a favorite folktale in storybook form

5. To classify a folktale as one (or more) of the four types

Materials

1. Blackboard or chart paper and marker

2. Writing paper

3. Construction paper

4. Crayons

Procedures

1. Ask the students what they like to do for entertainment, especially in the evenings at home. Reading, watching television, and playing video games (not necessarily in that order) are likely to be mentioned. Now ask them to imagine a world in which there are no computers, no televisions or radios, not even books. What would they do for entertainment? Perhaps they would do what human beings all over the world have done for thousands of years: tell stories.

2. Ask the students to name a few tales that they first heard as bedtime stories. Chances are, these will be **folktales** (others, such as Winnie the Pooh or Dr. Seuss stories, often resemble folktales, even if they are not as old). Make a list of the students' favorite folktales on the blackboard or chart paper.

Procedures *continued*

3. Most folktales can be classified as **sacred stories**, **legends**, **fairy tales**, or **fables**. (Sometimes a tale will fit into more than one category.) Construct a chart like the one below, using the students' examples to fill in the columns.

Sacred tales	Legends	Fairy tales	Fables
Adam and Eve	King Arthur	Cinderella	The Tortoise and the Hare
Mother Earth	Paul Bunyan	Jack and the Beanstalk	The Boy Who Cried Wolf
Jonah and the Whale	Loch Ness monster	Little Red Riding Hood	The Lion and the Mouse

4. Ask the class to think about why a tale fits into one category or another. What makes a legend, for example, different from a sacred story, a fairy tale, or a fable? (See **A Taxonomy of Tales**, below.)

5. Remind the students that they should imagine a world without computers, televisions, or even writing. How could people remember the important events of the past, if there were no videotapes or history books? How could older people pass on what they have learned about life, if there were no way to tape record it or write it down? The answer is that religion and history and the lessons of life had to be *recited*—that is, *spoken*—year after year, generation after generation. These **oral traditions** were easier to remember and more fun to learn when they took the form of *stories*, such as sacred stories, legends, fairy tales, and fables. Without these stories, the wisdom of the past could have been lost forever.

6. To keep them alive, folktales had to be recited on a regular basis.

The Tale of Mushkil Gusha should be recited once a *week*. Every Thursday night, to be exact. So, even if it is not Thursday night, read **The Tale of Mushkil Gusha**, below.

7. Discuss the story. Is it a sacred story, a legend, a fairy tale, or a fable? [It has elements of both a legend and a fairy tale.] What did the wood-cutter and his daughter learn in the story? What did the Princess learn?

8. Ask each student to choose a favorite folktale to turn into a storybook. Have the students write down their tales to the best of their memories and as neatly as possible, with a wide margin on the left side of each page. At the front of the text, each student should create a title page with his or her own name listed as the author. The text may be illustrated with scenes from the story. To make a cover for the book, fold a piece of construction paper over the text and bind it with staples on the left-hand side. The cover should display the title and author with an illustration from the story.

Procedures *continued*

9. Invite the students to read their stories to the rest of the class. Discuss each story in terms of the four types of folktale listed above. Does the story fit neatly into one of the four categories, or does it seem to fit more than one? To answer this question, it will help to consider the story's main characters. Are they superhuman beings, grown-ups, children, or animals? Also consider where and when the story takes place. Is it in the mythical past, a semi-historical world, an enchanted realm, or the animal kingdom? (See **A Taxonomy of Tales**, below.)

A Taxonomy of Tales

Sacred stories, legends, fairy tales, and fables can usually be distinguished according to these rules of thumb:

Sacred Stories have a religious quality lacking in legends, fairy tales, and fables. They are set beyond the world as we know it. They often include divine or semi-divine beings; if they are humans, as in the case of Jonah, they have a special relationship with a god or gods. The sacred stories of every culture and religion usually take place in the distant past, sometimes before the creation of the world, and often explain how the world came to be in its present form.

Legends, by contrast, take place in a more recent, post-creation world, and sometimes grow from actual historical events. Nevertheless, legendary figures often have superhuman qualities, such as great size or magical powers, and may be thought to survive even today in some haunted place or remote wilderness, such as Loch Ness, a desert island, or the North Pole.

Fairy tales do not always involve fairies, but usually include magic or enchantment of some kind. The heroes and heroines of fairy tales are often children or young adults who come into contact with extraordinary beings and powers. Fairy tale figures are usually considered to have lived in an indefinite place "once upon a time," and seldom haunt the world today.

Fables are relatively brief tales, often featuring animals as characters, designed to teach a moral lesson.

In the four types of folktale, the main characters fall along a continuum from gods to grown-ups, from children to animals:

Main characters

Sacred stories	gods and humans with a special relationship to a god
Legends	grown-ups (often with superhuman qualities)
Fairy tales	children (often with grown-up qualities)
Fables	animals (often with human qualities)

The four types of tale may also be distinguished in terms of their settings and their functions. Sacred stories are set in a time before the world as we know it, legends are set in a semi-historical world of human beings, fairy tales are set in an enchanted but recognizably human realm, and fables are set within or close to nature. Finally, in terms of function, sacred stories explain how the world came to be the way it is, legends glorify semi-historical persons or other mortals, fairy tales help children confront an adult world of mysterious powers, and fables convey moral lessons in a memorable, pithy form.

The Tale of Mushkil Gusha

(Adapted from *World Tales: The Extraordinary Coincidence of Stories Told in All Times, in All Places*, pp. 131-134, by Idries Shah, copyright (c) 1979 by Technographia, S.A. and Harcourt Brace and Company; reprinted by permission of Harcourt Brace and Company.)

Once upon a time, not a thousand miles from here, there lived a poor old wood-cutter. He was a widower, and his little daughter lived with him. Every day he used to go into the mountains to cut firewood, which he brought home and tied into bundles. Then he used to have breakfast and walk into the nearest town, where he would sell his wood and rest for a time before returning home.

One day, when he reached home very late, the girl said to him, "Father, I sometimes wish that we could have some nicer food, and more and different kinds of things to eat."

"Very well, my child," said the old man; "tomorrow I shall get up much earlier than I usually do. I shall go further into the mountains where there is more wood, and I shall bring back a much larger quantity than usual. I will get home earlier and I will be able to bundle the wood sooner, and

I will go into town and sell it so that we can have more money and I shall bring you back all kinds of nice things to eat."

The next morning the wood-cutter rose before dawn and went into the mountains. He worked very hard cutting wood and trimming it and made it into a huge bundle which he carried on his back to his little house.

When he got home, it was still very early. He put his load of wood down, and knocked on the door, saying, "Daughter, Daughter, open the door, for I am hungry and thirsty and I need a meal before I go to market."

But the door was locked. The wood-cutter was so tired that he lay down and was soon fast asleep beside his bundle. The little girl, having forgotten all about their conversation the night before, was fast asleep in bed. When he woke up a few hours later, the sun was high. The wood-cutter knocked on the door again and said, "Daughter, Daughter, come quickly; I must have a little food and go to market to sell the wood; for it is already much later than my usual time of starting."

But, having forgotten all about the conversation, the little girl had meanwhile got up, tidied the house, and gone out for a walk. She had locked the door assuming in her forgetfulness that her father was still in the town.

So the wood-cutter thought to himself, "It is now rather late to go into town, I will therefore return to the mountains and cut another bundle of wood, which I will bring home, and tomorrow I will take a double load to market."

All that day the old man toiled in the mountains cutting wood and shaping the branches. When he got home with the wood on his shoulder, it was evening.

He put down his burden behind the house, knocked on the door and said, "Daughter, Daughter, open the door for I am tired and I have eaten nothing all day. I have a double bundle of wood which I hope to take to market tomorrow. Tonight I must sleep well so that I will be strong."

But there was no answer, for the little girl when she came home had felt very sleepy, and had made a meal for herself and gone to bed. She had been rather worried at first that her father was not home, but she decided that he must have arranged to stay in town overnight.

Once again the wood-cutter, finding that he could not get into the house, tired, hungry, and thirsty, lay down by his bundles of wood and fell fast asleep. He could not keep awake, although he was fearful for what might have happened to the little girl.

Now the wood-cutter, because he was so cold and hungry and tired, woke very, very early the next morning, before it was even light.

He sat up and looked around, but he could see nothing. And then a strange thing happened. The wood-cutter thought he heard a voice saying: "Hurry, hurry! Leave your wood and come this way. If you need enough, and you want little enough, you shall have delicious food."

The wood-cutter stood up and walked in the direction of the voice. And he walked and he walked; but he found nothing.

By now he was colder and hungrier and more tired than ever, and he was lost. He had been full of hope, but that did not seem to have helped him. Now he felt sad, and he wanted to cry. But he realized that crying would not help him either, so he lay down and fell asleep.

Quite soon he woke up again. It was too cold, and he was too hungry, to sleep. So he decided to tell himself, as if in a story, everything that had happened to him since his little daughter had first said that she wanted a different kind of food.

As soon as he had finished his story, he thought he heard another voice, saying, somewhere above him, out of the dawn, "Old man, what are you doing sitting there?"

"I am telling myself my own story," said the wood-cutter.

"And what is that?" said the voice.

The old man repeated his tale. "Very well," said the voice. And then it told the old wood-cutter to close his eyes and to climb up a step. "But I do not see any step," said the old man. "Never mind, but do as I say," said the voice.

The old man did as he was told. As soon as he had closed his eyes, he found that he was standing up, and as he raised his right foot, he felt that there was something like a step under it. He started to ascend what seemed to be a staircase. Suddenly the whole flight of steps started to move, very fast, and the voice said, "Do not open your eyes until I tell you to do so."

In a very short time, the voice told the

old man to open his eyes. When he did he found that he was in a place which looked rather like a desert, with the sun beating down on him. He was surrounded by masses and masses of pebbles; pebbles of all colors: red, green, blue, and white. But he seemed to be alone. He look all around him, and could not see anyone, but the voice started to speak again.

"Take up as many of these stones as you can," said the voice, "Then close your eyes, and walk down the steps once more."

The wood-cutter did as he was told, and he found himself, when he opened his eyes again at the voice's bidding, standing before the door of his own house.

He knocked at the door and his little daughter answered it. She asked him where he had been, and he told her, although she could hardly understand what he was saying. It all sounded so confusing.

They went into the house, and the little girl and her father shared the last food they had, which was a handful of dried dates.

When they had finished, the old man thought he heard a voice speaking to him again, a voice just like the other one which had told him to climb the stairs.

The voice said, "Although you may not know it yet, you have been saved by Mushkil Gusha. Remember that Mushkil Gusha is always here. Make sure that every Thursday night you eat some dates and give some to any needy person, and tell the story of Mushkil Gusha to someone who will help the needy. Make sure that the story of Mushkil Gusha is never, never forgotten. If you do this, and if this is done by those to whom you tell the story, the people who are in real need will always find their way."

The wood-cutter put all the stones which he had brought back from the desert in a corner of his little house. They looked very much like ordinary stones, and he did not know what to do with them.

The next day he took his two enormous bundles of wood to market, and sold them easily for a high price. When he got home he took his daughter all sorts of delicious foods, which she had never tasted before. And when they had eaten it, the old wood cutter said: "Now I am going to tell you the whole story of Mushkil Gusha. Mushkil Gusha is 'the remover of all difficulties'. Our difficulties have been removed through Mushkil Gusha, and we must always remember it."

For nearly a week after that the old man carried on as usual. He went into the mountains, brought back wood, had a meal, took the wood to market and sold it. He always found a buyer without difficulty.

Now the next Thursday came, and, as is the way with humans, the wood-cutter forgot to repeat the tale of Mushkil Gusha.

Late that evening, in the house of the wood-cutter's neighbors, the fire had gone out. The neighbors had nothing with which to re-light the fire, and they went to the house of the wood-cutter. They said, "Neighbor, neighbor, please give us a light from those wonderful lamps of yours which we see shining through the window."

"What lamps?" said the wood-cutter.

"Come outside," said the neighbors, "and see what we mean."

So the wood-cutter went outside and then he saw, sure enough, all kinds of brilliant lights shining through the window from the inside.

He went back to the house, and saw that the light was streaming from the pile of pebbles which he had put in the corner. But the rays of light were cold, and it was not possible to use them to light a fire. So he went out to the neighbors and said, "Neighbors, I am sorry, I have no fire." And he banged the door in their faces. They were annoyed and confused, and went back to their house, muttering. They leave our story here.

The Tale of Mushkil Gusha *continued*

The wood-cutter and his daughter quickly covered up the brilliant lights with every piece of cloth they could find, for fear that anyone would see what a treasure they had. The next morning, when they uncovered the stones, they discovered that they were precious, luminous gems.

They took the jewels, one by one, to neighboring towns, where they sold them for a huge price. Now the wood-cutter decided to build for himself and for his daughter a wonderful palace. They chose a site just opposite the castle of the King of their country. In a very short time a marvelous building had come into being.

Now that particular King had a beautiful daughter, and one day when she got up in the morning, she saw a sort of fairy-tale castle just opposite her father's, and she was amazed. She asked her servants, "Who has built this castle? What right have these people to do such a thing so near to our home?"

The servants went away and made enquiries and they came back and told the story, as far as they could collect it, to the Princess.

The Princess called for the little daughter of the wood-cutter, for she was very angry with her, but when the two girls met and talked they soon became fast friends. They started to meet every day and went to swim and play in the stream which had been made for the Princess by her father. A few days after they first met, the Princess took off a beautiful and valuable necklace and hung it up on a tree just beside the stream. She forgot to take it down when they came out of the water, and when she got home she thought it must have been lost.

The Princess thought a little and then decided that the daughter of the wood-cutter had stolen her necklace. So she told her father, and he had the wood-cutter arrested; he confiscated the castle and declared forfeit everything that the wood-cutter had. The old man was thrown into prison, and the daughter was put into an orphanage.

As was the custom in that day, after a period of time the wood-cutter was taken from the dungeon and put in the public square, chained to a post, with a sign around his neck. On the sign was written: "This is what happens to those who steal from Kings".

At first people gathered around him, and jeered and threw things at him. He was most unhappy.

But quite soon, as is the way with humans, everyone became used to the sight of the old man sitting there by his post, and took very little notice of him. Sometimes people threw him scraps of food, sometimes they did not.

One day he overheard somebody saying that it was Thursday afternoon. Suddenly, he remembered that it would soon be the evening of Mushkil Gusha, the remover of all difficulties, and that he had forgotten to tell his tale for so many days. No sooner had this thought come into his head, than a charitable man, passing by, threw him a tiny coin. The wood-cutter called out: "Generous friend, you have given me money, which is of no use to me. If, however your kindness could extend to buying one or two dates and coming and sitting and eating them with me, I would be eternally grateful to you."

The other man went and bought a few dates, and they sat and ate them together. When they had finished, the wood-cutter told the other man the story of Mushkil Gusha. "I think you must be mad," said the generous man. But he was a kindly person who himself had many difficulties. When he arrived home after this incident, he found that all his problems had disappeared. And that made him start to think a great deal about Mushkil Gusha.

The Tale of Mushkil Gusha

continued

But he leaves our story here.

The very next morning the Princess went back to her bathing place. As she was about to go into the water, she saw what looked like her necklace down at the bottom of the stream. Just as she was about to dive in and try to get it back, she sneezed. Her head went up, and she saw that what she had thought was the necklace was only its reflection in the water. It was hanging on the bough of the tree where she had left it such a long time before. Taking the necklace down, the Princess ran excitedly to her father and told him what happened. The King gave orders for the wood-cutter to be released and given a public apology. The little girl was brought back from the orphanage, and everyone lived happily ever after.

These are some of the incidents in the story of Mushkil Gusha. It is a very long tale and it has never ended. It has many forms. Some of them are not called the story of Mushkil Gusha at all, so people do not recognize it. But it is because of Mushkil Gusha that his story, in whatever form, is remembered by somebody, somewhere in the world, day and night, wherever there are people. As his story had always been recited, so it will always continue to be told.

Cultural notes

1. The story of Mushkil Gusha (The Solver of Problems) is told throughout the Islamic world. It is most popular, and probably originated, in the regions that are now called India and Pakistan. Variations on the Mushkil Gusha theme can still be heard in East Africa, Yemen, Iran, and Afghanistan. The story appeals so broadly because it works both as a moral lesson and a spell. It is a story about the consequences of telling (or forgetting to tell) stories. Why do we tell stories, if not to solve problems and explain the mysteries of life? What would happen to us if we stopped telling the stories we knew? Like the wood-cutter and his daughter, we would suddenly find ourselves much poorer.

The Great Flood

Objectives

1. To appreciate sacred stories as the most basic kind of folktale

2. To learn about the mythology of Mesopotamia, the world's first civilization

3. To build a simple model of the Mesopotamian cosmos

4. To read a story of the Great Flood, part of the sacred tradition of many cultures

Materials

1. Globe (as large as possible)

2. A large sheet of blue construction paper

3. A flat disk of cardboard, poster board, or construction paper, in brown or another "earth tone," about 12" across

4. A clear plastic or glass bowl, large enough to cover the disk as a dome

5. Paint, magic markers, or stickers of stars and other celestial bodies (optional)

6. Several toy figures, such as miniature people or farm animals, small enough to fit comfortably under the dome

7. Three larger figures—two male and one female

8. Clay (optional)

Procedures

1. Gather the class around a large globe. Ask the students to find some familiar landmarks, such as their own state or hometown. Now ask them to trace the coastline surrounding North America. Ask them to imagine a world in which no one had ever been beyond this coastline. Without traveling overseas, how could people know that the earth is round? Explain that the globe represents our modern conception of the world, but that people in the past had very different conceptions.

2. On the globe, find Mesopotamia, the region between the Tigris and Euphrates Rivers in what is now called Iraq. Explain to the class that the world's first civilization developed in this region about 5,000 years ago.

3. The ancient Mesopotamians had a rich mythology. They thought of the earth as a flat circular disk surrounded by water. The earth was covered by the dome of heaven, and between the earth and heaven moved the wind. To represent this cosmos,

Procedures *continued*

build a simple model. Lay a sheet of blue construction paper on a table to represent the water. In the middle of the paper, place a flat disk of earth tone cardboard, poster board, or construction paper. Set several small toy figures on the disk to represent human beings and animals. Finally, cover the disk with a large transparent bowl to represent the dome of heaven. To enhance the effect, decorate the bowl with stars, clouds, the moon, or the sun. These may be drawn with water-soluble paint or magic marker; if available, stickers of stars or other celestial bodies might also be applied.

4. This cosmos was ruled by many gods and goddesses. Among the most important were:

   • **Ea**, Lord of Wisdom and the Waters

   • **Ninmah**, the Great Mother or Mother Earth

   • **Enlil**, Lord of the Atmosphere and Winds

To represent these deities, add three larger figures to the model. (If possible, place Ea on the "waters," Ninmah on the edge of the "earth," and Enlil on top of "heaven.")

5. According to one Mesopotamian myth, Ea and Ninmah created human beings from clay mixed with the blood of a god. If desired, have the students make clay figures of humans or gods to add to the model.

6. Read the Mesopotamian story, **The Great Flood**, below.

7. Discuss the story with the class. Have they heard a similar story before? Explain to the class that the story of the Great Flood is a **sacred tale** told in many cultures. Jews, Christians, and Muslims have their own version of this tale, known as the story of Noah's Ark.

The Great Flood

(Adapted from "Atranasis" and "The Epic of Gilgamesh" in *Myths from Mesopotamia: Creation, Flood, Gilgamesh and Others*, translated by Stephanie Dalley; reprinted by permission of Oxford University Press.)

Long ago, when the world had become too wide and the people too many, the country was as noisy as a bellowing bull. Enlil, Lord of the Air and Winds, was trying to sleep, but all the racket made him restless. Finally, when he could take it no more, he announced to the other gods,

The Great Flood *continued*

The noise of these humans has become too much!

I am losing sleep over their clamor.

Give the order that disease shall break out:

That will put an end to their noise straight away!

Let sickness, and headache, and famine, and flood

Blow in on them like a storm!

Just as Enlil was about to release sickness and headache and famine and flood upon the world, the wise god Ea took pity on humanity. From his home in the deep waters, Ea sent a breeze through the little reed hut of one thoughtful man, Utnapishtim. Utnapishtim was trying to sleep when he heard the breeze rustling in the rafters. Then the breeze spoke to him, and it was the voice of the wise god Ea:

Reed hut, reed hut, brick wall, brick wall,

Listen, reed hut, pay attention, brick wall:

Dismantle your house, build a boat instead.

Leave your possessions, and search out living things.

Forget your property, save lives instead!

Put aboard the seed of all living beings.

The boat that you build,

Should be sturdy and strong,

With decks above, decks below,

And a roof overhead,

So that Enlil cannot see inside it!

Utnapishtim kept his ear open to his god, and with the first light of morning began building a boat. The carpenter brought an axe, the reed-worker brought a stone, the young children brought oil and pitch, and the poor fetched what was needed. On the fifth day, the boat's form was laid out. Its circumference was one acre, and its walls were ten poles high. Then Utnapishtim loaded his boat with everything there was: loaded it with the seed of all living things, of cattle from the pastures, of wild beasts from the forests. And he loaded it with people, too: all kinds of craftsmen, and all his kith and kin.

Just when everyone was on board, a black cloud came up from the base of the sky. As Utnapishtim cut the rope to release the boat, the winds began to rage. As he sealed the door against the wind, a great eagle with a lion's head screamed across the heavens. This was Anzu, Enlil's servant, sent to tear the storm clouds with his talons. The storm bellowed on for seven days and seven nights, as Utnapishtim's boat bobbed upon the blackened seas, and the Great Flood swallowed up the land.

Even the gods were afraid of the Flood. They went up to heaven and cowered there like dogs. The goddess Ninmah, the Great Mother, watched the storm and wept. She began to wail so all the gods could hear:

Let daylight...let daylight...

Let it return and cast life upon the land!

How could I, in the assembly of gods,

Have agreed to such destruction?

Enlil was strong enough to give a wicked order.

Now he should be strong enough to take it back!

I myself gave birth to them,

And now I hear their cries, their cries...

My children, like sacrificial lambs!

Would a true god unleash the rolling sea

So that his children could drown like dragonflies?

The gods, humbled, sat there weeping. Their lips were closed so tight, they were covered with scabs. All the gods were sorry about the Flood — all, that is, but Enlil. He sat in a corner, away from the rest, secretly satisfied that he had destroyed the human race once and for all.

The Great Flood *continued*

But the human race was not destroyed. Utnapishtim, his kith and kin, still bobbed upon the blackened seas, when the tempest finally stopped. The storm clouds blew themselves out, the seas turned calm, and Utnapishtim peeked out from a porthole. Light, lovely daylight, fell upon his cheeks. The boat had come to rest on the peak of Mount Nimush, which rose only a few inches above the water. Utnapishtim looked for shores, for some limit to the sea, but the water spread in all directions, as far as the eye could see.

To find out if there was any dry land, Utnapishtim released a dove. The dove flew over the green waters for hours, then came back, because it could find no perching place. The next day, Utnapishtim released a swallow, but once again it came back, for no dry land could be found. On the third day, Utnapishtim released a raven. This time the bird saw the waters drawing back. Patches of land were emerging everywhere. The raven landed and ate and preened its feathers, and did not return to Utnapishtim's boat. Then the people knew they were saved, and they climbed upon the mountaintop to offer thanks to the gods.

But looking down from heaven, Enlil spied the boat and the people on the mountaintop, and he was enraged:

No human should have lived through the Flood!

No form of life should have survived!

We, the great gods, agreed,

Agreed upon a sacred oath!

Who has dared to tell the secrets of the gods

To humankind?

Enlil cast his gaze across the dome of heaven, and suddenly he knew the culprit.

Who but Ea would have done such a thing?

For Ea will do anything for humankind!

Then Ea made his voice heard in that assembly, and all the gods appreciated the wisdom of the words:

You, Enlil, great sage of the gods,

How could you have let this Flood upon the land?

If the land has grown too wide,

And humankind has grown too many,

You might have let a wolf among the people,

Let sickness and a lion's jaws take their toll

And bring quiet to the teeming multitudes.

With this flood you've overstepped the bounds,

The bounds that even gods must recognize.

As for me, I did not disclose the secrets of the gods

But merely sent advice upon the breeze,

Which Utnapishtim, a thoughtful man,

Heard rustling in his rafters.

Then even Enlil felt compassion for Utnapishtim, who had struggled so hard to save his family and friends and all the earth's living things. So Enlil descended to Mount Nimush, where the people were offering thanks. Utnapishtim and his wife kneeled before the god, who touched their foreheads and took them both by the hand, leading them up from that place. Then Utnapishtim and his wife were set down at the mouth of the rivers, where they dwelled forever like gods.

unit six

folktales and stories

Princes and jinn

Objectives

1. To discuss the importance of supernatural beings in all cultures

2. To learn about *jinn* and other supernatural beings in Arab culture

3. To read and discuss **The Bird of the Golden Feather**, a story of princes and jinn

4. To practice drawing

Materials

1. Drawing paper and crayons

Procedures

1. Ask the students if they've ever seen a ghost. Where do ghosts live? Where do they come from? What time of day or night do they appear? How do they look? How do they sound? Ask the class about other kinds of spirits, monsters, or things-that-go-bump-in-the-night. Even though these creatures are only make-believe, the thought of them can still scare us, especially in strange, dark places.

2. In the Middle East, many people believe in supernatural creatures called *jinn* (singular *jinni*). Ask the students how many have heard of Aladdin (or seen the movie of the same name). What comes out of Aladdin's lamp? How does the jinni appear? How does he act? Is he good or bad?

3. Not all jinn are like the jinni from Aladdin's lamp. Some are good and some are bad. Some remain invisible, some take the form of people, and still others appear as animals or monsters. The jinn are never far away. They live just beyond the human world, especially in lonely places, near a well or cave or abandoned house. Upon meeting a stranger in such a place, one should ask, "Are you *jinn* or *ins*?" ("Are you spirit or human?"). Evil jinn are known as *ghouls*. These creatures are usually wild and hairy in appearance, with long teeth, sometimes made of brass. Their passion is to eat people, yet ghouls can also be good-natured and sentimental. A persuasive hero may even be able to charm a ghoul into helping him, as seen in **The Bird of the Golden Feather**.

4. Read **The Bird of the Golden Feather**, below. (If the story is too long, it may be read over two days.)

Procedures *continued*

5. Discuss the story. Why did the ghouls help Prince Ala'i? Why didn't they kill him when he disobeyed their orders? (Remember that the ghoul shouts, "I would kill you now if, having carried you on my shoulder, I did not look upon you as a younger brother!") Who are the better brothers to the prince, his real brothers or the three ghouls? Who was truly evil, the horrible-looking ghouls or the two older brothers? At the end, why does Ala'i decline to have his two brothers killed?

6. Ask the students to name their favorite scene in the story. Why did they like this scene best? Who was their favorite character, and why?

7. Pass out drawing paper and crayons. Have the students draw their favorite scenes or their favorite characters. They should leave room at the bottom to label their drawings.

The Bird of a Golden Feather

(Adapted from *Arab Folktales*, pp. 80-88, by Inea Bushnaq, copyright (c) 1986 by Inea Bushnaq; reprinted by permission of Pantheon Books, a division of Random House, Inc.)

There was or there was not a king who had three sons. One day as he was sitting in the hall of his palace, a bird flew in and plucked a hair off the king's chin. "What kind of bird is this, I wonder," said the king. On the next day at the same time the bird returned and, in one darting movement, made off with another hair from the king's beard. "Why is this bird plaguing me?" said the king, angry now. On the third day when the bird swooped in at the open window, the king stood ~ and tried to catch it, but all he could grasp was one feather from its tail. Look, and what did he see? A feather of pure gold!

The king called for his minister and said, "O *wazir*, tell me what I must do about a bird who comes every morning and steals a hair off my chin. A little more of this and I shall go beardless!" The *wazir* answered, "O king of our age, this is a wonder never seen or told of before. It is a puzzle for no one but your three sons to solve. They must catch the Bird of the Golden Feather."

So what did the king do? Early next morning he gave his blessing to the three princes, who departed on their journey saying, "May Allah will it that we do not return without the bird with the beautiful feather!"

From city to city they traveled, laying down their heads in one place and raising them in the next until they had gone a distance of forty days. On the following noon they came to a parting of the ways. Here they found a smooth slab of stone on which was carved,

This way lies the Road of the Burning

This way lies the Road of the Drowning

This way lies the Road of No Returning

Wondering what they should do next, the princes stood in front of the stone and looked at the three paths before them. Then the youngest prince, Ala'i, spoke and said, "Brothers, let each of us choose a road to follow. But before we part, let us leave our rings beneath the stone until we have

returned once more to this place. Only so shall we know who has gone and who has come." So they pulled off their rings and hid them under the stone. Then they embraced each other and each headed off in a different direction.

Let the two older princes go their way, one along the Road of the Burning and the other on the Road of the Drowning. We shall stay with the youngest, Prince Ala'i.

Starting down the Road of No Returning, he walked swinging one hand before him and one hand behind, day after day, until he came to a mountain. One foot lifting him, one foot setting him down, he climbed step on step until he came to the top. But what is this thing that is like another mountain in the middle of the road? Why, a Ghoul, with hair as knotted as the nest of a bird and teeth hanging down to his chin! *Yammah!* O my mother!

But Ala'i had brought some mastic gum to chew on when he felt like something under his teeth, and he popped a lump of it into the monster's mouth and sweetened his tongue. "May Allah sweeten your days!" said the Ghoul, delighted. "Listen to me and let me carry you back, my son. The bird that you seek is difficult to catch." "As surely as I wish you a long life, uncle Ghoul," said Ala'i, "I cannot turn back—not if a hundred deaths await me." "Then you must consult my brother, who is older than I am by one day but wiser by an age," said the Ghoul, and showed Ala'i the way.

The second Ghoul was as horrible as the first. His hair was matted like the wool of a mattress before the carder has come, and it had grown so long that it covered his eyes. Ala'i trimmed it with his knife, and the Ghoul said, "You have restored my sight! May Allah give you clear vision in all that you do. Believe me when I say that the best help I can offer is to take you to my brother, who is older than I am by one day but wiser by an age." And without straying or turning either left or right, he took Ala'i to the third Ghoul.

The prince kissed this monster's hands and trimmed his nails and shaved his face until the third Ghoul was as pleased as his two brothers, and more. "Listen to one who knows," he said, "and let me carry you home." "I can only travel forwards; I do not know how to go back," said Ala'i, "and if death finds me on the way, then I have only met my destiny." "It is in Allah's hands, then," said the Ghoul. "Climb onto my back and I shall fly with you to the Garden of the Birdcages."

When they stood at the gate of the garden, the Ghoul said, "This far and no more can I come. You must enter alone. In the center of the orchard is an arbor covered with vines. Inside it, in a golden cage, hangs the bird you want. Take your bird in its cage, but touch nothing else inside the garden."

Fine. Ala'i made for the arbor in the middle of the orchard, as the Ghoul had told him. When he entered, it was not like passing from sunlight into shade, as in an ordinary grape arbor, but like walking from darkness into the heart of a lamp. For the whole place seemed to be lit by the bird's plumage, which was of shining gold. Ala'i took his bird in its cage and started back. But the eye is greedy. When the young prince saw the hundreds upon hundreds of birdcages hanging like ripe figs from the branches of the trees in the garden, and when he saw the birds with feathers of blue and yellow and red—well, he wanted one for himself. "Do I come this far every day?" he said.

But no sooner had he laid his hand on the second cage than a deafening cry filled the garden. Every bird in every tree opened its beak and began to call, "A stranger! A stranger!" On the instant an army of men surrounded Ala'i, and though he unsheathed his sword to fight them, they were too many. Very quickly they tied his hands and marched him to their king.

"Is this the dog who dares to steal our treasures?" said the king. "Cut off his head." But Ala'i spoke and said, "Will you shed royal blood for the sake of a bird? For as you are king and a son of kings, so am I the son of a king." The king thought and then said, "Since you are no common thief but a prince, I shall let you go. I am willing even to make you a gift of the Bird of the Golden Feather. But first you must bring me the Horse Who Leaves All Others Behind." "You shall have that horse," promised Ala'i, and returned to the Ghoul.

While the prince was still some distance away, the Ghoul began to shout and upbraid him. "I would kill you now if, having carried you on my shoulder, I did not look upon you as a younger brother! Didn't I tell you to take only the bird of gold and nothing else? Your greed has nearly cost you your life!" "What has happened is past," said Ala'i. "I shall have the bird as soon as I bring the king the Horse Who Leaves All Others Behind." But the Ghoul said, "Think neither of horse nor bird. Think only of returning home!"

Did Ala'i listen to the Ghoul? Of course not. He would rather face death than the disgrace of returning empty-handed! There was nothing for the Ghoul to do but take Ala'i to the Horse Who Leaves All Others Behind. At the gate of the stable the Ghoul said, "This time do not forget my advice. Go into the stall where the horse is tethered and saddle him with the saddle that is hanging there. But be sure to ride back to me without touching any of the things you see. Remember!" "I'll remember," said Ala'i and opened the gate.

He found the horse and did all that the

The Bird of a Golden Feather *continued*

Ghoul had told him. But just as he was riding away, his eye was caught by a row of swords and daggers hanging on the wall. They shone with the colors of precious gems, for their hilts were studded with jewels, and Ala'i longed to own a weapon so finely worked. "Who would know among so many if I took only one?" he said, and reached for a saber that pleased him. But he had hardly touched it when the whole building seemed to shout, "A stranger! A stranger!" In a minute a thousand men surrounded him and took him to the king.

"Kill the dog who tried to steal from us," said the king. And Ala'i said, "Tell me the price of your horse and I will give you more, for as you are a king, so am I the son of a king." The king then said, "Since you are a prince and wish for my horse, you may take it as a gift. But first you must bring me the One Who Excels All Maidens for Beauty, Badiat-ul-Jamal." "You shall have her," said Ala'i and left the king's presence.

The Ghoul was waiting for him with impatience. "How much longer, O Allah, is this youth destined to trouble me?" he said. And Ala'i told him, "I have but one wish more: I want to find the city of Badiat-ul-Jamal." "And I will take you to your own city, and to no other!" replied the Ghoul. Then Ala'i kissed the Ghoul's hands and said, "You have been like a father to me. Is it not ignoble to come this far and fail?" Well, when Ala'i begged in this way, could the Ghoul help but give in? No. He picked him up and flew with him to the land of Badiat-ul-Jamal.

Soon they stood at the outskirts of her city. The Ghoul lit a candle and said, "As long as you hold this in your hand, no one can see you. Walk through the city until you reach the palace. Enter the palace and look for the princess's chamber. You will find her lying on her bed. If her eyes are yellow — O misery and wretchedness! turn your back on her and return to me. But if her eyes are red, then yours is joy and happiness. Wrap the braids of her hair about your wrist and bring her with you."

When Ala'i stood at the princess' bedside, her eyes were red as blood. He twisted her hair in his hand and said, "Come, O Badiat!" Out of the palace gates, through the city streets, and beyond the city wall he led her without stopping once until he rejoined the Ghoul. The Ghoul lifted each of them onto one of his shoulders and flew straight to the land of the king who owned the Horse Who Leaves All Others Behind.

The Ghoul said, "Now take the girl to the king and he will give you the horse." "*Aywah!*" said Ala'i. "Let him keep the horse as long as he lives, for I shall never give up the princess. Allah bears witness to what I say!" "This cannot be!" said the Ghoul. "It shall!" said Ala'i. At last the Ghoul said, "Listen to me, Ala'i. I shall take the place of Badiat-ul-Jamal, and you can give me to the king. Tell him that the princess is weak from her journey, not only hungry but thirsty. Tell them to give her what food they have, but to be sure to offer her only rose water for her thirst; she must not drink anything else."

With a shake of his body, the Ghoul changed shape. What did he become? A sister to Badiat-ul-Jamal. How happy was the king when he caught sight of the Ghoul in this form! "Quickly take her to the palace," he said, and commanded his grooms to lead out the Horse Who Leaves All Others Behind for Ala'i. Before mounting, the prince explained to the king that Badiat-ul-Jamal was hungry and thirsty and that she could drink only rose water.

The palace slaves brought dishes filled with the daintiest foods for the Ghoul to dine on, as well as a pitcher of rose water. The Ghoul drank and asked for more. They brought him a larger jug, and what did he do? He jumped feet first into its mouth and plunged into the rose water and disappeared from sight.

The Ghoul caught up with Ala'i, who was riding the horse with the princess behind him. On and on they traveled till they came to the land of the Bird of the Golden Feather. Here the Ghoul stopped and said, "Now Ala'i, give the horse to the king and let us take the bird for your father." But Ala'i said, "This shall never be! I cannot give up a horse as strong and fast as this one." "If Allah wills a thing, it comes about," said the Ghoul. And he gave a violent shudder and transformed himself into a horse. "Ala'i," he said, "keep your horse and take me to the king. But remember to tell him that I feed on shelled almonds and drink only rose water."

The king was very pleased to receive so fine a horse and gladly handed Ala'i the cage with the Bird of the Golden Feather. "This is a horse like no other," said Ala'i. "He will accept only peeled almonds to eat and rose water to drink." Then he left. The grooms of the royal stable filled the Ghoul's trough with rose water, and the Ghoul bent his sleek horse's neck, curving like the moon's crescent, and dipped his nose into the rose water. Then, diving headfirst, he vanished, leaving not a trace.

Walk, walk, Ala'i and the Ghoul traveled with the princess and the bird and the horse till they came upon the second Ghoul. The second Ghoul accompanied them to the mountain where the first Ghoul lived, and from there Ala'i rode on alone, seating the princess behind him on the horse and holding the golden birdcage in his hand. At the parting of the ways, he looked under the stone slab and found one ring: his own. He knew then that his brothers had returned and retrieved their rings, and he began the journey back to his father's kingdom.

In the evening he came to a city. He rented a room in the *khan,* then walked through the crowded streets to take the air. Stopping at a food vendor's, what did he see? His oldest brother working in the kitchen, his face sooty from blowing on the smoky fire. Ala'i bought a dish of grilled meat and asked the shopkeeper if the hireling (meaning his brother) could carry it to the *khan. So* out they stepped together, Ala'i walking in front and his brother, who did not know it was he, a few steps behind carrying the food like a servant.

As soon as they were inside the *khan,* Ala'i threw his arms about his brother's shoulders and kissed him, saying, "I am Ala'i! Where is our third brother?" "He is working as an errand boy in a baker's shop," said the eldest prince and began to weep. Ala'i said, "There is no cause for sadness, O my brother, this is a day of joy. Take these twenty dinars and go to the baths with our brother. Buy fine clothes, the best you can find in the *suq,* and bring him to me."

Ala'i's oldest brother took the money and went running. He called for his brother at the baker's, and they both went to the bath and washed themselves and rested. After buying suits of striped silk and robes of camel's hair edged with threads of gold, they returned to the *khan.* Ala'i welcomed them and set a rich meal before them. "Praises and thanks be to Allah that I have found you," he said, "and that we have nothing but good news to tell our father who waits for us with his hand on his heart." And he entertained them with an account of all that had happened from the time he left them at the parting of the ways until he held them in his arms again. "You saved us from misery; we are yours to command, brother," said the older princes. And they all set out for their father's kingdom the next morning.

In the heat of the day they came to a well. Ala'i's brothers whispered to each other: "How can we free ourselves of this hero? It is far better that we older sons present the Bird of the Golden Feather to the king." They turned to Ala'i and said, "You are the slightest of us. Let us lower you into the well to bring up water to drink." Badiat-ul-Jamal, hearing them speak, warned Ala'i against his brothers, but he did not believe her. "How can they betray me? They are my brothers," he said, and began to tie the rope around his waist. Badiat-ul-Jamal said, "Wait. Do as you wish, but first take these three walnuts. In one there is a golden earring, in the second a golden bracelet, and in the third a folded gown made of the finest cloth of gold."

Then Ala'i was lowered into the well, where he filled the water bags for his brothers. When they had drunk and watered their animals, he said, "Pull me up." And they answered, "No. Die where you are, and may no one know that you have lived."

They left Ala'i in the well and resumed their journey home. But on the way the looks of the One Who Excels All Maidens for Beauty faded until she was changed into an ugly servant. The Bird of the Golden Feather lost his color and became plain as any other bird. And the Horse Who Leaves All Others Behind shrank and shriveled into a worn-down pack animal. Thus the two princes arrived at their father's palace. They kissed their father's hand, touched it to their foreheads, and said, "We have brought what you asked of us." The king was happy that they had returned safe and whole, but he asked, "Where is your brother?" They said, "May you live long: our brother died. We washed him and shrouded him and buried him by the wayside." The king said, "There is no power or strength except in God."

So much for the two princes. Now for their youngest brother. As he sat at the bottom of the well, he heard a sound above

him and saw a rope swinging down from its mouth. He caught it and shouted to the men who were holding the other end, "Pull me out!" The men were terrified to hear a voice in such a place and replied, "Who are you? *Jinn* or *Ins*?" "By Allah, I am a man," said Ala'i, and they lifted him out. Indeed they found he was a youth as pleasing to the eye as the sight of the full moon in the dark night. They heard his tale and gave him a horse and said, "May Allah make the road before you a smooth one."

When Ala'i neared the city of his father, he met a shepherd. "Uncle, will you give me your clothes in return for mine?" the prince said. The shepherd agreed, of course, counting it a blessing from Allah to be made richer without effort. As for Ala'i, he dressed himself in the shepherd's rags and looked as bedraggled as any urchin in the bazaar. He wandered into the goldsmiths' *suq* and entered the workshop of the master of their guild. He said, "Will you let me work for you?" The goldsmith asked, "Can you fetch and carry? Will you buy coal for my workshop and meat for my cookpot?" "Whatever you wish," said Ala'i.

Now, as soon as Ala'i had reached his father's city, the plain brown bird became golden again, and the drab workhorse became sleek and swift again, and the serving girl became the fair princess again, causing the hearts of the two princes to burn with love for her. They said to their father, "How long must we wait? We want to get married!" But when the king climbed up to the princess' quarters, she said, "I shall not marry any man until you bring me the mate of this earring."

So the king sent for the master of the goldsmiths' guild. He said, "I want you to make me an earring, a twin of one I have. It is not big or heavy but will fit into a walnut shell." "On my head and eye be it," said the master goldsmith. But when he saw the earring, he said, "No jeweler can make such a thing, it is not the work of men!" The king replied, "Bring me the mate tomorrow at this time, or I shall put out your eyes and cut off your head."

The master goldsmith gathered all the jewelers of the city into his shop and told them of the king's command. But when he showed them the earring, all turned their heads away and each returned to his work. So the master goldsmith sat in his shop and began to weep. When Ala'i found him thus, he asked him why he grieved. The goldsmith said, "I am mourning my own life, which will be cut off at noon tomorrow." And he told Ala'i all that had happened between him and the king. "Show me the trinket that is causing you so much sorrow," said Ala'i. As soon as he saw Badiat-ul-Jamal's earring, he began to laugh. He said, "When I was a small boy playing with knucklebones I could cast earrings like this, and better. Lock up the shop and leave me here; you shall have the earring's mate in the morning." The goldsmith said, "Do not make a joke of my troubles. If all the jewelers in the city have not the skill for the work, will you be able to do it?" "If I can't," said Ala'i, "I shall offer my own head to the executioner's sword instead of yours." So his master left him.

Next morning Ala'i took the second earring out of the walnut the princess had given him and presented the pair to the master goldsmith. When he looked and could not tell which was old and which was new, the master was overjoyed. He ran to the king with the earrings and received a rich reward.

The king took the jewelry to the princess and said, "Now will you choose one of my sons for a husband?" When the princess saw the second earring, she knew that Ala'i was near. She said, "First let the man who brought this earring make me a bracelet to match the one on my arm." And she gave the king her bracelet.

The master goldsmith had hardly begun to enjoy his good fortune when he was summoned to the palace again. He returned to his shop with the bracelet in his hand and his head bowed in despair. Ala'i asked him why he was still sad now that he had grown rich from the king's reward. Unable to lift his sorrowing eyes from the ground, the goldsmith showed him the bracelet. "Is this all that is clouding your happiness?" asked Ala'i. "This is my work, not yours. Leave the bracelet with me overnight, and you shall have its twin in the morning."

Well, the next day the goldsmith received an even greater purse of gold from the king. But the princess still refused to choose a husband until the king had matched her *kaftan* made of cloth of gold. The goldsmith said, "O king of our time, is not this rather work for the tailors?" The king replied, "Take it to the ironmongers if you wish, but bring me another like it by tomorrow."

The goldsmith begged Ala'i to help him, and Ala'i matched the princess' gown with the dress of gold gossamer so fine it fitted into the walnut. When the king took it to Badiat-ul-Jamal, she said, "Now I am ready to choose one of the princes to be my bridegroom. But which one? Let them ride and show their skill on horseback, and I shall marry the winner.

The city was decorated with flags and banners, and the criers walked the streets announcing a royal wedding after three days and a display of horsemanship in which all the young men of the city could take part. The sons of ministers and the sons of pashas flocked on their horses to the open ground before the palace. Ala'i bought a horse for himself and joined them.

There was racing, shooting at targets from a galloping horse, and jousting. And in every sport Ala'i beat all the young men, including the two princes. Word reached

The Bird of a Golden Feather *continued*

the king that a youth of the people had unhorsed his sons and beaten all contenders. He called for his horse and rode out to meet the hero and challenge him. But when he came near, he saw that it was his youngest son Ala'i. He kissed the youth between the eyes and said, "Are you alive, O my loved one?" And Ala'i described to him all that he had done from the day that he left his father's palace. The king said, "You shall sit on my throne and rule over me and your brothers, O Ala'i. Take your revenge! Kill them if you wish!" But Ala'i said, "No. Today I shall marry Badiat-ul-Jamal. A wedding cannot be stained with blood." And he ordered the celebrations to begin.

So Ala'i married the princess and ruled justly over the people to the end of his days.

Mulberry, mulberry, That makes two.
I've told my story, So must you.

Cultural notes

1. According to the Quran, God created human beings from clay, angels from light, and jinn from fire. Jinn are commonly said to be "spirits." They are neither human nor angelic; they are neither exclusively good or consistently bad. Their world is parallel to the human world — it has its own cities and nations and histories — and most of the time it is hidden from view. Some people believe the jinn can assume human and animal forms and take part in the affairs of this world. Stories about "genies" and "magic lamps" are fanciful attempts to explain the relationship between human society and the unseen forces that shape it.

2. "The Bird of the Golden Feather" is a legend about the responsibilities of a good brother, especially a good older brother. Notice that the three human brothers are mirrored by the three ghoulish brothers. While the ghouls respect each other and cooperate, the two older princes plot to betray their younger brother. This malicious scheme is what destroys the beauty of the princess, the bird, and the horse, until the good brother returns to set things right. One important quality required of a brother is mercy: just as the ghoul spares the prince's life early in the story, the prince spares the lives of his older brothers at the end.

3. To see how the relationship between older and younger brothers is dealt with in sacred tales, refer to the story of Joseph (and his coat of many colors), which is told by Jews, Christians, and Muslims.

4. For an excellent discussion of how folktales reflect the ideals and realities of family relations in the Arab world, see the introduction to *Speak, Bird, Speak Again: Palestinian Arab Folktales*, by Ibrahim Muhawi and Sharif Kanaana.

Enchanted animals and foolish humans

(Note: This lesson may be presented over two consecutive days.)

Objectives

1. To compare and contrast three stories of enchanted animals and foolish humans

2. To learn that very similar stories can come from quite different sources and have quite different endings

3. To discuss what makes humans foolish and what makes them wise

4. To practice critical thinking and writing by answering worksheet questions about the three stories in this lesson

Materials

1. "Puss in Boots," pp. 20-25 in *A Treasury of Fairy Tales*, edited by Michael Foss (or any other standard version of this tale)

2. *Sitti and the Cats: A Tale of Friendship*, by Sally Bahous

Procedures

1. Ask the students how many know the story "Puss in Boots." Because many will have heard the story but may not remember it in detail, offer to read it again to refresh their memories.

2. Discuss "Puss in Boots." What seems to be the moral of the story? (See **Cultural notes**.) Did the miller's son *deserve* his good fortune? Was he a wise man? Was he a good man? Does the story suggest that trickery is a legitimate way to success?

3. Read **The Beggar and the Gazelle**, below.

4. Discuss the story. In what ways is it similar to "Puss in Boots"? In what ways is it different? [Unlike the miller's

son in "Puss in Boots," Mustapha loses all the good things he once had.] Why did Mustapha's wife desert him? Why did he lose his fortune and find himself a beggar once again?

5. What seems to be the moral of the story? What does the story say about friendship, gratitude, and loyalty?

(Note: If desired, the lesson may be continued the next day. To resume the lesson, remind the students of "Puss in Boots" and **The Beggar and the Gazelle**. Ask them to think about the morals of those two stories before reading the next one.)

6. Read *Sitti and the Cats: A Tale of Friendship*.

Procedures *continued*

7. Discuss the story. What was the first thing Sitti did with her silver and gold? [She thought of the needs of her friends and neighbors who had helped her when she was not so fortunate.] Why did Im Yusuf get wasps and bees in her bags, rather than silver and gold? [Because she was selfish and impolite, rather than generous and friendly. According to the magic of the cats, she got what she deserved.]

8. Suggest to the class that wisdom often consists of seeing oneself as just a small part of a family, a community, or the world as a whole (see **Cultural notes**). By putting the good of the community before her own selfish wishes, Sitti sets an example for us all.

9. Have the students compare and contrast the three stories in this lesson by answering the questions on the **worksheet** below (for model answers, see **Teacher's key**).

Enchanted Animals and Foolish Humans

We have read three stories in this lesson:

Puss in Boots
The Beggar and the Gazelle
Sitti and the Cats

Please answer the following questions comparing these three stories:

1. What do all three stories have in common?

2. Who is the main character in each tale?

3. What is the magical animal in each tale?

4. Where does each story take place?

5. What happens to the main characters in each story?

6. Of all the humans in the three stories, who is the most foolish?

7. How is Im Yusuf similar to Mustapha the beggar?

8. How is Im Yusuf *different* from Mustapha?

9. Of all the humans in the three stories, what makes Sitti the wisest?

10. Why does Sitti seem to deserve her treasures, while the miller's son does not?

Teacher's key

Enchanted Animals and Foolish Humans

1. What do all three stories have in common? *All feature a poor person encountering a magical animal capable of granting great wealth.*

2. Who is the main character of each tale? *A miller's son with a very small inheritance, a beggar sleeping on an outdoor oven, and an old widow who must gather twigs and sticks to stay warm.*

3. What is the magical animal in each tale? *A cat wearing boots, a talking gazelle, and the Queen of a whole community of cats.*

4. Where does each story take place? *In the European countryside; in the camp of an Arab sheikh; and in a Palestinian village.*

5. What happens to the main characters in each story? *The miller's son prospers, Mustapha loses all his wealth and becomes a beggar once again, Sitti lives happily and shares her wealth with Im Yusuf, who learns her lesson and becomes a much more pleasant person.*

6. Of all the humans in the three stories, who is the most foolish? *Mustapha (in "The Beggar and the Gazelle") or Im Yusuf (in "Sitti and the Cats").*

7. How is Im Yusuf similar to Mustapha the beggar? *Both are selfish and do not appreciate their friends.*

8. How is Im Yusuf *different* from Mustapha? *Unlike Mustapha, she learns her lesson in time and lives happily to the end of her days.*

9. Of all the humans in the three stories, what makes Sitti the wisest? *She puts the good of the community before her own selfish wishes.*

10. Why does Sitti seem to deserve her treasures, while the miller's son does not? *She gains her wealth through generosity, rather than trickery.*

The Beggar and the Gazelle

(Adapted from *World Tales: The Extraordinary Coincidence of Stories Told in All Times, in All Places*, pp. 218-221, by Idries Shah, copyright (c) 1979 by Technographia, S.A. and Harcourt Brace and Company; reprinted by permission of Harcourt Brace and Company.)

Once upon a time there was a poor beggar who slept on the outside oven of a rich man's kitchen. One morning he was awakened by the cries of a vendor who was calling, "Gazelles! Gazelles! Buy my fine miniature gazelles!"

The beggar said, "There is no one awake at this hour in the rich man's house. Cease from your noise until a more civilized hour, brother."

The gazelle-seller, who had several of the poor creatures in a cage on top of a donkey cart, replied, "Would you like to buy one of these fine gazelles?" "I have only a handful of coppers," said the beggar. "What would I do with a gazelle, anyway?" And he climbed down off the oven to talk to the gazelle-seller.

At that moment one of the small animals poked its head out of the cage and said in a low voice to the beggar, whose name was Mustapha, "Buy me, and you will not be sorry."

Mustapha was so astonished that he said to the gazelle-seller, "Here is all I have in the world: three copper coins. Can I buy this gazelle with its head out of the cage for that?"

"Take it and be blessed!" cried the man, and released the gazelle. "As I shall otherwise only have to feed the thing, I shall let it go for whatever you can give me." Then he closed the cage again, took three coppers from Mustapha, and went on his way to the nearest coffee house.

"Well," said Mustapha to the gazelle, "what about it? I have bought you, and now I have nothing left in the world, until I can beg some coins from the rich men who enter the mosque at the time of the midday prayer."

"You will not regret buying me," said the gazelle, "for I shall make your fortune."

"How is that?" cried Mustapha, "and what shall I do next?"

"Do nothing, simply stay here until I return," said the gazelle, and it trotted away.

The Beggar and the Gazelle *continued*

The tattered beggar scratched his head. He would probably never see the wretched animal again, he thought. How did he allow himself to be so deluded as to give his three copper coins for a talking gazelle? Probably the creature was bewitched, and might bring him bad luck. Deep in thought, he sat down again on the oven to wait until the rich man's servants woke, hoping that perhaps they would throw out some food that he could eat.

Meanwhile, the gazelle ran on until it reached the tent of a noble sheikh. It bowed to him and said, "O Sheikh of a Thousand Tents, I am the slave of a great and noble merchant, whose caravan has just been attacked and plundered by thieves. Could you please send some clothes for him to put on, so that he will not have to appear before you completely naked when he comes to pay you a visit?"

"Certainly, good gazelle," said the Sheikh, "My servant shall give you a white linen shirt and a robe of the finest camel hair to take to your master. And when he has recovered from his shock, let him come here to my encampment, so that I may cause a sheep to be roasted in his honor."

So the gazelle thanked the Sheikh and said, "I was to bring you this emerald in payment of any clothes which you might send, as my master does not wish to accept your kindness for nothing." Thereupon the gazelle placed an emerald without flaw at the feet of the Sheikh, and bounded away with the clothes upon its back.

The Sheikh was delighted at the value of the gift, and resolved that if the man did appear he would offer him the hand of his daughter, for he was apparently a person of great substance.

The gazelle went back to Mustapha and said, "Look, I have brought you clothes from a rich sheikh. Cast off your rags, bathe in the river, and put on these magnificent garments."

The beggar was amazed, and said, "How in the world did you manage to do this? Never in my life have I seen such beautiful clothes."

"Do as I tell you," said the gazelle, "and I shall get you a rich wife as well. Did you not give me back my liberty by buying me from the man who had put me in a cage?" He transformed the beggar into a man who could sit in a royal court without shame.

"Now, follow me," said the gazelle, and trotted off into a ruined building. "Look under the third brick on the left and you will see a treasure."

Sure enough, as Mustapha lifted the brick he saw the gleam of gold and precious stones in a cavity below. He filled his pockets and his money-belt, until he had as much as he could carry.

"What a piece of luck!" cried the beggar. "I shall never have to go without anything for the rest of my days."

"Not if you marry into the family of the Sheikh of a Thousand Tents," said the gazelle. "Buy yourself a horse, and boots, and we shall set out for the noble Sheikh's oasis at once."

An hour later Mustapha, mounted on a beautiful white horse, followed the gazelle as it sped along like the wind before him. Soon they reached a dip in the sand, and in the distance, beside some tall palm trees, were some black tents.

"Wait here," said the gazelle, "until I come for you; and remember that you are now the Sheikh Abu Zakaat, a rich merchant whose caravan was set upon by thieves and plundered."

"I understand," said Mustapha. "I shall stay here until you return."

The gazelle then descended into the valley of the oasis and, presenting himself to the Sheikh of a Thousand Tents, let fall a priceless ruby without flaw at his feet, saying, "My master, the noble Sheikh Abu

The Beggar and the Gazelle *continued*

unit six

folktales and stories

Zakaat, sends you blessings and peace, and requests that he may call upon you at once, to thank you for the clothes you sent him after his recent misfortune. In the meantime, here is a small token of his regard which he wishes to give to your daughter as a mark of his respect."

"Excellent gazelle!" cried the Sheikh. "Let your master hasten here as fast as he can. I am eager to meet him. He should start thinking of himself as my son-in-law from this moment on."

The gazelle returned to Sheikh Abu Zakaat and told him what the Sheikh of a Thousand Tents had said, and soon the one-time beggar and the rich and venerable Sheikh were sitting together and drinking coffee like old friends. By nightfall, when the sheep had been roasted and eaten, the Sheikh of a Thousand Tents came to the delicate subject of his daughter. "My Son," said he, placing his hand on Sheikh Abu Zakaat's arm, "I am glad that I have kept my daughter unmarried until you came along, for I can think of no more suitable match for her. I shall arrange for the marriage rites to be solemnized tomorrow, and she shall come to you with her servants and her finery all complete."

At this news, Sheikh Abu Zakaat was delighted and thanked his lucky stars for bringing him such fortune.

Next day, at the wedding, he was congratulated by every member of the tribe, who each piled gifts before the happy pair. The bridal feast went on for twelve hours, and at last they were led to a black tent hung with rare carpets and decorated with lamps of burnished brass set with coral. While they slept, the gazelle lay across the threshold, keeping watch.

The months passed, and the tribe moved to another oasis, so the Sheikh of a Thousand Tents gave his daughter and new son-in-law his palace in the desert to live in until his return. There were tinkling

fountains in blue-tiled courtyards, carved wooden balconies, vast rooms with painted pillars. Sheikh Abu Zakaat became more and more conceited, and forgot completely what he owed to the gazelle. He spent all day playing dice with his friends.

One day the gazelle went to his master's wife and said, "Lady, ask my master if he will give me a bowl of dates and honey, prepared with his own hands, for I am feeling ill, and fear that I may die."

So the girl went to her husband and said, "Peace be upon you, Husband. Please give the gazelle a bowl of dates and honey prepared with your own hands. It is ill and fears that it may die."

And the man answered, "Foolish one, do not worry about the animal. Did I not buy it for only a few pence? Take no notice, and leave me to my game of dice."

Then the girl went back to the gazelle, which was lying on the ground looking very weak and thin, and said, "I cannot get your master to come. Shall I prepare you the mixture myself so that you will get better?

The gazelle said, "No, mistress, thank you, I would rather that my master did it. Please go back to him and beg him for my sake to do as I ask, or I shall die."

So she ran back to Sheikh Abu Zakaat and said "Come quickly: the gazelle begs you to do as it asks, or indeed it will die, for it is now so weak and thin lying on the ground."

But again her husband would not do anything, and told her to go to the gazelle and give it a bowl of milk herself.

When the girl got back to where the gazelle was lying she saw its eyes were very dull, and when she had told it the Sheikh was not coming, it dropped its head and died.

That night, lying in his luxurious palace, the man who had been a beggar said to his wife, "What happened to the

The Beggar and the Gazelle *continued*

gazelle? You did not come back to tell me."

And she answered sadly, "It died, and I am so grieved at the way you disregarded the poor creature's pleas that I have decided when my father comes back I shall return to his tents, for I no longer love you."

"Foolish woman!" cried the Sheikh. "Go to sleep, and in the morning you will have forgotten all about this matter." Within a few moments he was snoring.

In the middle of the night he had a dream. He thought he saw the gazelle again, and its eyes were very sad. "Why did you not bring me a bowl of dates and honey when I begged you to do so? Had

you forgotten that you owed all your good fortune to me? I was grateful because you bought my liberty back for me. Why could you not show me one act of kindness when I was in need?"

"I asked my wife to take you a bowl of milk!" cried Sheikh Abu Zakaat, feeling suddenly very ashamed of himself.

"It was not the same thing," said the gazelle, faintly, and it disappeared.

In a great fright Sheikh Abu Zakaat sat up, and found himself Mustapha the beggar again, dressed in tatters, sitting against the outdoor oven of a rich man's house in the moonlight.

Cultural notes

1. "Puss in Boots," according to Idries Shah (*World Tales*, p. 218), is originally an Eastern tale, and is well known in Zanzibar and East Africa as well as the Middle East. It made its way to Italy in the sixteenth century, and was translated from French into English in 1697. Shah explains some of the differences between the Western and Eastern versions:

   The tale has annoyed many people in the West, because they have disliked ... its supposed lack of a moral. On the surface, of course, it looks as if a beggar (or a young miller without a penny, as in the 'Puss in Boots' version) has no right to the advantages obtained for him by a cat, through trickery. But in the Eastern telling it is easier to understand that the animal stands for the fate which constantly gives humanity (in spite of its unworthiness) great opportunities. The ingratitude of the main figure is thus characteristic of man's forgetfulness of a debt. The defection of the Princess symbolizes the withdrawal of the advantages which subsist, according to this idea, only when appreciated by a worthwhile person.

   In *Sitti and the Cats*, the kind of selfishness displayed by Mustapha the beggar is found again in the character of Im Yusuf. This time, however, the selfish character is balanced by a generous one, Sitti, who helps Im Yusuf to repent and become a more pleasant person. Sally Bahous, the author of the tale, explains how good and evil are portrayed in traditional Palestinian stories (*Sitti and the Cats*, p. iv):

   Good characters are those who display the characteristics necessary for living in small communities; generosity, friendliness and never selfishness. Indeed evil is often defined in these fairy tales as selfishness, and good is defined as putting the good of community and others before self.

Cinderella stories

(Note: This lesson may be presented over two consecutive days.)

Objectives

1. To learn the basic elements of a story: setting, characters, and plot

2. To see that the same basic story may be told in different ways in different cultures

3. To understand how folktales gradually change through their retelling

4. To read two Arab tales similar to the Western story of Cinderella

Materials

1. Blackboard or chart paper and marker

2. Tape recorder (optional)

Procedures

1. Introduce the class to the basic elements of a story. Write the following three elements on the blackboard or chart paper and discuss each one with the class.

   Setting: Where and when does the story take place?

   Characters: Who is the hero or heroine of the story? Who are the other main characters? Are they good or bad? How is each character described?

   Plot: What happens in the story? What is the most exciting part? How does the story end?

2. Ask the students if they know the tale of Cinderella. Tell them to think silently about the story in terms of the three elements listed above: Where does "Cinderella" take place? Who

are the main characters? What are they like? What do they do and say? What happens to them?

3. Before discussing these questions, the students should divide into small groups. Anyone who does not know the story well should join up with others who think that they do.

4. Have each group choose a storyteller. After the group has discussed the tale thoroughly, the storyteller will present the group's version of Cinderella to the rest of the class.

5. The groups should move apart and work independently, discussing the story as quietly as possible. (Anything overheard by another group may be used by that group to improve their own version of the story.) Without consulting any text and without writing anything down,

Procedures *continued*

the students should try to recollect the story of Cinderella as accurately as possible.

6. After a fixed amount of time, have the students finish up and prepare to present their version to the class. Emphasize that each storyteller, without using notes, must tell the story exactly as the group remembers it.

7. Have the storytellers draw lots to determine the order in which they will tell their tales. Then have all the storytellers wait outside the room. Emphasize that they should wait quietly, without speaking to their classmates. It is important that each storyteller present the tale without having heard how the other storytellers have presented it.

8. If a tape recorder is available, consider taping the stories so that parts may be played back at the end. Otherwise, have the students write down whatever they notice about each version of the tale. Ask them to pay attention to setting, characters, and plot.

9. Invite the first storyteller in to tell the tale. When each storyteller is finished, he or she may remain in the room while the next storyteller is invited in. Ask the students to save their comments until all the storytellers have finished.

10. Discuss the similarities and differences among the presentations. Where was each version set? Who were the main characters? What did they say (or not say) to each other? What were the main events? Did any version leave out an important character or event? Did any version introduce a completely new element?

11. Storytellers should not feel bad if they have changed the story or left something out. Explain to the class that different versions of the same story always exist side-by-side, even within the same classroom. Whenever someone tells a story, he or she changes it to some degree, because all people are creative and no one has a perfect memory (see **Cultural notes**).

12. Over time, these small changes may add up, so that the original story changes into a new one. This new story is likely to resemble the original one, just as children tend to resemble their parents. (Note: If desired, the lesson may be continued the next day.)

13. Read **Jameela** and **Sackcloth**, below.

14. Discuss the stories with the class. How are Jameela and Sackcloth similar to each other? How are they different? How are they similar to Cinderella? How are they different?

15. See if the class can explain why such similar stories might be found in such different cultures. Have the students recall their own experiences in telling the tale of Cinderella.

"Jameela"

(Adapted from "Jbene," in *Speak, Bird, Speak Again: Palestinian Arab Folktales*, pp. 122-125, by Ibrahim Muhawi and Sharif Kanaana, copyright (c) 1988, The Regents of the University of California; reprinted by permission of the University of California Press.)

Once upon a time there was a girl who was so beautiful the other girls in the village became jealous of her. One day her so-called friends came to her and said, "Jameela, let's go pick dates together."

With permission from their parents, Jameela and the other girls set out on their adventure.

When the girls reached the orchard, the oldest one said, "We're too big to climb to the highest branches. Who will go up the tree for us?" And she looked right at Jameela.

Jameela was the youngest and the best-behaved among them. "I'll climb it," she said, and scampered up the tree. For an hour or more, Jameela picked dates and dropped them to her friends below.

"We'll fill your basket for you," they called up to Jameela. But while they filled their own baskets with delicious dates, they filled hers up with snails.

As the sun was setting, Jameela's so-called friends said, "It's getting dark; we can't wait for you." Then they left her up in the tree with nothing but a basket full of snails. Night fell, and Jameela was afraid to climb down in the dark.

Meanwhile, her mother wondered where she was. Her mother asked Jameela's friends, but they said, "Jameela didn't come with us."

Later that night a horseman came by. The horse approached the tree but backed away in fear. Looking up in the tree, the horseman saw the girl. "Come down!" he cried, but she would not because she was afraid.

"I swear by Allah your safety is guaranteed," he called to her, and only then did the girl dare to climb down. The horseman sat Jameela behind him on the saddle and took her home at midnight.

When she arrived home, she was so ashamed she did not wake her mother or anyone else in the house. Instead she disguised herself as a servant girl and slept downstairs with the sheep and camels.

In the morning, Jameela's family thought she was a servant. Instead of welcoming her home with open arms, they sent her out to graze the animals. Every day after that, while her family grieved for their beautiful daughter, Jameela roamed alone with the herds. As she walked along, she would sing:

"O birds that fly
Over mountains high!
Greet my mother and my father
And say, "Jameela's a shepherd now.
Sheep she grazes, and camels too.
And she rests in the shade of the vine."

Then she would cry, and the birds would cry, and the sheep and camels would stop grazing and cry.

After weeks of this, the horseman — who was in fact a mighty prince — noticed that all the animals in the kingdom were coming home from the pasture without having eaten. They were getting thinner day by day. "By Allah," he thought, "I must follow the herds and find out what is the matter."

So the next day he veiled his face to protect it from the sun and followed the herds until they reached their grazing ground. There he heard Jameela sing out,

"O birds that fly
Over mountains high!
Greet my mother and my father
And say, "Jameela's a shepherd now.
Sheep she grazes, and camels too.
And she rests in the shade of the vine."

"Jameela" *continued*

Then she started crying, and the birds cried with her. The herds all stopped grazing and stood in their tracks and cried. Everything around her cried, and the mighty prince himself stood there and cried.

In the evening, Jameela herded the animals home. With his face still veiled, the prince called to her, "Shepherdess! Come here and tell the truth. Who are you, and why do you weep?"

"My name's Jameela," she answered, and then she told him the whole story of her so-called friends, and the basket full of snails, and the noble horseman who had saved her. She wiped the soot from her face, and behold! she was as lovely as a desert flower.

Then the prince removed his veil, and Jameela saw that he was not only a mighty prince, but the very horseman who had saved her.

So the two were wed. They arranged festivities and beautiful nights. Once she was married, Jameela brought her mother and father to stay in the prince's palace. I was there, and have just returned.

Now the bird of this tale has flown!

"Sackcloth"

(Adapted from *Speak, Bird, Speak Again: Palestinian Arab Folktales*, pp. 127-130, by Ibrahim Muhawi and Sharif Kanaana, copyright (c) 1988, The Regents of the University of California; reprinted by permission of the University of California Press.)

There once was a princess who had a terrible quarrel with her father the king. She was so angry and confused that she ran away from home. After wandering many roads, sleeping here and waking there, she became lonely and a little frightened. One evening, as the sky grew dark and a storm was blowing up, she glimpsed the lights of a city in the distance. With hunger driving her, she trudged through the wind and rain till she came to the walls of a magnificent palace.

"Thanks be to Allah!" she cried. "Here I'll find shelter and something to eat." She was about to knock at the great wooden gate, when she stopped and took a long look at herself. Her fine silk gown was soaked and muddy, her shoes were covered with grime, even her hair was wet and dishevelled.

"I look like an ordinary servant girl," she thought to herself. "No one will believe I am a princess!" Too exhausted and discouraged to go on, she collapsed right there outside the gate, and slept straight through until morning.

With first light she woke and began to wonder what to do. Though the rain had stopped, her gown was still damp and the air was chill. "I must find some dry clothes," she thought to herself, yet she was still too shy to knock at the front gate. The entire palace was encircled by a massive wall, far too high for her to climb. All the princess could do was walk along the wall, wishing she had the courage to knock. Every once in a while she could smell the delicious aroma of breakfast being served inside. "I'm so hungry," she thought to herself, but there was no way into the palace.

Just as she was beginning to despair, she discovered a small back entrance used by the servants. There in a junk pile she found an empty sack, of very plain and coarse material, but just her size. Working quickly, she cut holes for her arms and neck, and soon had a simple dress of sackcloth. When no one was looking, she slipped into her new clothes and hid her old ones behind a loose stone in the palace wall.

The princess had just stashed her muddy shoes when a servant girl came out the back door to dump some leftover food. By the look of the leftovers, the princess knew this must be a palace of great wealth. Inside they would be warm and satisfied, cleaning up from a great breakfast banquet, and here she sat in a sackcloth, too hungry to resist! With the servant girl looking on in astonishment, the princess fell upon the scraps of food and set to eating.

"Oh my!" cried the servant, rushing back inside. "There's a weird sight out here, the strangest-looking person, and she's eating the leftovers!"

"Go call her, and bring her to me!" the queen commanded.

So the princess was brought inside, and they asked her many questions.

"Who are you, girl? How did you get here? Are you human or jinn?"

"By Allah," said the princess, "I'm human, and the choicest of the race. But Allah has made me the way I am."

"What skills do you have?" they asked. "What can you do?"

"I don't have any skills in particular," she answered. "But I can help in the kitchen, peeling onions and passing things over when needed."

So they put her to work in the kitchen, and soon all the other servants were saying, "Here comes Sackcloth! There goes Sackcloth!" They were happy to have Sackcloth around, but she was so ashamed of her appearance, she stayed in the kitchen and never went out.

One day there was a wedding in the city, and the entire household of the palace was invited. In the evening the servants were preparing to go to the celebration. For the next three nights there would be dancing and feasting.

"Hey Sackcloth!" they called, "Don't you want to come with us?"

"No, Allah help me!" she exclaimed. "I can't go to weddings or anything else like that. You go and have a good time, but I'll stay here."

The king's household and all the servants went to the celebration, and no one was left at home except Sackcloth. Waiting till they were well on their way, she found her old clothes where she had stashed them in the palace wall. She washed her silken gown and shined her shoes till they were as good as new, then bathed and brushed her long black hair. Lovely as a princess again, she set out for the celebration.

At the wedding party, the men were celebrating on one side of the house, and the women on another. Men were not allowed to see the women dance, and women were not allowed to see the men. Slipping into the women's side, the princess found them singing and clapping in a circle. Each woman would take turns dancing in the middle, a colorful handkerchief in each hand. When her turn came, the princess took the handkerchiefs and danced to her heart's content. No one had ever seen such a lovely gown or such a beautiful dancer.

The queen turned to one of her servants and asked, "Who is that noble girl?"

"I don't know, mistress," replied the servant girl with awe. "I've never seen her —or anyone like her — before." No one recognized the beautiful dancer as Sackcloth, the poor maid in the palace kitchen.

Then, when she'd had her fill of dancing, the princess simply dropped the handkerchiefs and slipped away into the night. No one knew where she had come from or where she went.

Returning home, she put on her sackcloth and went to sleep. When the servants came home from the celebration, they started taunting her.

"What! Are you sleeping?" they cried. "If you'd come to the wedding, you would have seen a beautiful girl who danced and danced, and then left without anyone knowing who she was or where she went."

Meanwhile, the queen came home and told her son all about the mysterious girl.

"Dear son," she said, "if only you could find that girl, you might ask for her hand in marriage. There is no more noble woman in all the world!"

"I have an idea," said the prince. "Tomorrow night, I will disguise myself in women's clothes, and you take me to the women's celebration. If anyone should ask, tell them, 'This is my sister's daughter. She's here visiting us, and I brought her to see the dance.'"

The queen agreed, and the next night she took her "sister's daughter" to the dance. Sackcloth, meanwhile, gave them enough time to get there, then changed into her gown and followed. Again she entered the circle of women and danced and danced, a colorful handkerchief in each hand. Observing from the sidelines, the prince was captivated by her beauty, but dared not reveal himself at the women's celebration. So, when the princess had danced to her heart's content, she slipped away again into the night. Returning home, she put on her sackcloth and went to sleep.

The next night, the prince went back to the house where the celebration was taking place, but he did not go into the men's side or the women's side. Instead, he hid outside and waited for the mysterious girl. Soon the princess arrived, went in and danced, then pulled herself together and slipped away. This time,

however, as she started back to the palace, the prince followed her, keeping a safe distance so that she wouldn't see him. Imagine his surprise when she led him back to his own home! Once she was inside, the prince slipped through the back door and spied the mysterious girl, now fast asleep, wearing an old sackcloth instead of a silken gown.

In the morning, the prince announced to his servants, "I don't want any of you to bring my food today. I will take my breakfast only from Sackcloth, and I want her to share it with me."

When the astonished servants told Sackcloth, she cried, "Oh, for the sake of Allah! I can't do it! I'm so disgusting, how could the prince have breakfast with me?"

Nevertheless, the servants prepared the meal, arranged it on a tray, and gave it to Sackcloth. She carried the tray halfway up the stairs, then pretended to slip and dropped the whole breakfast on the floor.

"I'm sorry, master!" she cried. "Didn't I tell you, I can't carry anything?"

"You must make a new breakfast," the prince commanded, "and bring it up to me immediately."

With a second tray, she came up to the landing at the top of the stairs, slipped, and dropped the whole breakfast again.

"This is not getting you anywhere," said the prince. "You must keep bringing breakfasts and dropping them until you manage to come up here on your own."

With the third tray, she limped into the room, leaning here and there, until she managed to set the breakfast before the prince.

"Come sit here," said the prince. "Let's eat this breakfast together."

"Please, master!" she protested, "Just look at me. Surely I must disgust you. How can you dine with a poor servant in a sackcloth?"

"You must take it off!" cried the prince.

"Sackcloth" *continued*

"How long have you been living here, pretending to be Sackcloth, when you are the most beautiful, the most noble woman in the world!" Then he called in the queen, and she called in the servants, and they took Sackcloth to be bathed and dressed in a royal gown, woven from golden thread and encrusted with precious gems. When she reappeared, radiant in all her finery, everyone agreed that the beautiful girl at the dance was none other than Sackcloth, whom they had known as a common kitchen maid.

Then the princess told the story of her terrible quarrel with her father the king and all the sadness of her journey. The prince immediately dispatched messengers to tell the king that his daughter was alive and well, and to ask for her hand in marriage. Word soon came back that the king would attend the wedding in person.

"For forty days," the public crier announced, "no one is to eat or drink except in the royal palace!" And on a beautiful spring morning, the prince and princess were wed, with kings and queens and servants all rejoicing as one.

Cultural notes

1. In an oral tradition, no version of a tale is entirely "right" or definitive, because each teller changes the story slightly, whether on purpose or accidentally. Without writing, stories like **Jameela, Sackcloth,** and "Cinderella" evolve over time. There is no authoritative text against which the story can be checked for accuracy. With sacred stories, however, accuracy may be more important. The religious significance of a story may compel people, even in a strictly oral tradition, to standardize its form by precisely memorizing each line and verse.

The strong and the clever

Objectives

1. To introduce the eastern Mediterranean as a gateway between Europe and Asia

2. To read a fable by Aesop, a legendary storyteller of ancient Greece

3. To read a related fable that came to Europe from India by way of the Middle East

4. To discuss how strangers of different talents and skills can learn to cooperate and trust one another

Materials

1. World map

2. "The Lion and the Mouse," pp. 42-43 in Aesop's Fables, retold by Robert Mathias (or any other standard version of this fable)

Procedures

1. Ask the students to find Greece on the world map. Explain that ancient Greece is usually considered the birthplace of Western civilization. Yet from earliest times Greece was also in contact with the Middle East and Africa. On the map, point out Egypt, Syria, and Asia Minor (now Turkey), all close neighbors of Greece in the eastern Mediterranean. Over land and sea, the cultures of the Middle East strongly influenced Greek civilization and were influenced by it in turn. Suggest to the students that the Mediterranean has been a gateway between Africa, Europe and Asia, with important cultural traditions passing all around.

2. Ask the students if they have heard of Aesop, the famous storyteller of ancient Greece. No one knows if Aesop really existed, but according to legend, he lived in the sixth century B.C. By birth, Aesop may not have been Greek at all, but Asian or African. He is described as a slave, perhaps from Phrygia (western Turkey) or Abyssinia (Ethiopia), with a very dark complexion. In any case, he seems to have traveled widely, which may have given him the experience and wisdom to create some of the world's greatest stories.

3. Aesop's stories are called fables. Fables are relatively brief tales, often featuring animals as characters,

Procedures *continued*

designed to teach a moral lesson. Ask the students if they already know some of Aesop's fables. Among the most famous are "The Hare and the Tortoise," "The Town Mouse and the Country Mouse," "The Ant and the Grasshopper," and "The Boy Who Cried Wolf." Invite the students to retell their favorite fables for the rest of the class.

4. One of the best known of Aesop's fables is "The Lion and the Mouse." Read the fable to the class, without revealing the moral of the story.

5. Discuss the fable. What seems to be the moral? ["Kindness given, to great or humble, is seldom wasted," or simply, "The weak can sometimes help the strong."] What makes the lion seem strong and the mouse seem weak? What can the mouse do that the lion cannot? How did the mouse and the lion both benefit by becoming friends and exchanging favors, rather than remaining enemies?

6. Now explain to the class that similar fables are found in many other cultures, including those of the Middle East. On the world map, point out India, Iran, and Iraq. Some of the most famous fables in world literature came from India to Iran and Iraq, where they were first translated into Arabic (see **Cultural notes**). Eventually these Arabic tales made their way to Europe, where they were translated into many Western languages. One of these fables is called **The Ringdove**.

7. Read **The Ringdove**, below, from *Kalila wa Dimna*.

8. Discuss **The Ringdove**. What are some of the similarities between this tale and Aesop's story of "The Lion and the Mouse"? [The mouse's ability to gnaw through a hunter's ropes is a key to both tales, and in both, the various animals benefit by cooperating rather than competing.] What are some of the differences? ["The Lion and the Mouse" shows how two individuals can come to cooperate and help each other. **The Ringdove** goes further and suggests how several individuals can form a circle of friends, all cooperating as a team and relying on each other's various talents. Not only the mouse, but each of the other animals has a special ability: the crow can fly, the gazelle can run swiftly, and the tortoise can swim.]

9. Ask the students if they belong to a group of friends like the crow, the mouse, the tortoise, and the gazelle. What special abilities does each friend have that the others do not? How do such friends help each other? What can friends accomplish as a group that they would not be able to do individually? (Use team sports as a metaphor.)

10. What seems to be the moral of **The Ringdove**? What does it say about "how strangers of alien cultures can come to love and trust one another?" If desired, discuss the relevance of the fable to our own lives in the United States.

The Ringdove

(Reproduced from *Kalila wa Dimna: Fables from a Fourteenth-Century Arabic Manuscript*, Esin Atil, Washington, D.C.: Smithsonian Institution Press, 1981, pp. 33 and 35, by permission of the publisher.)

The king said to the philosopher that he would like to know how a man is received into brotherhood among his fellows and how strangers of alien races can come to love and trust one another.

The philosopher answered that nothing is equal in value to brotherhood because brothers can help in times of trouble, rescue one another from hidden snares, and protect their kin from enemies, like the crow, the mouse, the tortoise, and the gazelle.

There was a fertile region with abundant grass and trees frequented by fowlers and hunters. An old and wise crow lived in a tree that was particularly large and rich in foliage. One day the crow saw a hunter spreading a net below the tree and covering it with safflower seeds. Soon a flock of doves flew in. Their leader, a ringdove, spotted the seeds but did not notice the net. When the doves landed on the ground to feast on the seeds, the snare was drawn and they were caught in the net.

The ringdove suggested that the group unite and fly away together before they were caught by the hunter. The birds followed his advice, flapped their wings in unison, and took off with the net just as the hunter was approaching.

The crow decided to follow them. The doves flew over hills and houses with the hunter in hot pursuit. They eventually lost the man and landed near a burrow where a mouse lived. The ringdove called her friend, Zirak, the mouse, who came out of his burrow and saw the birds entangled in the net. He began to gnaw the ropes and finally cut through the snare. The doves rejoiced at being freed; they congratulated each other and thanked the mouse before flying off. Zirak returned to his home.

The crow, impressed by the friendship between the ringdove and the mouse, decided to stay on. He called out to Zirak and told the mouse that he would like them to be friends. Zirak, knowing well that crows are the natural enemies of mice, was slightly apprehensive at first but became convinced of the crow's sincerity and accepted his offer of brotherhood. A strong bond soon developed between the two, and they came to rely on one another. The crow, noticing that their homes were too close to men, suggested that they move to another area. He knew of a secluded region full of vegetation and water where his friend, the tortoise, lived. The mouse agreed and the crow took him by the tail and flew to the pond of the tortoise. The three friends enjoyed each other's company and passed their days in peace and happiness.

One day a gazelle came running into their neighborhood and frightened them. The tortoise dove into the water, the mouse scurried into his burrow, and the crow took flight and hid in a tree. When they saw that no one was pursuing the gazelle and that the animal was merely thirsty, they came out of hiding. The gazelle told them that he was running away from hunters. The friends asked him to join them and live in their peaceful place. The gazelle moved in, enjoyed good company and ample food and drink.

It became the custom of the four friends to meet every day, talk about their lives and experiences, and share their meal together. One day the gazelle failed to show up and the crow, the mouse, and the tortoise were worried that some misfortune had befallen him. The crow took to the air, searched for the gazelle, and saw that he was caught in a hunter's net.

The Ringdove *continued*

He reported what he had seen to the mouse and the tortoise, who then set out to rescue their friend. When they reached the gazelle, the mouse began to gnaw the net and eventually freed him. The gazelle turned to the tortoise and said that if the hunter came back, he could run away, the crow could fly, and the mouse could hide; but, the slow and defenseless tortoise would probably be caught. As they were talking, the hunter arrived; the gazelle, the crow, and the mouse ran away and hid, but the tortoise, who could not move fast enough, was captured by the man. The hunter bound him and took him away, slung over his shoulders.

The friends, distressed by the loss of their brother, devised a plan to free him. They decided that if the gazelle pretended to be wounded and lay down with the crow who would appear to lick his wound, they might deceive the hunter. The gazelle followed their plan and lay down in the path of the hunter with the crow over him; the mouse hid nearby and they waited for the man. When the hunter arrived and saw them, he let go of the tortoise and went after the gazelle. The crow took flight and the gazelle jumped up and ran, luring the hunter away from the tortoise. The mouse quickly went to the tortoise and severed the ropes binding him.

By the time the hunter returned, the friends were safely far away. The man was disappointed and ashamed of himself for having lost his catch. He had become quite leery of this region and moved onto another area. The crow, the mouse, the tortoise, and the gazelle rejoiced; they embraced and kissed each other, greatly relieved that now they could live in complete peace and happiness.

Cultural notes

1. For a history of *Kalila wa Dimna*, see pp. 9-10 and 55-60 in *Kalila wa Dimna: Fables from a Fourteenth-Century Arabic Manuscript*, by Esin Atil. For present purposes, the history of the book can be briefly summarized. The fables are traditionally attributed to an Indian sage named Bidpai, who may have lived in the fourth century B.C. More likely, however, *Kalila wa Dimna* is a compilation of classic folktales, first written down in Kashmir around A.D. 300. The book was brought from India to Persia (Iran) by a physician named Burzoe. At the request of the Persian king, Burzoe translated the book from Sanskrit into Pahlavi (Middle Persian) around A.D. 570.

   Almost two hundred years later, *Kalila wa Dimna* was translated into Arabic by Ibn al-Muqaffa, a native of southern Iran who adopted Islam and became secretary to the Abbasid Caliph in Iraq. His translation is the oldest surviving version of the book, and one of the finest examples of classical Arabic prose. Over the following centuries, new translations were produced and beautifully illustrated in Islamic courts throughout the Middle East. Aside from the Quran itself, *Kalila wa Dimna* became the most famous and beloved book in Islamic literature.

   By the thirteenth century A.D., the Arabic fables had made their way to Spain, where they were translated into Old Spanish. With the invention of printing, an Italian version of *Kalila wa Dimna* was one of the first books to be produced. Subsequent European works such as *La Fontaine's Fables* were undoubtedly influenced by *Kalila wa Dimna*. In the Middle East and beyond, this collection of fables ranks as one of the most popular and important books in history.

Jokes and Joha tales

Objectives

1. To understand joking as an important part of storytelling

2. To practice public speaking by telling jokes

3. To read some humorous tales from the Arab world, including three popular "Joha" tales

4. To perform a short play based on one of the included stories

Materials

[No special materials required.]

Procedures

1. Ask the students if they know any good jokes. Invite them to tell their favorite jokes to the rest of the class.

2. Explain that joking is an important part of storytelling. Many folktales take the form of jokes or humorous narratives. **The Silent Couple** and **The Boots of Hunayn**, below, may be read as examples. Both of these stories come from the Arab world, although various other versions are told from Scotland to Sri Lanka (see **Cultural notes**).

3. In the Middle East, some of the most popular folktales are jokes about a man named Joha (also called Jiha, Goha, Jawha, Jeha, and so on). Sometimes Joha is portrayed as a clever trickster, sometimes as a bumbling fool (see **Cultural notes**). For a sample of the ridiculous yet lovable Joha, read **Joha and the Hundred Eggs** and **Joha Rides the Bus**, below. These are simple jokes which children around the world can understand and enjoy.

4. Next, read **What Will People Say?**, below. Discuss the tale. What is the moral of the story? Ask the students if they have ever tried to please everybody, and ended up pleasing no one. What do they think is the best way to act: Should you always do what you want, regardless of what people think? Under what conditions should you give in to the opinions of others? When should you do things your own way, even if others do not like it?

5. If desired, adapt any of the three stories — **The Silent Couple**, **The Boots of Hunayn**, or **What Will People Say?** — as a short play to be performed by the class. If the class is large, divide it into work groups. One group may be assigned to develop a script, another to create the scenery and props, and another to play the parts. Preparations for the play may be as simple or as elaborate as time allows.

Procedures *continued*

6. If possible, perform all three stories. In this case, have the students rotate their jobs, so that they help write the script for one play, create scenery and props for another, and act in the third.

Joha and the Hundred Eggs

(Adapted from *Arab Folktales*, Inea Bushnaq, copyright (c) 1986 by Inea Bushnaq; reprinted by permission of Pantheon Books, a division of Random House, Inc.)

In the Middle Ages, Harun Al Rasheed was Caliph, leader of the entire Islamic world. His royal court was filled with fascinating people from all over the world, but his favorite companion was a simple man named Joha. No matter what the situation, Joha could always make the Caliph laugh.

Once, as a joke on Joha, Harun Al Rasheed gave a hundred eggs to the hundred members of his royal court and ordered each person to put an egg on his chair and sit down. Later, when Joha arrived, the Caliph stood up and said, "I command each of you to lay an egg for me this morning." And sure enough, every last one of the courtiers produced an egg, except for Joha. For a moment, Joha was at a loss. Then he threw back his head and began to crow, "Cock-a-doodle-doo!" Loud and shrill. "What's the matter with you, Joha?" asked the Caliph. "O master and protector, with a hundred hens in this chamber, don't you think you need at least one rooster?"

For his quick answer, Harun Al Rasheed rewarded Joha with a hundred coins of gold.

Joha Rides the Bus

(Retold by Milad Amir)

Joha was a simple man. He was not too tall, but not too short. He was not too large, but not too small. He was not too fat, but not too thin. He was not too young, but not too old. In fact, Joha was not too much of anything at all.

Joha was also not too rich, owning very little except for a donkey named Baseet (simple), whom he treated as a friend. Baseet accompanied Joha everywhere.

One day, after a long nap under a simple palm tree, reading a simple book about simple things, Joha felt tired, too tired for the long ride home on Baseet in the middle of the noonday sun. He decided to take the bus.

At the nearest bus stop, Joha straddled Baseet and boarded the bus. He greeted the bus driver and all the passengers he passed as he rode to the back of the bus. The other passengers were amazed. They had never seen a man riding a donkey on a bus. Even Baseet himself was surprised. "Joha has really done it this time!" he thought.

After many stops and many turns, the bus arrived at Joha's house. As Joha rode off the bus, the driver shouted after him, "Where is your fare?" Joha replied simply, "Fare? What fare? I didn't ride your bus. I was riding my donkey!"

As the bus driver pondered these words, Joha rode away without paying. He wasn't such a simple man after all, was he?

What will people say?

(Adapted from *Lands, Peoples and Communities of the Middle East*, by Juanita W. Soghikian, Middle East Gateway Series, copyright (c) 1981; reproduced by permission of the Swedenburg Family Trust.)

unit six

folktales and stories

Joha had a young son named Abdullah. As the little boy grew, Joha noticed that Abdullah had trouble making decisions. He worried so much about what people might say that he stopped doing anything at all. Joha decided that something had to be done to teach his son the foolishness of his worries.

One day, Joha prepared his donkey for a journey to the market in the next town. He called Abdullah to him. "Son," said Joha, "I am going to the Thursday market. I want you to walk along behind me and help me when I get there."

Joha climbed onto his donkey and away he went, with Abdullah running along the road, as he had been told to do.

After a few minutes, they came to a group of women who were filling their water cans at the village fountain. Just as Joha guessed they would do, the women called out to him.

"Heartless man!" they shouted. "Why do you ride the donkey while your poor child has to run behind in the dust?"

"Ah," murmured Joha, "Maybe they are right. Come, Abdullah, you ride the donkey and I will walk."

With that, Joha got off the donkey and his son climbed up to ride. Soon they came to a field where some men were eating their lunch of bread, olives, and yogurt. One of the men yelled at Joha. "Foolish man!" he shouted. "Why do you walk in the hot, midday sun while your strong son rides the donkey? You are spoiling him! You cannot teach him good manners and respect for his elders that way! *You* should be riding the donkey!"

Abdullah looked pale and confused. He was worried about what the men thought of him. He immediately slipped down from the donkey's back and handed the reins to his father. "Here, Baba. You were right the first time. You should be the one to ride."

But Joha said, "No, we will both ride the donkey." So up they climbed onto the donkey's back and started once more toward town.

It was not long before they met a man who loved donkeys. As he drew up aside Abdullah and Joha, he scolded them. "How can you both be so thoughtless and mean to your poor, skinny little donkey? Two of you are much too heavy for him!"

Now Abdullah was even more confused and very close to tears. He did not know what to do. But Joha said calmly, "Maybe this man is right. We will both get down and walk beside the donkey into town. That way, if we meet any more people, they cannot criticize either of us!"

So ... on they went. Soon enough, they met a party of young men who liked to joke and play tricks. One called out, "Ya, Baba! How is it that you make that poor donkey walk before you? He looks so tired he might die! Why don't you carry the poor creature?" Then the young men laughed and slapped one another's backs and went their merry way up the road.

Joha knew his donkey was healthy and strong enough to carry people and other burdens, but to teach his fearful son a lesson, he said, "Perhaps those men are right. Come, Abdullah. Help me cut a strong branch from that tree over there."

Abdullah was puzzled about what his father was going to do, but he was glad that his father was paying attention to what people said. He immediately followed Joha to the tree.

After cutting the branch and making it into a long pole, Joha took some strong rope and tied together the front legs of the anxious, struggling donkey. Then he tied the donkey's hind legs. Finally, he slipped the pole between the donkey's legs so the two ends of the branch stuck out at either end.

"Now, Abdullah," said Joha, "we will turn the donkey upside down, so he hangs by his legs from the pole. You will carry one end of the pole over your shoulder, and I will carry the other end over mine. That way, we can carry the donkey to town and he will not be tired!"

Abdullah was speechless, but he did as his father said. Slowly and painfully, the father and son carried the donkey into the market square...

What will people say? *continued*

and there, suddenly, the whole town seemed to roar with laughter. Fingers pointed and people jeered at the hapless men and their donkey. Wearily, Abdullah put down his burden and accepted a drink of water from his father.

"Abdullah, my son," said Joha, "I hope that you will never forget today's lesson. You can suffer much and gain little if you worry about what other people say. You must understand: *there is no way you can please everyone.*"

The Silent Couple

(Adapted from *World Tales: The Extraordinary Coincidence of Stories Told in All Times, in All Places*, p. 124, by Idries Shah, copyright (c) 1979 by Technographia, S.A. and Harcourt Brace and Company; reprinted by permission of Harcourt Brace and Company.)

Once upon a time there was a newly-married couple, still dressed in their wedding finery, relaxing in their new home after the last of the guests had left their wedding feast.

"Dear husband," said the young bride, "do go and close the door to the street. Someone has left it open."

"*Me* shut it?" said the groom, "a bridegroom in his splendid costume, with a priceless robe and a dagger studded with jewels? How could I be expected to do such a thing? You must be out of your mind. Go and shut it yourself."

"So!" shouted the bride, "you expect me to be your slave: a gentle, beautiful creature like me, wearing a dress of finest silk. How could you suggest that I get up on my wedding day and close a door which looks onto the public street? Impossible."

They were both silent for a moment or two, and the bride suggested that they should make the problem the subject of a contest. Whoever spoke first, they agreed, should be the one to shut the door.

There were two sofas in the room, and the pair settled themselves face to face, one on each, sitting mutely, looking at each other.

They had been in this posture for two or three hours when a party of thieves came and noticed that the door was open. The robbers crept into the silent house, which seemed so deserted, and began to load themselves with every portable object they could find.

The bridal couple heard them come in, but each thought that the other should attend to the matter. Neither of them spoke or moved as the burglars went from room to room, until at length they entered the sitting room and at first failed to notice the utterly motionless couple.

Still the pair sat there, while the thieves collected all the valuables, and even rolled up the carpets under them. Mistaking the idiot and his stubborn wife for wax dummies, they stripped them of their personal jewels ... and *still* the couple said nothing at all.

The thieves made off, and the bride and her groom sat on their sofas throughout the night. Neither would give up.

When daylight came, a policeman on his beat saw the open street door and walked into the house. Going from room to room he finally came upon the pair and asked them what was happening. Neither man nor wife deigned to reply.

The policeman called massive reinforcements, and the swarming custodians of the law became more and more enraged at the total silence of the couple, which seemed a blatant show of disrespect.

The officer in charge at last lost his temper and called out to one of his men: "Give that man a blow or two, and get some sense out of him!"

At this the wife could not restrain herself: "Please, kind officers," she cried, "do not strike him. He is my husband!"

"I won!" shouted the fool immediately, "so *you* have to shut the door!"

The Boots of Hunayn

(Adapted from *World Tales: The Extraordinary Coincidence of Stories Told in All Times, in All Places*, p. 224, by Idries Shah, copyright (c) 1979 by Technographia, S.A. and Harcourt Brace and Company; reprinted by permission of Harcourt Brace and Company.)

There was once a desert Arab who rode into town and saw a pair of boots for sale in the market. He went into the shop and made an offer for them, but Hunayn the shoemaker stuck to his price, and in the end the infuriated bedouin stamped out of the shop. "The price you ask is equal to the value of my camel," he snorted.

Now the shoemaker was deeply offended by the rude behavior and rough language of this desert Arab, and decided that he would not let him get away with such insults. The Arab had mounted his camel and was moving along the trail towards the tents of his tribe. The shoemaker, knowing where his would-be

customer had come from, picked up the boots and went by short-cuts to a point the Arab would eventually have to pass. There he placed one boot on the sand.

Then the Shoemaker went a mile or more further along the road and dropped the other boot, hiding himself to watch what would happen, for he had a plan.

Presently the Arab came along, and saw the first boot lying on the ground. He said to himself, "That is one of the boots of Hunayn, the cobbler; if only it was a pair, I would dismount and take them away for nothing." And he went on his way. After all, what was the use of one boot?

Soon afterwards, the Arab came upon the second boot. He thought, "What a pity

The Boots of Hunayn *continued*

I did not take up the first one; then I would have a pair." Then it occurred to him that he could go back for the first boot; then he would have them both.

The bedouin was some way from his own tents and did not want to tire his camel, so he hobbled it and ran back to the place where he had seen the first boot.

The shoemaker came out of hiding and, leaving the second boot where it was, he made off with the Arab's camel.

When the Arab arrived back to the place where he had left his camel, he found it missing. Thinking it must have strayed, he made his way back to the tents of his people.

"What have you brought back from town?" his fellow bedouins asked, as he limped into the settlement.

"Only the boots of Hunayn" said the miserable man.

The moral of the story: Be careful of what you want; you might get it.

Cultural notes

1. **The Silent Couple**, according to Idries Shah (*World Tales*, p. 124), "is one of the world's most widely distributed folktales. It is found in Turkey and Sri Lanka, in Venice and Kashmir, in Arabia and Sicily, and quite possibly many other places as well." Even in Scotland, there is a remarkably similar ballad entitled "The Barring of the Door."

2. **The Boots of Hunayn** is a Middle Eastern parable, again found all over the world. The version in *World Tales* (p. 224) is adapted from Ibn Khallikan's monumental *Wafayaat*, written in the thirteenth century AD. Its famous author was himself of Central Asian descent, and the story of Hunayn's boots was no doubt a familiar tale in his homeland.

3. A brief history of Joha and his Turkish counterpart, Nasradeen Hodja, is provided by Paul Lunde (in *Arab World Notebook*, pp. 173-74):

   Some modern Turkish scholars consider Nasreddin Hodja a historical personality... born in 1208 ... It seems likely that the name "Joha" was much earlier than the Turkish Nasreddin. In fact, Joha originally seems to have been an entirely different person, a Bedouin renowned for his simplicity. What seems to have happened is that Nasreddin and Joha coalesced into one person sometime in the 16th century... In each country into which he has been adopted, the stories told about him naturally reflect the temperament of the people. When stories are told in the countryside, Joha is usually portrayed as a simple peasant. In the cities, his personality is more complex. Sometimes he is a fool and sometimes he has the cunning of a Yankee city slicker ... It has been suggested that Cervantes got the idea, and perhaps even the name, for his great work Don Quixote from Joha stories. ("Joha" or "Goha" can even be heard in the name "Quixote" — pronounced "Kihote" at that time.) After all, Cervantes spent some years as a prisoner in Algiers, and what better way to while away the time in a dreary cell than by exchanging Joha stories with one's jailer?

   (originally published in *Aramco World* magazine, May-June 1971)

Middle East Outreach Programs

American-Arab Anti-Discrimination Committee
4201 Connecticut Ave. NW, Suite 300
Washington, D.C. 20008
Tel: 202.244.2990
Fax: 202.244.3196
Email: ADC@adc.org
Website: www.adc.org

AMIDEAST
1730 M Street, NW, Suite 1100
Washington, D.C. 20036-4505
Tel: 202.776.9600
Fax: 202.776.7000
Email: inquiries@amideast.org
Website: www.amideast.org

AWAIR
2137 Rose
Berkeley, CA 94709
Tel: 510.704.0517
Email: awair@igc.org

Columbia University
Middle East and Asian Languages and Cultures
602 Kent Hall, Mail Code 3928
1140 Amsterdam Avenue
New York, NY 10027
Tel: 212.854.2556
Fax: 212.854.5517
Email: jr650@columbia.edu
Website: www.columbia.edu

Council on Islamic Education
P.O. Box 20186
Fountain Valley, CA 92708
Tel: 714.839.2929
Fax: 714.839.2714
Email: info@cie.org

Fordham University
Middle East Program
678 Faber Hall
441 East Fordham Road
Bronx, NY 10458
Tel: 718.817.3953
Fax: 718.817.3972
Email: entelis@fordham.edu
Website: www.fordham.edu/facts/iped/

Georgetown University
Center for Contemporary Arab Studies
ICC 241
Washington, D.C. 20057-1020
Tel: 202.687.5793
Fax: 202.686.7001
Email: ccasinfor@gunet.georgetown.edu
Website: www.georgetown.edu\sfs\programs\ccas

Harvard University
The Center for Middle Eastern Studies
1737 Cambridge Street
Cambridge, MA 02138
Tel: 617.495.4055
Fax: 617.496.8584
Email: mideast@fas.harvard.edu
Website: www.fas.harvard.edu/~mideast

MERIP
1500 Massachusetts Avenue, NW, Suite 119
Washington, D.C. 20005
Tel: 202.223.3677
Fax: 202.223.3604
Email: twalz@merip.org
Website: www.merip.org

New York University
Hagop Kevorkian Center for Near Eastern Studies
50 Washington Square South
New York, NY 10012
Tel: 212.998.8877
Fax: 212.995.4144
Email: kevorkian.center@nyu.edu
Website: www.nyu.edu/gsas/program/neareast/
center.html

Ohio State University
Department of Near Eastern Languages
and Cultures
1735 Neil Avenue
Columbus, Ohio 43210
Tel: 614.292.9255
Fax: 614.292.1262
Email: noble.3@osu.edu
Website: www.cohums.ohio-state.edu/NELC/
nelc.htm

Portland State University
Middle East Studies Center
Office of International Affairs
Sixth Avenue Building
1950 S.W. Sixth Ave.
Portland, OR 97207
Tel: 503.725.3455
Fax: 503.725.5320
Email: lutzkere@pdx.edu
Website: www.oaa.pdx.edu/International/
    MiddleEast

Princeton University
Department of Near Eastern Studies
110 Jones Hall
Princeton, NJ 08544-1008
Tel: 609.258.4281
Fax: 609.258.1242
Email: jwwein@princeton.edu
Website: www.princeton.edu/neareast

SUNY Binghamton
The Institute of Global Cultural Studies
P.O. Box 6000 LNG-100
Binghamton, NY 13905
Tel: 607.777.4494
Fax: 607.777.2642
Email: igcs@binghamton.edu
Website: http://igcs.binghamton.edu

University of Arizona
Center for Middle Eastern Studies
Franklin Building, Room 204
1011 East 5th Street
Tucson, AZ 85721
Tel: 520.621.5450
Fax: 520.621.9257
Email: mideast@u.arizona.edu
Website: www.arizona.edu/cmesua

University of California at Berkeley
Center for Middle Eastern Studies
372 Stephens Hall, #2314
Berkeley, CA 94720-2314
Tel: 510.642.8208
Fax: 510.643.3001
Email: cmes@uclink4.berkeley.edu
Website: www.ias.berkeley.edu/cmes

University of California at Los Angeles
Center for Near Eastern Studies
10286 Bunche Hall
P.O. Box 951480
Los Angeles, CA 90095-1480
Tel: 310.825.1181
Fax: 310.206.2046
Email: swilliams@isop.ucla.edu
Website: www.isop.ucla.edu/cnes

University of California at Santa Barbara
Global and International Studies Program
    Islamic and Near Eastern Studies
Santa Barbara, CA 93106-7131
Tel: 805. 893.7860
Fax: 805.893.8003
Email: gisp@alishaw.ucsb.edu
Website: www.gisp.ucsb/ines.htm

University of Chicago
The Department of Near Eastern Languages
    and Civilizations
1155 East 58th Street
Chicago, IL 60637
Tel: 773.702.9512
Fax: 773.702.9853
Email: ne-lc@uchicago.edu
Website: www.uchicago.edu/

University of Michigan
Center for Middle Eastern and North African
    Studies
1080 South University Avenue, Suite 4640
Ann Arbor, MI 48109-1106
Tel: 734.764.0350
Fax: 734.764.8523
Email: cmenas@umich.edu
Website: www.umich.edu/~inet/cmenas

University of Pennsylvania
The Middle East Center
838-839 Williams Hall
36th and Spruce Streets
Philadelphia, PA 19104-6305
Tel: 215.898.6335
Fax: 215.573.2003
Email: info@mec.sas.upenn.edu
Website: www.upenn.edu.mec.sas

Middle East
Outreach Programs continued

University of Texas
The Center for Middle Eastern Studies
Austin, TX 78712
Tel: 512.471.3881
Fax: 512.471. 7834
Email: cmes@menic.utexas.edu
Website: www.dla.utexas.edu/depts/cmes

University of Utah
Middle East Center
260 S. Central Campus Drive
Salt Lake City, UT 84112
Tel: 801.581.6181
Fax: 801.581.6183
Email: mec@mail.hum.utah.edu
Website: www.utah.edu/mec

University of Washington
The Henry M. Jackson School of International
    Studies
225 Thomson Hall Box 353650
Tel: 206.543.4227
Fax: 206.685.0668
Email: burrowes@u.washington.edu
Website: http://jsis.artsci.washington.edu

Wayne State University
Department of Near Eastern and Asian Studies
437 Manoogian Hall
College of Liberal Arts
Detroit, MI 48202
Tel: 313.577.3015
Fax: 313.577.3266
Email: neareasternstudies@wayne.edu
Website: www.wayne.edu

Bibliography

ACCESS (Anan Ameri and Dawn Ramey, eds.), 2000. *Arab American Encyclopedia.* Detroit: UXL, The Gale Group.

Alexander, Sue, 1983. *Nadia the Willful.* New York: Alfred A. Knopf, Inc.

Al Faruqi, Isma'il R., 1984. *Islam.* Brentwood, Maryland: International Graphics.

Asch, Frank, 1984. *Just Like Daddy.* New York: Simon & Schuster Trade.

Baer, Edith, 1992. *This is the Way We Go to School.* New York: Scholastic, Inc.

Bahous, Sally, 1993. *Sitti and the Cats: A Tale of Friendship.* Niwot, Colorado: Roberts Rinehart Publishers.

Beaton, Margaret, 1988. *Syria.* Chicago: Children's Press.

Bennett, Olivia, 1985. *A Family in Egypt.* Minneapolis: Lerner Publications Co.

Brill, Marlene Targ, 1987. *Libya.* Chicago: Children's Press, Inc.

Butterfly Books, 1983. *Camels.* Beirut: Librairie Du Liban.

1986. *Arab Horses.* Beirut: Librairie Du Liban.

1991. *Khaled and Aida.* Beirut: Librairie Du Liban.

Burgoyne, Diane Turnage, 1982. *Amina and Muhammad's Special Visitor.* Spring Valley, California: Middle East Gateway Series.

Carter, John, 1990. *The Arabian Desert.* New York: State Mutual Book & Periodical Service, Ltd.

Cross, Wilbur, 1982. *Egypt.* Chicago: Children's Press, Inc.

Dutton, Roderic, 1987. *An Arab Family.* Minneapolis: Lerner Publications Co.

Heide, Florence Parry and Judith Heide Gilliland, 1990. *The Day of Ahmed's Secret.* New York: Lothrop, Lee & Shepard Books.

1992. *Sami and the Time of the Troubles.* New York: Clarion Books.

Hintz, Martin, 1985. *Morocco.* Chicago: Children's Press, Inc.

Morris, Ann, 1989. *Hats, Hats, Hats.* New York: Lothrup, Lee & Shepard Books.

Nye, Naomi Shihab, 1994. *Sitti's Secrets.* New York: Four Winds Press.

Sales, Francesc, 1989. *Ibrahim.* New York: J.B. Lippincott.

Soghikian, Juanita Will, 1981. *Lands, Peoples and Communities of the Middle East.* Spring Valley, California: Middle East Gateway Series.

Steward, Judy, 1986. *A Family in Morocco.* Minneapolis: Lerner Publications Co.

Wood, Audrey, 1984. *The Napping House.* San Diego: Harcourt Brace Jovanovich, Publishers.